Lecture Notes in Computer Science   8910

Commenced Publication in 1973
Founding and Former Series Editors:
Gerhard Goos, Juris Hartmanis, and Jan van Leeuwen

More information about this series at http://www.springer.com/series/8379

Maciej Koutny · Serge Haddad
Alex Yakovlev (Eds.)

Transactions on Petri Nets and Other Models of Concurrency IX

 Springer

Editor-in-Chief

Maciej Koutny
School of Computing Science
Newcastle University
Newcastle upon Tyne
UK

Guest Editors

Serge Haddad
École Normale Supérieure de Cachan
Cachan
France

Alex Yakovlev
Newcastle University
Newcastle upon Tyne
UK

ISSN 0302-9743   ISSN 1611-3349   (electronic)
Lecture Notes in Computer Science
ISBN 978-3-662-45729-0   ISBN 978-3-662-45730-6   (eBook)
DOI 10.1007/978-3-662-45730-6

Library of Congress Control Number: 2014957728

Springer Heidelberg New York Dordrecht London

Printed on acid-free paper

Springer-Verlag GmbH Berlin Heidelberg is part of Springer Science+Business Media
(www.springer.com)

Preface by Editor-in-Chief

The 9th Issue of LNCS Transactions on Petri Nets and Other Models of Concurrency (ToPNoC) contains revised and extended versions of a selection of the best papers from the workshops held at the 34th International Conference on Application and Theory of Petri Nets and Concurrency (Petri Nets 2013, Milan, Italy, during 24–28 June 2013), and 13th International Conference on Application of Concurrency to System Design (ACSD 2013, Barcelona, Spain, during 8–10 July 2013). It also contains one paper submitted directly to ToPNoC.

I would like to thank the two guest editors of this special issue: Serge Haddad and Alex Yakovlev. Moreover, I would like to thank all authors, reviewers, and the organizers of the Petri Nets 2013 and ACSD 2013 conferences satellite workshops, without whom this issue of ToPNoC would not have been possible.

July 2014   Maciej Koutny

LNCS Transactions on Petri Nets and Other Models of Concurrency: Aims and Scope

ToPNoC aims to publish papers from all areas of Petri nets and other models of concurrency ranging from theoretical work to tool support and industrial applications. The foundations of Petri nets were laid by the pioneering work of Carl Adam Petri and his colleagues in the early 1960s. Since then, a huge volume of material has been developed and published in journals and books as well as presented at workshops and conferences.

The annual International Conference on Application and Theory of Petri Nets and Concurrency started in 1980. The International Petri Net Bibliography maintained by the Petri Net Newsletter contains close to 10,000 different entries, and the International Petri Net Mailing List has 1,500 subscribers. For more information on the International Petri Net community, see: http://www.informatik.uni-hamburg.de/TGI/PetriNets/

All issues of ToPNoC are LNCS volumes. Hence, they appear in all main libraries and are also accessible in LNCS Online (electronically). It is possible to subscribe to ToPNoC without subscribing to the rest of LNCS.

ToPNoC contains:

- revised versions of a selection of the best papers from workshops and tutorials concerned with Petri nets and concurrency;
- special issues related to particular subareas (similar to those published in the *Advances in Petri Nets* series);
- other papers invited for publication in ToPNoC; and
- papers submitted directly to ToPNoC by their authors.

Like all other journals, ToPNoC has an Editorial Board, which is responsible for the quality of the journal. The members of the board assist in the reviewing of papers submitted or invited for publication in ToPNoC. Moreover, they may make recommendations concerning collections of papers for special issues. The Editorial Board consists of prominent researchers within the Petri net community and in related fields.

Topics

System design and verification using nets; analysis and synthesis, structure and behavior of nets; relationships between net theory and other approaches; causality/ partial order theory of concurrency; net-based semantical, logical and algebraic calculi; symbolic net representation (graphical or textual); computer tools for nets; experience with using nets, case studies; educational issues related to nets; higher level net models; timed and stochastic nets; and standardization of nets.

Applications of nets to: biological systems; defense systems; e-commerce and trading; embedded systems; environmental systems; exible manufacturing systems; hardware structures; health and medical systems; office automation; operations research; performance evaluation; programming languages; protocols and networks; railway networks; real-time systems; supervisory control; telecommunications; cyber physical systems; and workow.

For more information about ToPNoC see: www.springer.com/lncs/topnoc.

Submission of Manuscripts

Manuscripts should follow LNCS formatting guidelines, and should be submitted as PDF or zipped PostScript files to ToPNoC@ncl.ac.uk. All queries should be addressed to the same e-mail address.

LNCS Transactions on Petri Nets and Other Models of Concurrency: Editorial Board

Preface by Guest Editors

This volume of ToPNoC contains revised and extended versions of a selection of the best workshop papers presented at the 34th International Conference on Application and Theory of Petri Nets and Other Models of Concurrency (Petri Nets 2013) and 13th International Conference on Application of Concurrency to System Design (ACSD 2013).

We, Serge Haddad and Alex Yakovlev, are indebted to the Program Committees of the workshops and in particular their chairs. Without their enthusiastic work this volume would not have been possible. Many members of the Program Committees participated in reviewing the extended versions of the papers selected for this issue. The following workshops were asked for their strongest contributions:

- PNSE 2013: InternationalWorkshop on Petri Nets and Software Engineering (chairs: Daniel Moldt and Heiko Rölke)
- ModBE 2013: International Workshop on Modeling and Business Environments (chair: Daniel Moldt)
- ART 2013: InternationalWorkshop on Applications of Region Theory (chairs: Robin Bergenthum and Josep Carmona)

The best papers of these workshops were selected in close cooperation with their chairs. The authors were invited to improve and extend their results where possible, based on the comments received before and during the workshop. The resulting revised submissions were reviewed by three to have referees. We followed the principle of asking for fresh reviews of the revised papers, i.e., from referees who had not been involved initially in reviewing the original workshop contribution. All papers went through the standard two-stage journal reviewing process and eventually seven were accepted after rigorous reviewing and revising. Presented are a variety of high-quality contributions, ranging from specification, validation, verification, and synthesis based on Petri nets and other models of concurrency.

The paper "Decidability of k-Soundness for Workow Nets with an Unbounded Resource" by Vladimir A. Bashkin and Irina A. Lomazova studies an extension of workow nets, called resource workow nets (RWF-net), which is supplied with an additional set of initially marked resource places. More specifically, they study a particular kind of proper termination denoted k-soundness. They establish the decidability of both marked and unmarked k-soundness for a restricted class of RWF-nets with a single unbounded resource place (1-dim RWF-nets). In addition, they present an algorithm for computing the minimal k-sound resource for a given sound 1-dim RWF-net.

The paper "Modeling Distributed Private Key Generation by Composing Petri Nets" by Luca Bernardinello, Görkem Kılınç, Elisabetta Mangioni, and Lucia Pomello presents a Petri net model of a protocol for the distributed generation of id-based private keys. These keys can then be used for secure communications. The components of the system are built as refinements of a common interface, by applying a formal operation based on a class of morphisms between Elementary Net Systems. Thus, the authors derive behavioural properties of the composed system without building it explicitly, by exploiting properties of the given morphisms.

The paper "Software Engineering with Petri Nets: a Web Service and Agent Perspective" by Tobias Betz, Lawrence Cabac, Michael Duvigneau, Thomas Wagner, and Matthias Wester-Ebbinghaus develops complex Petri net-based software applications according to the multi-agent paradigm. Agent-internal as well as agent-spanning processes are implemented directly as (high-level) Petri nets. These nets are essential parts of the resulting software application alongside other parts (operational and declarative ones), which are implemented using traditional ways of programming. The authors emphasize the benefit of having Petri net models serve as conceptual models that progressively refine the constructed system from simple models to well-defined specifications of the systems.

The paper "Modeling Organizational Structures and Agent Knowledge for Mulan Applications" by Lawrence Cabac, David Mosteller, and Matthias Wester-Ebbinghaus presents a service-oriented view on the organizational structure of multi-agent systems. This view is supported by new modeling techniques and tools described in this paper. The conceptual basis underlying the models and tools is provided by an ontology model, with its means for the agents to communicate about roles and dependencies and for the organizational structure to ensure self-adaptation, which is particularly important for multi-agent systems.

The paper "A Canonical Contraction for Safe Petri Nets" by Thomas Chatain and Stefan Haar extends the contraction of sets of events called facets in the context of occurrence nets and propose a canonical contraction of general safe Petri nets. On occurrence nets, the construction coincides with the facets abstraction. Furthermore, the contraction preserves the maximal semantics in the sense that the maximal processes of the contracted net are in bijection with those of the original net.

The paper "Symbolic termination and conuence checking for ECA rules" by Xiaoqing Jin, Yousra Lembachar, and Gianfranco Ciardo investigates formal verification techniques to guarantee properties of Event-condition-action (ECA) rules that are widely used in reactive systems and active database systems. The authors tackle with the nondeterministic and concurrent semantics of ECA rule execution. They propose an approach to analyze the dynamic behavior of a set of ECA rules, by first translating them into an extended Petri net and then studying the termination and conuence. The applied symbolic algorithms greatly improve scalability.

The paper "Tissue Systems and Petri Net Synthesis" by Jetty Kleijn, Maciej Koutny, and Marta Pietkiewicz-Koutny tackles the problem of synthesis of tissue systems, which are a computational abstraction of the chemical reactions and transport of molecules in a tissue. The synthesis proceeds with the initial specification being given in terms of observed and desired behaviors expressed by transition systems. The paper solves the synthesis problem for Petri nets using the notion of regions, and offers a method and algorithm of synthesis when the topology of the system is initially given. It then moves to the discussion of the case when such a topology is unknown and has to be determined.

As guest editors, we would like to thank all authors and referees who have contributed to this issue. Not only is the quality of this volume the result of the high scientific value of their work, but we would also like to acknowledge the excellent cooperation throughout the whole process that has made our work a pleasant task.

We are also grateful to the Springer/ToPNoC team for the final production of this issue.

July 2014

Serge Haddad
Alex Yakovlev

Organisation of This Issue

Guest Editors

Serge Haddad   ENS Cachan, France
Alex Yakovlev   Newcastle University, UK

Co-chairs of the Workshops

Robin Bergenthum   University of Hagen, Germany
Josep Carmona   Polytechnic University of Catalonia, Spain
Daniel Moldt   University of Hamburg, Germany
Heiko Rölke   University of Hamburg, Germany

Referees

Eric Badouel
Luca Bernardinello
Didier Buchs
Patrick Delfmann
Jörg Desel
Raymond Devillers
Amal El Fallah Seghrouchni
Sami Evangelista
Jorge Figueiredo
Stefan Haar
Serge Haddad
Xudong He
Kunihiko Hiraishi

Kaïs Klai
Hanna Klaudel
Michael Köhler-Bumeier
Maciej Koutny
Lars Michael Kristensen
Johan Lilius
Robert Lorenz
Berndt Muller
Wojciech Penczek
Laure Petrucci
Kent Inge Fagerland Simonsen
Alexei Sharpanskykh
Ferucio Laurentiu Tiplea

Contents

Contents

Decidability of k-Soundness for Workflow Nets with an Unbounded Resource

Vladimir A. Bashkin[1] and Irina A. Lomazova[2]($\boxtimes$)

[1] Yaroslavl State University, Yaroslavl 150000, Russia
v_bashkin@mail.ru
[2] National Research University Higher School of Economics (HSE),
Moscow 101000, Russia
ilomazova@hse.ru

Abstract. A resource workflow net (RWF-net) is a workflow net, supplied with an additional set of initially marked resource places. Resources can be consumed and/or produced by transitions. Neither the intermediate nor final resource markings are constrained, hence a net can have an infinite number of different reachable states.

An RWF-net with k tokens in the initial place and a certain number of resource tokens in resource places is called k-sound if it properly terminates with k tokens in the final place and, moreover, adding any extra initial resource does not violate its proper termination. An unmarked RWF-net is k-sound if it is k-sound for some initial resource. In this paper we prove the decidability of both marked and unmarked k-soundness for a restricted class of RWF-nets with a single unbounded resource place (1-dim RWF-nets). We present an algorithm for computing the minimal k-sound resource for a given sound 1-dim RWF-net.

Keywords: Petri nets · Workflow · Soundness · Modeling · Verification

1 Introduction

Petri nets is a popular formalism for modeling and analysis of distributed systems. In this paper we consider workflow systems, or, to be more precise, workflow processes. To model workflow processes a special subclass of Petri nets, called WF-nets [1,2], is used.

In the context of WF-nets a crucial correctness criterion is soundness [1,3]. We say that a workflow case execution terminates properly, iff its firing sequence (starting from the initial marking with a single token in the initial place) terminates with a single token in the final place (i.e. there are no "garbage" tokens after the termination). A model is called sound iff a process can terminate properly starting from any reachable marking.

This work is supported by the Basic Research Program of the National Research University Higher School of Economics.

© Springer-Verlag Berlin Heidelberg 2014
M. Koutny et al. (Eds.): ToPNoC IX, LNCS 8910, pp. 1–18, 2014.
DOI: 10.1007/978-3-662-45730-6_1

Soundness of WF-nets is decidable [1]. Moreover, a number of decidable variations of soundness are defined and studied, such as structural soundness [25] and soundness of nested models [20]. The important generalizations of classical soundness are k-soundness and generalized soundness [18,19]. A WF-net is k-sound if, starting with k tokens in the initial place, it always properly terminates with k tokens in the final place. Hence this notion allows handling multiple individual processes (cases) in a WF-net. The classical soundness then coincides with 1-soundness.

One of important aspects of workflow development concerns resource management. In classical Petri nets one can distinguish places, corresponding to control flow states, and places, representing different kinds of resources. Then many interesting Petri net analysis problems arise, such as bisimulation equivalent resource replacement [9–11], as well as specific resource-oriented modeling [7,8,13–15]. Resource places can be also used for representing channels in services interaction, or inter-organizational workflow. Then checking resource conformance can be used for verifying compatibility of services [22].

In business process management resources are executives (people or devices), raw materials, finances, etc. Different resource extensions of the base formalism of WF-nets with different versions of soundness criteria were introduced for taking resources into account. In [5,6] a specific class of WFR-nets with decidable soundness was studied. In [19,24] a more general class of Resource-Constrained Workflow Nets (RCWF-nets) was defined. Informally, the authors impose two constraints on resources. First, they require that all resources that are initially available are available again after terminating of all cases. Second, they also require that for any reachable marking, the number of available resources does not override the number of initially available resources.

In [19] it was proven that for RCWF-nets with a single resource type generalized soundness can be effectively checked in polynomial time. In [24] it was proven that generalized soundness is decidable in RCWF-nets with an arbitrary number of resource places (by reducing to the home-space problem).

In all mentioned papers resources are assumed to be permanent, i.e. they are used (blocked) and released later on. Resources are never created, nor destroyed. Hence the process state space is explicitly bounded.

To study a more general case of arbitrary resource transformations (that can arise, for example, in open and/or adaptive workflow systems), in [12] we defined a notion of WF-nets with resources (RWF-nets). RWF-nets extend RCWF-nets from [19] in such a way that resources can be generated or consumed during a process execution without any restrictions. For RWF-nets we defined notions of resources and controlled resources and studied the problem of soundness-preserving resource replacement (this problem is important for adaptive workflows).

Unfortunately, even 1-sound RWF-nets are not bounded in general, hence existing soundness checking algorithms cannot be applied here. In [12] the decidability of soundness for RFW-nets was declared as an open problem.

In this paper we consider a restricted case — RWF-nets with a single resource place (1-dim RWF-nets). One resource type is sufficient for many practical applications (memory or money are typical examples of such resources). Note that 1-dim RWF-nets are, generally speaking, not bounded and hence this case cannot be reduced to finite-state WF-nets with resources, such as RCWF- or WFR-nets. We use graph-theoretic properties of RWF-net control automaton to prove decidability of k-soundness for marked, as well as unmarked 1-dim RWF-nets. We present also an algorithm for computing minimal k-sound resource for a given sound 1-dim RWF-net.

A preliminary version of this work has been published in [16], where decidability of 1-soundness for RWF-nets was studied. Here we have extended the obtained results to k-soundness and classical soundness.

The paper is organized as follows. In Sect. 2 basic definitions of multisets and Petri nets are given. In Sect. 3 we give definitions of sound RWF-nets. In Sect. 4 the class of 1-dim RWF-nets is defined and studied, algorithms for checking marked k-soundness, k-soundness and finding the minimal k-sound resource are given. In Sect. 5 we consider classical soundness. Section 6 contains some conclusions.

2   Preliminaries

Let S be a finite set. A *multiset* m over a set S is a mapping $m : S \to Nat$, where Nat is the set of natural numbers (including zero), i. e. a multiset may contain several copies of the same element.

For two multisets m, m' we write $m \subseteq m'$ iff $\forall s \in S : m(s) \leq m'(s)$ (the inclusion relation). The sum, the union and the subtraction of two multisets m and m' are defined as usual: $\forall s \in S : (m + m')(s) = m(s) + m'(s), (m \cup m')(s) = max(m(s), m'(s)), (m - m')(s) = m(s) \ominus m'(s)$ (where $\ominus$ denotes the truncated subtraction). By $\mathcal{M}(S)$ we denote the set of all finite multisets over S.

Non-negative integer vectors are often used to encode multisets. Actually, the set of all multisets over finite S is a homomorphic image of $Nat^{|S|}$.

We write a^k for a multiset, containing k copies of element a.

Let P and T be nonempty disjoint sets of *places* and *transitions* and let $F : (P \times T) \cup (T \times P) \to Nat$. Then $N = (P, T, F)$ is a *Petri net*. A *marking* in a Petri net is a function $M : P \to Nat$, mapping each place to some natural number (possibly zero). Thus a marking may be considered as a multiset over the set of places. A *marked net* (N, M_0) is a Petri net $N = (P, T, F)$ together with some initial marking $M_0 \in \mathcal{M}(P)$.

Pictorially, P-elements are represented by circles, T-elements by boxes, and the flow relation F by directed arcs. Places may carry tokens represented by filled circles. A current marking M is designated by putting $M(p)$ tokens into each place $p \in P$. Tokens residing in a place are often interpreted as resources of some type consumed or produced by a transition firing. A simple example, where tokens represent molecules of hydrogen, oxygen and water respectively is shown in Fig. 1.

For a transition $t \in T$ an arc (x, t) is called an *input arc*, and an arc (t, x) — an *output arc*; the *preset* $^\bullet t$ and the *postset* $t^\bullet$ are defined as the multisets over P such that $^\bullet t(p) = F(p, t)$ and $t^\bullet(p) = F(t, p)$ for each $p \in P$. A transition $t \in T$ is

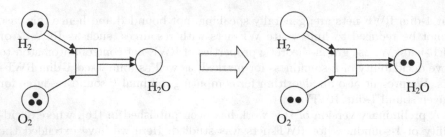

Fig. 1. A chemical reaction

enabled in a marking M iff $\forall p \in P\ M(p) \geq F(p,t)$. An enabled transition t may *fire* yielding a new marking $M' =_{def} M - {}^\bullet t + t^\bullet$, i. e. $M'(p) = M(p) - F(p,t) + F(t,p)$ for each $p \in P$ (denoted $M \xrightarrow{t} M'$, or just $M \to M'$). We say that M' is reachable from M iff there is a sequence $M = M_1 \to M_2 \to \cdots \to M_n = M'$. For a Petri net N by $\mathcal{R}(N, M_0)$ we denote the set of all markings reachable from its initial marking M_0.

3   WF-Nets with Resources

In Petri nets with resources we divide Petri net places into control and resource ones.

Definition 1. A *Petri net with resources is a tuple* $N = (P_c, P_r, T, F_c, F_r)$, *where*

- P_c *is a finite set of control places;*
- P_r *is a finite set of resource places,* $P_c \cap P_r = \emptyset$;
- T *is a finite set of transitions,* $P_c \cap T = P_r \cap T = \emptyset$;
- $F_c : (P_c \times T) \cup (T \times P_c) \to Nat$ *is a multiset of control arcs;*
- $F_r : (P_r \times T) \cup (T \times P_r) \to Nat$ *is a multiset of resource arcs;*
- $\forall t \in T\ \exists p \in P_c : F_c(p,t) + F_c(t,p) > 0$ *(each transition is incident to some control place).*

Note that all transitions are necessarily linked to control places — this guarantees the absence of "uncontrolled" resource modifications.

A marking in a Petri net with resources is also divided into control and resource parts. For a multiset $c + r$, where $c \in \mathcal{M}(P_c)$ and $r \in \mathcal{M}(P_r)$, we write $c|r$.

Definition 2. *For a net N a resource is a multiset over P_r. A controlled resource is a multiset over $P_c \cup P_r$.*

Workflow nets (WF-nets) are a special subclass of Petri nets designed for modeling workflow processes. To study resource dependencies in workflow systems we consider WF-nets with resources.

Definition 3. *A Petri net with resources N is called a* WF-net with resources *(RWF-net) iff*

1. *There is one source place $i \in P_c$ and one sink place $o \in P_c$ s. t. $^\bullet i = o^\bullet = \emptyset$;*
2. *Every node from $P_c \cup T$ is on a path from i to o, and this path consists of nodes from $P_c \cup T$.*

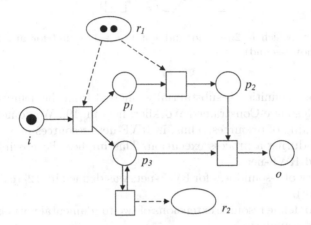

Fig. 2. WF-net with resources

Figure 2 represents an example of a RWF-net, where resource places r_1 and r_2 are depicted by ovals, resource arcs — by dotted arrows.

Every RWF-net $N = (P_c, P_r, T, F_c, F_r)$ contains its *control subnet* $N_c = (P_c, T, F_c)$, which forms a RWF-net with the empty set of resources.

A classical workflow net models a single case of a process (a single token in the input place i). In this paper we consider a more general notion that allows handling of multiple cases in the WF-net [18,19].

Definition 4. *Let $k \in \mathbf{N}$ be a natural parameter. A marked RWF-net $(N, c|r)$ is called k-sound iff*

$$\forall s \in \mathcal{M}(P_r), \ \forall M \in \mathcal{R}(N, c|r + s) \ \text{we have} \ \exists s' \in \mathcal{M}(P_r) : \ o^k|s' \in \mathcal{R}(N, M).$$

Remark 1. Note that just like in the case of RCWF-nets (Lemma 11 in [18]) this definition implies the proper completion: $c'|r' \in \mathcal{R}(N, M) \Rightarrow (c' = o^k \lor c' \cap o = \emptyset)$.

Definition 5. *An (unmarked) RWF-net N is called k-sound iff $(N, i^k|r)$ is k-sound with some $r \in \mathcal{M}(P_r)$.*

Soundness of a RWF-net means that, first, this workflow net can terminate properly from any reachable state, and, additionally, adding any extra resource does not violate the proper termination property.

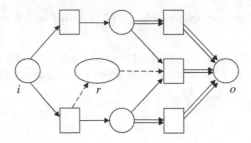

Fig. 3. RWF-net, which is $2n$-sound and not $(2n + 1)$-sound for any $n \in Nat$ (in particular it is not 1-sound)

Note that our definition is substantially different from the definition of sound RCWF-nets (Resource-Constrained Workflow net) in [19]. We do not forbid creating and spending of resources. Thus, in RWF-nets resources may be produced and consumed during a process execution. This implies the possible unboundedness of sound RWF-nets.

The property of 1-soundness for RWF-nets was defined in [12] (called resource *soundness* there).

Here we also define resource extensions of two fundamental notions of *classical* and *generalized* soundness:

Definition 6. *Let N be an (unmarked) RWF-net, $r \in \mathcal{M}(P_r)$. N is called (classical) sound with a resource r iff $(N, i|r)$ is 1–sound and, additionally, there are no dead transitions in $(N, i|r)$.*

Definition 7. *Let N be an (unmarked) RWF-net, $r, s \in \mathcal{M}(P_r)$. N is called generalized sound iff N is k-sound for any $k \in \mathbf{N}$.*

Figure 3 represents an example of an RWF-net, k-sound for some k, but not generalized sound.

Further we use k-soundness as a basic one. Classical soundness will be studied in Sect. 5, generalized soundness will be discussed in Sect. 6.

The following statement is similar to Lemma 5 in [19].

Proposition 1. *If a marked RWF-net $(N, c|r)$ is k-sound, then its control subnet (N_c, c) is also k-sound.*

Proof. The proof is by contradiction. Let $(N, c|r)$ be a k-sound RWF-net and let the net (N_c, c) be not k-sound. Then there exists a marking $c' \in \mathcal{R}(N_c, c)$, such that either the final marking o^k is not reachable from c', or $o \in c'$ and $c' \neq o^k$.

Since for the control subnet the control marking c' is reachable from the initial marking c via some sequence of firings, we can always take a resource s, sufficiently large to support the same sequence of firings for $(N, c|r + s)$ and to reach the same control state c'. If for the control subnet the final state o^k was not reachable from c', then adding resource places can't make it reachable for the net with resources $(N, c|r + s)$, in contradiction with k-soundness of $(N, c|r)$.

If otherwise $o \in c'$ and $c' \neq o^k$, then we also obtain a contradiction with k-soundness of $(N, c|r)$, since the control state c' is reachable for $(N, c|r + s)$.

The converse statement is not true: there may be RWF-nets with k-sound control subnets, for which sound resources do not exist. An example of such a net is given in Fig. 4.

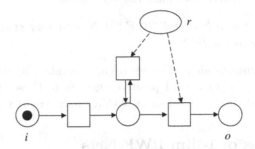

Fig. 4. RWF-net with a 1–sound control subnet, which is not 1–sound for any resource

Let N be a RWF-net. By $C^k(N)$ we denote *the set of all control markings reachable in* (N_c, i^k), i. e. $C^k(N) = \mathcal{R}(N_c, i^k)$.

Proposition 2. *If an RWF-net N is k-sound, then*

1. *for any reachable control marking $c' \in C^k(N)$ there exists a resource r', such that $(N, c'|r')$ is k-sound;*
2. *for any two control markings $c_1, c_2 \in C^k(N)$ we have $c_1 \not\subseteq c_2$ and $c_2 \not\subseteq c_1$.*

Proof. (1) Similarly to the proof of the Proposition 1 we can always take a sufficiently large initial resource $r + s$.

(2) Suppose this is not true. Assume that for some $c_1, c_2 \in C^k(N)$ we have $c_2 = c_1 + c'$ for some $c' \neq \emptyset$. From the first statement of this proposition it follows that there exist resources r_1 and r_2 s. t. RWF-nets $(N, c_1|r_1)$ and $(N, c_2|r_2)$ are k-sound. Then nets $(N, c_1|r_1 + r_2)$ and $(N, c_2|r_1 + r_2)$ are also k-sound. Thus the final marking $o^k|r'$ is reachable from the marking $c_1|r_1 + r_2$, and (due to the monotonicity property for Petri nets) the marking $o^k + c'|r'$ is reachable from the larger marking $c_2|r_1 + r_2$ — contradiction with the k-soundness for RWF-net $(N, c_2|r_1 + r_2)$.

From the second statement of Proposition 2 and the well-known Dickson's lemma we obtain the following

Corollary 1. *For a k-sound RWF-net N the set $C^k(N)$ of all its reachable control markings is finite.*

Note 1. Since the control subnet of a k-sound RWF-net N is bounded, the set $C^k(N)$ can be effectively constructed (e.g. by constructing a coverability tree).

Definition 8. *Let N be a RWF-net, $c \in C^k(N)$. We define:*

1. *$res^k(c) =_{def} \{r \in \mathcal{M}(P_r) \mid (N, c|r)$ is k-sound$\}$ — the set of all k-sound resources for c;*
2. *$mres^k(c) =_{def} \{r \in res(c) \mid \nexists r' \in res(c) : r' \subset r\}$ — the set of all minimal k-sound resources for c.*

Then from Dickson's Lemma we immediately obtain:

Proposition 3. *For any k-sound RWF-net N and any control marking $c \in C^k(N)$ the set $mres^k(c)$ is finite.*

The questions of computability of $mres^k(c)$ and decidability of k-soundness for RWF-nets remain open. In Sect. 4 positive answers to these two questions are given for a restricted case — RWF-nets with a single resource place.

4 k-Soundness of 1-dim RWF-Nets

Let $N = (P_c, P_r, T, F_c, F_r)$ be an RWF-net with $P_r = \{p_r\}$, i.e. with just one resource place. By 1-dim RWF-nets we denote the subclass of RWF-nets with single resources. An example of such a net is given in Fig. 5. In the following sections we consider only 1-dim RWF-nets.

If a control subnet of N is not k-sound, then N is also not k-sound. So, *further we assume that the control subnet of N is k-sound, and hence bounded.*

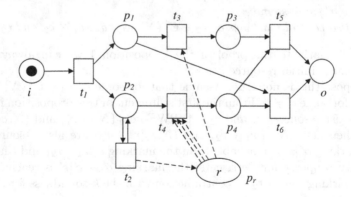

Fig. 5. 1-dim RWF-net $(N_1, i|r)$

4.1   Control Automaton

It is easy to note that a bounded control subnet can be represented as an equivalent finite automaton (a transition system). In this control automaton states (nodes) are exactly the elements of $C^k(N)$, with two distinguished nodes – a source node i^k and a sink node o^k. There is a transition (c_1, c_2) with a label t

in this automaton whenever a transition firing $c_1 \xrightarrow{t} c_2$ is possible in the control subnet of an RWF-net. Additionally, every transition t of the automaton is labeled by an integer $\delta(t)$, defining a "resource effect" of transition firing. A positive $\delta(t)$ means that the firing of t increments the marking of a (single) resource place p_r by $\delta(t)$, a negative $\delta(t)$ means that t is enabled in a state $(c|r)$ iff $r(p_r) \geq |\delta(t)|$, and that the firing of t decrements the resource by $|\delta(t)|$. Formally,

$$\delta(t) =_{\text{def}} \begin{cases} -F_r(p_r, t) & \text{for } F_r(p_r, t) > 0; \\ F_r(t, p_r) & \text{for } F_r(t, p_r) > 0. \end{cases}$$

The value $\delta(t)$ is called an *effect* of t (denoted *Eff*(t)). Note that for simplicity we exclude loops, when both $F_r(p_r, t) > 0$ and $F_r(t, p_r) > 0$; such loops can be simulated by two sequential transitions.

A *support* of t is the amount of the resources required for a firing of t. It is defined as:

$$Supp(t) =_{\text{def}} \begin{cases} 0, & \delta(t) \geq 0; \\ |\delta(t)|, & \delta(t) < 0. \end{cases}$$

Thus, an RWF-net (N, i^k) can be transformed into a control automaton $Aut^k(N)$, which can be considered as a one-counter net (e.g. [4]) or, alternatively, a 1-dim Vector Addition System with States (VASS [21]) with a specific workflow structure: one source state, one sink state, and every state is reachable from the source state, as well as the sink is reachable from every state. Note that the control automaton $Aut^k(N)$ is behaviorally equivalent to (N, i^k) in the branching-time semantics.

Consider an example depicted in Fig. 6. This is a control automaton for the 1-dim RWF-net from Fig. 5. States are denoted by octagons, labeled with the corresponding control markings of the net. Transitions are labeled with the corresponding names and effects.

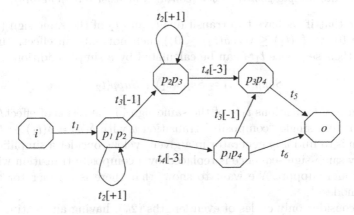

Fig. 6. Control automaton for (N_1, i)

A control automaton (a one-counter net) is a digraph with arcs labeled by integers. Recall some basic notion from graph theory.

A *walk* is an alternating sequence of nodes and arcs, beginning and ending with a node, where each node is incident to both the arc that precedes it and the arc that follows it in the sequence, and where the nodes that precede and follow an arc are the head and the tail of this arc.

We consider only non-empty walks, containing at least one arc.

A walk is *closed* if its first and last nodes coincide.

A *path* is a walk where no arcs are repeated (nodes may be repeated).

A *simple path* is a path where no nodes are repeated.

A *cycle* is a closed path.

A *simple cycle* is a closed path where no nodes are repeated (except the first/last one).

A walk in a control automaton corresponds to some sequence of firings in 1-dim RWF-net. Now we inductively define an effect and a support of a walk.

Let t be a transition and σ a walk, such that the ending node of t is the beginning node of the first transition of σ. Let $t\sigma$ denote a walk, constructed by linking t and σ. We define:

$$Eff(t\sigma) =_{\text{def}} Eff(t) + Eff(\sigma); \quad Supp(t\sigma) =_{\text{def}} Supp(\sigma) \ominus Eff(t),$$

where $\ominus$ denotes the truncated subtraction. Note that if the effect is negative, it increases the support, if it is positive, it decreases the support.

A *positive* (resp., *negative*) *walk* is a walk with a positive (resp., negative) effect. Obviously, the effect of a cycle does not depend on a choice of a starting node.

A node q is called *a positive generator*, iff there exists a simple positive path from q to q (a simple positive cycle) with a zero support.

Lemma 1. *Any simple positive cycle contains at least one generator.*

Proof. Note that if we have two transitions t_1 and t_2 of the same sign $((\delta(t_1) \geq 0 \land \delta(t_2) \geq 0) \lor (\delta(t_1) \leq 0 \land \delta(t_2) \leq 0))$ then not only an effect, but also a support of their sequence $t_1 t_2$ can be calculated by a simple addition:

$$Supp(t_1 t_2) = Supp(t_1) + Supp(t_2).$$

So a sequence of transitions $t_1 t_2$ of the same sign in the terms of effect/support is equivalent to a single "composite" transition u with $\delta(u) = \delta(t_1) + \delta(t_2)$.

Our aim is to find *any* generator in a given cycle. Consider a simplified cycle, where every same-sign sequence is replaced by a composite transition with their total effect and support. We want to show, that there is a generator amongst remaining nodes.

So, we consider only cycles of even lengths $(2k)$, having alternating positive and negative arcs. The case of $k = 1$ is obvious. Consider an arbitrary k.

First note, that for any nonnegative sequence $\sigma = t_1^+ t_1^- t_2^+ t_2^- \ldots t_k^+ t_k^-$ with $\delta(t_i^+) > 0$ and $\delta(t_i^-) < 0$ there is some $1 \leq j \leq k$ such that $\delta(t_j^+) \geq |\delta(t_j^-)|$ (otherwise $Eff(\sigma) = \sum_{i=1}^{k}(\delta(t_j^+) - |\delta(t_j^-)|) < 0$).

Consider a subsequence $\theta = t_j^+ t_j^- t_{j+1}^+$ (in the case of $j = k$ we take t_1^+ instead of t_{j+1}^+). Since the positive effect of t_j^+ is larger then the support of t_j^-, we have

$$Eff(\theta) = Eff(t_j^+) + Eff(t_j^-) + Eff(t_{j+1}^+) > 0 \quad \text{and} \quad Supp(\theta) = 0.$$

So we replace a sequence θ by a single positive transition u with $\delta(u) = \delta(t_j^+) + \delta(t_j^-) + \delta(t_{j+1}^+)$, omitting two intermediate nodes.

This transformation of a given cycle reduces its length by 2, but preserves effect and support properties. It can be repeated $k - 3$ more times, producing a cycle with two nodes and an obvious generator.

A node q is called *a negative generator*, iff there exists a simple negative path θ from q to q (a simple negative cycle), such that $Supp(\theta) = -Eff(\theta)$.

Lemma 2. *Any simple negative cycle contains at least one generator.*

Proof. The proof is similar to the previous one. Consider a cycle with alternating positive and negative arcs, represented as:

$$\sigma = t_1^+ t_1^- t_2^+ t_2^- \ldots t_k^+ t_k^-.$$

There is some $1 \leq j \leq k$ such that $\delta(t_j^+) \leq |\delta(t_j^-)|$ (otherwise $Eff(\sigma) = \sum_{i=1}^{k}(\delta(t_j^+) - |\delta(t_j^-)|) > 0$).

Consider a subsequence $\theta = t_{j-1}^- t_j^+ t_j^-$ (in the case of $j = 1$ we take t_k^- instead of t_{j-1}^-). Since the support of t_j^- is larger then the positive effect of t_j^+, we have

$$Eff(\theta) = Eff(t_{j-1}^-) + Eff(t_j^+) + Eff(t_j^-)$$

$$= -(Supp(t_{j-1}^-) + Supp(t_j^-) - Eff(t_j^+)) = -Supp(\theta).$$

So we replace a sequence θ by a single negative transition u with $\delta(u) = \delta(t_{j-1}^-) + \delta(t_j^+) + \delta(t_j^-)$, omitting two intermediate nodes. Just like in the previous lemma, this transformation reduces the length of cycle by 2, but preserves effect and support properties.

4.2 Decidability of k-Soundness for Marked Nets

Let $(N, i^k | r_0)$ be an initially marked 1-dim RWF-net. By abuse of notation we denote by N^k also the control automaton of (N, i^k), represented as a one-counter net. Recall that $i^k \in C^k(N)$ denotes the initial control state, $r_0 \in Nat$ denotes the initial value of a counter (the single resource place), and $\mathcal{R}(N, (i^k | r_0))$ denotes the set of all reachable states.

Note that a marked RWF-net $(N, i^k | r_0)$ with a k-sound control subnet is not k-sound if and only if it does not always terminate with a final control state o^k for some larger initial resource $r_0 + s$:

$$\exists(c|r) \in \mathcal{R}(N, i^k | r_0 + s) \quad \text{such that} \quad (o^k | s') \notin \mathcal{R}(N, c|r) \quad \text{for any} \quad s' \in Nat.$$

So we consider both kinds of possible undesirable (not properly terminating) behaviors of a Petri net, namely, deadlocks and livelocks.

Definition 9. *A state* $(c|r) \in C^k(N) \times Nat$ *is a* deadlock *iff* $c \neq o^k$ *and there is no transition* $t \in T$ *s.t.* $(c|r) \xrightarrow{t} (c'|r')$ *for some* c', r'.

A finite set $L \subset C^k(N) \times Nat$ *of states is a* livelock *iff*

1. $|L| > 1$;
2. *for any* $(c|r), (c'|r') \in L$ *there is a finite transition sequence* $\sigma \in T^*$ *s.t.* $(c|r) \xrightarrow{\sigma} (c'|r')$;
3. *for any* $(c|r) \in L$ *and* $t \in T$ *s.t.* $(c|r) \xrightarrow{t} (c''|r'')$ *we have* $(c''|r'') \in L$.

A livelock state *is a state that belongs to some livelock.*

Note that by definition $(o^k|r) \notin L$ for any $r;$.

Proposition 4. *If a state* $(c|r)$ *is a deadlock then for any* $t \in T$ *s.t.* $c \xrightarrow{t} c'$ *we have* $Supp(t) > r$.

Proof. Straightforward.

Note that Proposition 4 implies $\delta(t) < 0$ and hence we obtain:

Corollary 2. *If a state* $(c|r)$ *is a deadlock then:*

1. $\forall t \in T$ *s.t.* $c \xrightarrow{t} c'$ *for some* c' *we have* $\delta(t) < 0$;
2. $r < min\{|\delta(t)| : c \xrightarrow{t} c'$ *for some* $c'\}$.

So deadlocks can occur (1) just for control states with only negative outgoing transitions; (2) only for a finite number of different resources – when there are no enough resources for firing any of the successor transitions.

Proposition 5. *The set of deadlock states is finite.*

Proof. The set of "potential deadlock" control states (nodes with only negative outgoing transitions) is finite. For a given "potential deadlock" control state the set of applicable deadlock states (natural numbers smaller than the smallest required resource for a successor transition) is also finite.

Hence, all deadlocks can be detected by checking control states with only negative outgoing transitions.

Now let us consider livelocks.

Proposition 6. *If* $L \subset C^k(N) \times Nat$ *is a livelock then there is a state* $(c|r) \in L$ *and a negative transition* $t \in T$ *with* $c \xrightarrow{t} c'$, *such that* $\delta(t) < -r$.

Proof. Straightforward, since the control subnet of RWF-net N is k-sound.

Proposition 7. *The set of livelocks is finite.*

Proof. First note that if $(c|r), (c|r + x) \in L$ with $x > 0$ then L is not a livelock. Indeed, in this case the transition sequence $(c|r) \xrightarrow{\sigma} (c|r + x)$ corresponds to a positive cycle that can generate an infinite number of states — a contradiction with the finiteness of the number of livelocks. So, every control state can occur in a given livelock at most once.

Now assume the converse: there are infinitely many livelocks. Then there are infinitely many livelocks with the same set of control states, which differ only in their resource value. Hence, this set includes a livelock with an arbitrarily large resource, and we can take a livelock with a resource big enough to reach the final state o^k. This implies that o^k belongs to the livelock — a contradiction with the definition of a livelock.

Thus, all livelocks can be easily detected by checking finite systems of states, closed under transition firings (strongly connected components) and satisfying the property from Proposition 6.

Theorem 1. *k-soundness is decidable for marked 1-dim RWF-nets.*

Proof. The following proof is similar to the proof of decidability of structural soundness in [25]

For a given 1-dim RWF-net N construct the modified RWF-net $\overline{N}$ by adding a new initial place $\overline{i}$, a new intermediate place u and three new transitions, as depicted in Fig. 7. The original 1-dim RWF-net $(N, i^k|r)$ is k-sound iff neither deadlocks nor livelocks are reachable in 1-dim RWF-net $(\overline{N}, \overline{i}^k|r)$ (otherwise some sufficiently large initial resource would produce the same undesirable situation in the given net N).

Since the sets of deadlocks and livelocks are finite and computable, the problem of k-soundness of a marked 1-dim RWF-net can be reduced to a finite number of instances of a reachability problem for a 1-counter Petri net. This reachability problem is decidable.

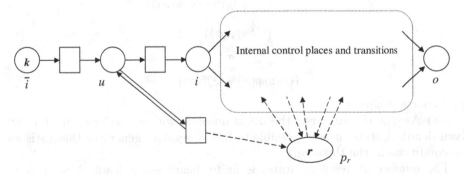

Fig. 7. Modified RWF-net $\overline{N}$

4.3   Decidability of k-Soundness for Unmarked Nets

Theorem 1 gives us only a semidecision procedure for k-soundness of a net. One can check the soundness of a given initial marking, but if the answer is negative, it is not known whether there exists a larger sound resource.

Corollary 2 gives us only a necessary condition of a deadlock, reachable from *some* initial marking. Now we prove a stronger theorem, which gives a sufficient and necessary condition for existence of a soundness-violating deadlock (i.e. a deadlock that is reachable from an infinite number of different initial markings).

Theorem 2. *An unmarked 1-dim RWF-net is not k-sound with deadlocks iff there exist a deadlock state $(c|r)$, a negative generator q and a simple path $q \xrightarrow{\sigma} c$ such that $Supp(\sigma) + Eff(\sigma) \leq r$.*

Proof. ($\Leftarrow$) It is sufficient to show that for any (large enough) initial resource r_0 there exists a larger initial resource $r_0 + x$, such that a deadlock is reachable from $(i^k|r_0 + x)$.

Consider an arbitrary (large enough) initial resource r_0 s.t.

$$(i^k|r_0) \xrightarrow{\tau} (q|s)$$

for some path τ and resource s (it is always possible to find such a resource since the control net is k-sound, and therefore any control state is reachable for some sufficiently large initial resource). Let $\theta = qc_1 \ldots c_j q$ be a simple negative cycle with generator q, i.e. $Supp(\theta) = -Eff(\theta)$. Denote $z = s \bmod Supp(\theta)$ and consider a larger initial resource $r_0 + z + Supp(\sigma)$.

We have

$$(i^k|r_0 + z + Supp(\sigma))$$

$$\downarrow \tau$$

$$(q|s + z + Supp(\sigma))$$

$$\downarrow \theta^{\left((s+z)/Supp(\theta)\right)}$$

$$(q|Supp(\sigma))$$

$$\downarrow \sigma$$

$$(c|Supp(\sigma) + Eff(\sigma))$$

and hence a deadlock.

($\Rightarrow$) Assume the converse: the net is unsound with a deadlock, but for any given deadlock state, it is impossible to find a negative generator that satisfies the conditions in the theorem.

The number of deadlock states is finite, hence some deadlock state $(c|r)$ is reachable from an infinite number of different initial states (initial resource values).

Every transition sequence $\sigma = t_1.t_2.\ldots.t_n$ from $(i^k|r_0)$ to $(c|r)$ corresponds to a walk σ in the control automaton graph. Since there are infinitely many deadlock-generating initial states, the set of corresponding walks is also infinite. Each of these walks can be decomposed as:

$$\sigma = \rho(\theta)^k\tau,$$

where ρ is a path, θ is a simple cycle and τ is an acyclic simple path.

Let us show that among these walks there is a walk with a negative last cycle θ. Indeed, if the last cycle is positive (or neutral) with an effect x, we can consider a larger initial resource $r_0 + x * k_{n-1}$ and a shorter walk

$$\sigma' = \rho\tau,$$

having the same ending — a deadlock. Now, the new walk σ' can be decomposed into a path, a simple cycle and a simple path, then the last cycle, if it is positive, can be removed by increasing the initial resource, and so on. At the end of this process we will obtain either a walk with a negative "last cycle" or a completely acyclic walk (simple path from i^k to c). There are only finitely many acyclic paths in the graph, but infinitely many deadlock-generating initial markings (and hence deadlock-generating walks from i^k to c), so we necessarily obtain a walk with a negative last cycle.

Consider such a deadlock-walk σ'', ending with a suffix $\theta^k\tau$, where θ is a negative cycle and τ is acyclic. Let $\theta = c_1 c_2 \ldots c_i \ldots c_m c_1$, where c_i is a negative generator (from Lemma 2 such c_i always exists). The path $((c_i \ldots c_m c_1)\tau)$ is simple (remember that we decompose "from the right to the left" and hence $\theta\tau$ cannot contain cycles other than θ). Since the final state of the whole walk σ'' is $(c|r)$, for any suffix ϕ of σ'' we have

$$Supp(\phi) + Eff(\phi) \leq r.$$

It holds for $((c_i \ldots c_n c_1)\tau)$ as well. But this is a simple path that leads from a negative generator to a deadlock control state – Q.E.D.

A result similar to Theorem 2 is valid for livelocks:

Theorem 3. *An unmarked 1-dim RWF-net is not k-sound with livelocks iff there exist a livelock state $(c|r)$, a negative generator q and a simple path $q \xrightarrow{\sigma} c$ such that $Supp(\sigma) + Eff(\sigma) \leq r$.*

Proof. Similar to Theorem 2.

Corollary 3. *k-soundness is decidable for unmarked 1-dim RWF-nets.*

Proof. All simple (negative) cycles can be found by Tarjan algorithm, deadlock and livelock states — by searching for states, satisfying Propositions 4 and 6 respectively. The set of simple paths is finite (and easily computable).

4.4   Computability of the Minimal k-Sound Resource

Now we propose a plain (and hence, may be, not the most effective) algorithm for computing the minimal resource r such that $(N, i^k|r)$ is k-sound:

One tests k-soundness for incremented values of r until success. Note that this method can be applied only to k-sound nets, while k-soundness of the unmarked net can be checked with the algorithm given in Corollary 3.

5   Classical Soundness

Like in the previous chapter, we consider only nets with sound control subnets (now it is *classical soundness*).

It is easy to see that the additional requirement of absence of dead transitions (Definition 6) is not substantial:

Proposition 8. *N is 1-sound with a resource r iff N is (classical) sound with a resource r + s for some finite resource s.*

Proof. ($\Rightarrow$) One can take $r+s$ as a smallest 1-sound resource s.t. every transition t can be eventually enabled in $(N, i|r + s)$.

($\Leftarrow$) One can take empty s.

Hence classical soundness is decidable for 1-dim RWF-nets (both marked and unmarked), and, moreover, minimal classical sound resources can be effectively computed.

The similar reasoning is valid for all weaker notions, such as relaxed soundness [17], easy soundness [26] and lazy soundness [23].

6   Conclusion and Further Work

In this paper workflow nets with unbounded resources (RWF-nets), when resources can be generated and consumed without any restrictions, were studied. The k-soundness property for such nets means, that for some initial resource, k concurrent cases can terminate properly from any reachable state, and adding extra resources will not violate this property.

We have proven that k-soundness is decidable for the restricted case of a RWF-net with a single (unbounded) resource place (both for marked and unmarked cases), and that the minimal sound resource can be effectively computed. The decidability proof is based on representing a workflow net with an unbounded resource as a one-counter finite automaton. Structural properties of such automata were then used for checking k-soundness.

The proposed algorithms use reductions to the reachability problem for unbounded Petri nets and hence cannot be considered efficient. However, the inefficiency could be unavoidable, since RWF-nets are expressively rather close to ordinary Petri nets (VASS).

Based on the similar approach the resource extension of classical soundness was defined and proven to be decidable.

The further research will concern decidability of soundness for the general case of RWF-nets. Note, that when a RWF-net has two, or more unbounded resource places, it cannot be represented as a one-counter finite automaton. So, the technique presented here cannot be directly extended to several resources, and some new ideas are needed.

It would be also interesting to consider some other notions of soundness for infinite-state workflow nets, such as structural and generalized soundness [3].

The authors would like to thank the anonymous reviewers for their helpful comments and corrections.

References

1. van der Aalst, W.M.P.: The application of Petri Nets to workflow management. J. Circuits Syst. Comput. **8**(1), 21–66 (1998)
2. van der Aalst, W.M.P., van Hee, K.M.: Workflow Management: Models. MIT Press, Methods and Systems (2002)
3. van der Aalst, W.M.P., van Hee, K.M., ter Hofstede, A.H.M., Sidorova, N., Verbeek, H.M.W., Voorhoeve, M., Wynn, M.T.: Soundness of workflow nets: Classification, decidability, and analysis. Formal Aspects Comput. **23**(3), 333–363 (2011)
4. Abdulla, P.A., Čerans, K.: Simulation is decidable for one-counter nets. In: Sangiorgi, D., de Simone, R. (eds.) CONCUR 1998. LNCS, vol. 1466, pp. 253–268. Springer, Heidelberg (1998)
5. Barkaoui, K., Petrucci, L.: Structural analysis of workflow nets with shared resources. In: van der Aalst, W.M.P., Michelis, G., Ellis, C.A. (eds.) Proceedings of Workflow Management: Net-based Concepts, Models, Techniques and Tools (WFM'98). Computing Science Reports, vol. 98/7, pp. 82–95. Eindhoven University of Technology, Eindhoven (1998)
6. Barkaoui, K., Ben Ayed, R., Sbaï, Z.: Workflow soundness verification based on structure theory of Petri Nets. Int. J. Comput. Inf. Sci. **5**(1), 51–61 (2007)
7. Bashkin, V.A.: Formalization of semantics of systems with unreliable agents by means of nets of active resources. Programm. Comput. Softw. **36**(4), 187–196 (2010)
8. Bashkin, V.A.: Modular nets of active resources. Automatic Control Comput. Sci. **46**(1), 1–11 (2012)
9. Bashkin, V.A., Lomazova, I.A.: Petri Nets and resource bisimulation. Fundamenta Informaticae **55**(2), 101–114 (2003)
10. Bashkin, V.A., Lomazova, I.A.: Resource similarities in Petri Net models of distributed systems. In: Malyshkin, V.E. (ed.) PaCT 2003. LNCS, vol. 2763, pp. 35–48. Springer, Heidelberg (2003)
11. Bashkin, V.A., Lomazova, I.A.: Similarity of generalized resources in Petri Nets. In: Malyshkin, V.E. (ed.) PaCT 2005. LNCS, vol. 3606, pp. 27–41. Springer, Heidelberg (2005)
12. Bashkin, V.A., Lomazova, I.A.: Resource Equivalence in Workflow Nets. In: Proceedings of CS&P'2006 on Concurrency, Specification and Programming, vol. 1., pp. 80–91. Humboldt-Universitat zu Berlin, Berlin (2006)
13. Bashkin, V.A., Lomazova, I.A.: Resource driven automata nets. Fundamenta Informaticae **109**(3), 223–236 (2011)
14. Bashkin, V.A., Lomazova, I.A.: Modelling multiagent systems with the help of generalized nets of active resources. Cybern. Syst. Anal. **47**(2), 202–209 (2011)
15. Bashkin, V.A., Lomazova, I.A.: Cellular resource-driven automata. Fundamenta Informaticae **120**(3–4), 243–257 (2012)
16. Bashkin, V.A., Lomazova, I.A.: Soundness of Workflow Nets with an Unbounded Resource is Decidable. In: Joint Proceedings of PNSE'13 and ModBE'13. CEUR Workshop Proceedings, vol. 989, pp. 61–75. CEUR-WS.org (2013)
17. Dehnert, J., Rittgen, P.: Relaxed soundness of business processes. In: Dittrich, K.R., Geppert, A., Norrie, M. (eds.) CAiSE 2001. LNCS, vol. 2068, pp. 157–170. Springer, Heidelberg (2001)
18. van Hee, K.M., Sidorova, N., Voorhoeve, M.: Generalised soundness of workflow nets is decidable. In: Cortadella, J., Reisig, W. (eds.) ICATPN 2004. LNCS, vol. 3099, pp. 197–215. Springer, Heidelberg (2004)

19. van Hee, K.M., Serebrenik, A., Sidorova, N., Voorhoeve, M.: Soundness of resource-constrained workflow nets. In: Ciardo, G., Darondeau, P. (eds.) ICATPN 2005. LNCS, vol. 3536, pp. 250–267. Springer, Heidelberg (2005)
20. van Hee, K., Oanea, O., Serebrenik, A., Sidorova, N., Voorhoeve, M., Lomazova, I.A.: Checking properties of adaptive workflow nets. Fundamenta Informaticae **79**(3–4), 347–362 (2007)
21. Hopcroft, J.E., Pansiot, J.J.: On the reachability problem for 5-dimensional vector addition systems. Theor. Comput. Sci. **8**, 135–159 (1979)
22. Lomazova, I.A., Romanov, I.V.: Analyzing compatibility of services via resource conformance. Fundamenta Informaticae **128**(1–2), 129–141 (2013)
23. Puhlmann, F., Weske, M.: Interaction soundness for service orchestrations. In: Dan, A., Lamersdorf, W. (eds.) ICSOC 2006. LNCS, vol. 4294, pp. 302–313. Springer, Heidelberg (2006)
24. Sidorova, N., Stahl, C.: Soundness for resource-contrained workflow nets is decidable. IEEE Trans. Syst. Man Cybern. Syst. **43**(3), 724–729 (2013)
25. Tiplea, F.L., Marinescu, D.C.: Structural soundness of workflow nets is decidable. Inf. Process. Lett. **96**(2), 54–58 (2005)
26. van der Toorn, R.A.: Component-based software design with Petri Nets: An approach based on inheritance of behavior. Ph.D. Thesis, Eindhoven University of Technology, Eindhoven, The Netherlands (2004)

Modeling Distributed Private Key Generation by Composing Petri Nets

Luca Bernardinello[1]([⊠]), Görkem Kılınç[1],
Elisabetta Mangioni[1,2], and Lucia Pomello[1]

[1] Dipartimento di Informatica Sistemistica e Comunicazione,
Università degli studi di Milano - Bicocca,
Viale Sarca, 336 - Edificio U14, 20126 Milano, Italy
bernardinello@disco.unimib.it
[2] Istituto per la Dinamica dei Processi Ambientali,
Consiglio Nazionale delle Ricerche (CNR-IDPA),
Piazza della Scienza, 1 - Edificio U1, 20126 Milano, Italy

Abstract. We present a Petri net model of a protocol for the distributed generation of id-based private keys. Those keys can then be used for secure communications. The components of the system are built as refinements of a common interface, by applying a formal operation based on a class of morphisms between Elementary Net Systems. It is then shown that we can derive behavioural properties of the composed system without building it explicitly, by exploiting properties of the given morphisms.

Keywords: Petri nets · Morphisms · Local state refinement · Composition · Distributed private key generation

1 Introduction

In [1] we proposed a way to compose Elementary Net (EN) Systems by identifying conditions, places, and events. The identification is ruled by a pair of morphisms from the two components to an *interface*. The interface is an EN System which can be seen as specifying the protocol of interaction between components, or a common abstraction.

This framework was first defined relying on N-morphisms, originally introduced in [2,9]. Later, the same operation was defined over a new class of morphisms, called α-morphisms (see [1]).

An α-morphism from an EN System N_1 to an EN System N_2 corresponds to a relation of refinement: some subnets of N_1 refine conditions of N_2. This refinement may require that some events be duplicated. Such morphisms are defined and discussed in Sect. 3.

When composing two EN Systems, N_1 and N_2, over an interface N_I, the two morphisms towards the interface specify how each component refines parts of the interface. An uninterpreted example is given in Sect. 4.

© Springer-Verlag Berlin Heidelberg 2014
M. Koutny et al. (Eds.): ToPNoC IX, LNCS 8910, pp. 19–40, 2014.
DOI: 10.1007/978-3-662-45730-6_2

One of the claimed advantages of this approach to design is the ability to derive properties of the composed systems from properties of the components and of the morphisms, without the need to actually build and analyze the composed system.

Ideally, one would like to derive behavioral properties, like liveness and safety properties, by analyzing only the structure of the models involved, thus avoiding the potentially high cost of computing the reachable markings. This is not always possible. Hence, the method we propose uses some behavioral information about components and interface; however, this is limited to only a part of the models, and does not involve the whole system model.

Another significant advantage of α-morphisms is that model checking becomes easier provided that some additional requirements are satisfied. More detailed explanation is given in Sect. 3 and a model checking example is sketched in Sect. 6.

Here, we test these ideas on a protocol for distributed generation of id-based cryptographic keys. The protocol, described in more detail in Sect. 5, requires the cooperation of several *private key generators* (PKGs) so that a client can build a private key. Basically, n PKG nodes come together to generate a master key pair consisting of a private and a public key. After that, each PKG node has a share for the master key pair. A client who wants to have a private key applies to k available PKG nodes. Each PKG node calculates a piece of the client's private key by using the unique id-string of the client and the share of the master private key which is held by that specific PKG node. On receiving k pieces, the client continues to extract its private key. The so called bulletin board is responsible for the initialization of the components in the system and broadcasting the public parameters. During both the distributed generation of the master key pair and the extraction of the clients' private keys, a verification can be performed by using the commitment values and public keys held and broadcast by the bulletin board. The id-based distributed private key generation protocol was proposed in [3]; an improved version is presented in [4]. In [5], a Petri net model for the protocol to be implemented on industrial control systems is presented.

In the next section, basic definitions related to EN Systems are recalled. Section 3 recalls the formal definition of α-morphisms and the properties they preserve or reflect and which are used in the rest of the paper. The definition of an operation of composition of EN Systems, based on α-morphisms, is informally recalled in Sect. 4 on the basis of an uninterpreted example. In the same section, the main result relating behavioral properties of the composed system to behavioral properties of its components is recalled. Section 5 presents the distributed private key generation protocol which is modeled by Petri nets in Sect. 6. In the same section, we analyze behavioral properties of the model. The paper is closed by a short concluding section.

2   Preliminary Definitions

In this section, we recall the basic definitions of net theory, in particular Elementary Net Systems and unfoldings [11].

A *net* is a triple $N = (B, E, F)$, where B is a set of *conditions* or local states, E is a set of *events* or transitions such that $B \cap E = \emptyset$, and $F \subseteq (B \times E) \cup (E \times B)$ is the *flow relation*.

We adopt the usual graphical notation: conditions are represented by circles, events by boxes and the flow relation by arcs. The set of elements of a net will be denoted by $X = B \cup E$.

The *preset* of an element $x \in X$ is ${}^\bullet x = \{y \in X | (y, x) \in F\}$; the *postset* of x is $x^\bullet = \{y \in X | (x, y) \in F\}$; the *neighborhood* of x is given by ${}^\bullet x^\bullet = {}^\bullet x \cup x^\bullet$. These notations are extended to subsets of elements in the usual way: i.e., let $A \subseteq X$, ${}^\bullet A = \bigcup_{x \in A} {}^\bullet x$.

For any net N we denote the *in-elements* of N by ${}^\circ N = \{x \in X : {}^\bullet x = \emptyset\}$ and the *out-elements* of N by $N^\circ = \{x \in X : x^\bullet = \emptyset\}$. When in-elements or out-elements are only conditions, we call them respectively, *in-conditions* or *out-conditions*.

A net $N' = (B', E', F')$ is a *subnet* of $N = (B, E, F)$ if $B' \subseteq B, E' \subseteq E$, and $F' = F \cap ((B' \times E') \cup (E' \times B'))$. Given a subset of elements $A \subseteq X$, we say that $N(A)$ is the *subnet of N identified* by A if $N(A) = (B \cap A, E \cap A, F \cap (A \times A))$.

A *State Machine* is a connected net such that each event e has exactly one input condition and exactly one output condition: $\forall e \in E, |{}^\bullet e| = |e^\bullet| = 1$.

Elementary Net (EN) Systems are a basic system model in net theory. An *Elementary Net System* is a quadruple $N = (B, E, F, m_0)$, where (B, E, F) is a net such that B and E are finite sets, self-loops are not allowed, $\forall e \in E : {}^\bullet e \cap e^\bullet = \emptyset$, isolated elements are not allowed, and the *initial marking* is $m_0 \subseteq B$.

A subnet of an EN System N identified by a subset of conditions A and all its pre- and post-events, $N(A \cup {}^\bullet A^\bullet)$, is a *Sequential Component* of N if $N(A \cup {}^\bullet A^\bullet)$ is a State Machine and if it has only one token in the initial marking.

An EN System is *covered* by Sequential Components if every condition of the net belongs to at least a Sequential Component. In this case we say that the system is *State Machine Decomposable (SMD)*.

Let $N = (B, E, F, m_0)$ be an EN System, $e \in E$ and $m \subseteq B$. The event e is *enabled* at m, denoted $m\,[e\rangle$, if ${}^\bullet e \subseteq m$ and $e^\bullet \cap m = \emptyset$; the occurrence of e at m leads from m to m', denoted $m\,[e\rangle\,m'$, iff $m' = (m \setminus {}^\bullet e) \cup e^\bullet$. We also say that e *fires* at m.

Let ϵ denote the empty word in E^*. The firing rule is extended to sequences of events by setting $m\,[\epsilon\rangle\,m$ and $\forall e \in E, \forall w \in E^*, m\,[ew\rangle\,m' = m\,[e\rangle\,m''[w\rangle\,m'$; w is called *firing sequence*.

A subset $m \subseteq B$ is a *reachable marking* of N if there exists a $w \in E^*$ such that $m_0\,[w\rangle\,m$. The *set of all reachable markings* of N is denoted by $[m_0\rangle$.

An EN System is *contact-free* if $\forall e \in E, \forall m \in [m_0\rangle : {}^\bullet e \subseteq m$ implies $e^\bullet \cap m = \emptyset$. An EN System covered by Sequential Components is contact-free [11]. An event is called *dead* at a marking m if it is not enabled at any marking reachable from m. A reachable marking m is called *dead* if no event is enabled at m. An EN System is *deadlock-free* if no reachable marking is dead.

The semantics of an EN System can be given as its *unfolding*. The unfolding is an acyclic net, possibly infinite, which records the occurrences of its elements in all possible executions.

In order to define occurrence nets, firstly we need to define the relation #. Let $N = (B, E, F)$ be a net, and let $x, y \in X$. We say that x and y are in # relation, if there exist two distinct events $e_x, e_y \in E$ such that $e_x F^* x$, $e_y F^* y$, and ${}^\bullet e_x \cap {}^\bullet e_y \neq \emptyset$, where F^* is the reflexive and transitive closure of F.

An *occurrence net* is a net $N = (B, E, F)$ such that if $e_1, e_2 \in E, e_1{}^\bullet \cap e_2{}^\bullet \neq \emptyset$ then $e_1 = e_2$; F^* is a partial order; for any $x \in X, \{y : yF^*x\}$ is finite; $\#_N$ is irreflexive and the minimal elements with respect to F^* are conditions. Occurrence nets were introduced in [8,11].

A branching process of an EN System N is an occurrence net whose elements can be mapped to the elements of N. Let $N = (B, E, F, m_0)$ be an EN System, and $\Sigma = (P, T, G)$ be an occurrence net. Let $\pi : P \cup T \to B \cup E$ be a total map. The pair (Σ, π) is a *branching process* of N if $\pi(P) \subseteq B$, $\pi(T) \subseteq E$; π restricted to the minimal elements of Σ is a bijection on m_0; for each $t \in T$, π restricted to ${}^\bullet t$ is injective and π restricted to $t^\bullet$ is injective and for each $t \in T$, $\pi({}^\bullet t) = {}^\bullet(\pi(t))$ and $\pi(t^\bullet) = (\pi(t))^\bullet$.

The *unfolding* of an EN System N, denoted by $Unf(N)$, is the maximal branching process of N, namely the unique, up to isomorphism, branching process such that any other branching process of N is isomorphic to a subnet of $Unf(N)$. The map associated to the unfolding will be denoted u and called *folding*.

Bisimulation relations have been introduced as equivalence notions with respect to event observation [7]. The observability of events of a system is defined by using a labelling function which associates the same label to different events, when viewed as equal by an observer, and the label τ to unobservable events. Let $N = (B, E, F, m_0)$ be an EN System, $l : E \to L \cup \{\tau\}$ be a labelling function where L is the alphabet of observable actions and $\tau \notin L$ the unobservable action. Let ϵ denote the empty word both of E^* and L^*. The function l is extended to a homomorphism $l : E^* \to L^*$ in the following way:

$$l(\epsilon) = \epsilon$$

$$\forall e \in E, \forall w \in E^*, l(ew) = \begin{cases} l(e)l(w) & \text{if } l(e) \neq \tau \\ l(w) & \text{if } l(e) = \tau \end{cases}$$

The pair (N, l) is called *Labelled* EN System.

Let $m, m' \in [m_0\rangle$ and $a \in L \cup \{\epsilon\}$; then:

- a is enabled at m, denoted $m \, (a\rangle$, iff $\exists w \in E^* : l(w) = a$ and $m \, [w\rangle$;
- if a is enabled at m, then the occurrence of a can lead from m to m', denoted $m \, (a\rangle \, m'$, iff $\exists w \in E^* : l(w) = a$ and $m \, [w\rangle \, m'$.

Weak bisimulation is defined as a relation between reachable markings of Labelled EN Systems [10].

Let $N_i = (B_i, E_i, F_i, m_0^i)$ be an EN System for $i = 1, 2$, with the labelling function $l_i : E_i \rightarrow L \cup \{\tau\}$. Then (N_1, l_1) and (N_2, l_2) are *weakly bisimilar*, denoted $(N_1, l_1) \approx (N_2, l_2)$, iff $\exists r \subseteq [m_0^1\rangle \times [m_0^2\rangle$ such that:

- $(m_0^1, m_0^2) \in r$;
- $\forall (m_1, m_2) \in r, \forall a \in L \cup \{\epsilon\}$ it holds

$$\forall m_1' : m_1 (a) \, m_1' \Rightarrow \exists m_2' : m_2 (a) \, m_2' \wedge (m_1', m_2') \in r$$

and (vice versa)

$$\forall m_2' : m_2 (a) \, m_2' \Rightarrow \exists m_1' : m_1 (a) \, m_1' \wedge (m_1', m_2') \in r$$

Such a relation r is called *weak bisimulation*.

3 α-morphisms

In this section we present the formal definition of α-morphisms for State Machine Decomposable Elementary Net Systems (SMD-EN Systems) and the structural and behavioral properties that α-morphisms preserve and reflect. For a comparison of α-morphisms with other notions introduced in the literature, see [1].

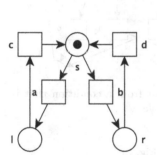 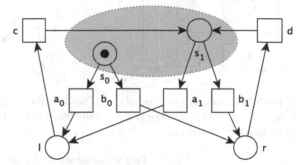

(a) An Elementary Net System

(b) Part of the bubble is not generated by one of the pre-events of the bubble

Fig. 1. A net and one of its refinements

The proposed approach is motivated by the attempt to define a refinement operation preserving behavioural properties on the basis of structural and only local behavioural constraints. The additional restrictions, with respect to general morphisms, aim, on one hand, to capture typical features of refinements, and on the other hand to ensure that some behavioural properties of the abstract model still hold in the refined model.

An α-morphism can map a subnet to a single place, which is then considered as an abstraction of that subnet. In this case, the subnet will be called a *bubble*. So, in general, the existence of an α-morphism from N_1 to N_2 means that N_1 can be seen as a refinement of N_2, where some places are replaced by more detailed subnets, or, viceversa, that N_2 is an abstraction of N_1.

The formal definition of α-morphism, given in this section, puts some restrictions on the structure and the behaviour of subnets mapped to a single place, and on the way these subnets are linked to the rest of the net. These restrictions are informally explained below, with the help of simple examples. The rest of the section comprises the related formal definitions, and deals with behavioural properties which are preserved or reflected by α-morphisms.

Regarding the restrictions mentioned above, we require that a bubble does not contain an initialization part; in Fig. 1b we can see a refinement of the net of Fig. 1a in which the bubble contains an initialization part that will be executed only once. Moreover, each final marking of the bubble must have all the possibilities of the corresponding abstract condition (for a counterexample

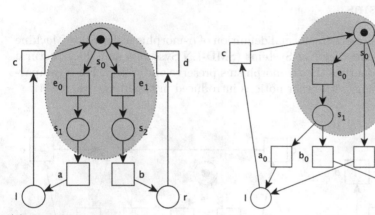

(a) Each final marking of the bubble has only part of the post-events of the abstract condition

(b) The flow can exit from a condition that is not final in the bubble

Fig. 2. Two refinements of the net of Fig. 1a

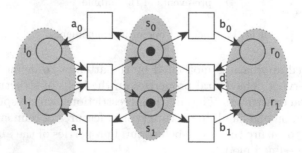

Fig. 3. A refinement of the net of Fig. 1a in which no sequential component contains all the pre- and post-events of the bubble of s

see Fig. 2a). We also do not want that a token can exit (enter) from (in) the bubble before the bubble reaches its end (after the bubble already starts) and you can see a counterexample in Fig. 2b. Finally, we require that all the pre- and post-events of a bubble must be part of the same sequential component; a counterexample is shown in Fig. 3.

The formal definition is stated as follow.

Definition 1. *Let* $N_i = (B_i, E_i, F_i, m_0^i)$ *be a SMD-EN System, for* $i = 1, 2$. *An* α-*morphism from* N_1 *to* N_2 *is a total surjective map* $\varphi : X_1 \to X_2$ *such that:*

1. $\varphi(B_1) = B_2$;
2. $\varphi(m_0^1) = m_0^2$;
3. $\forall e_1 \in E_1$, *if* $\varphi(e_1) \in E_2$, *then* $\varphi({}^\bullet e_1) = {}^\bullet\varphi(e_1)$ *and* $\varphi(e_1{}^\bullet) = \varphi(e_1){}^\bullet$;
4. $\forall e_1 \in E_1$, *if* $\varphi(e_1) \in B_2$, *then* $\varphi({}^\bullet e_1{}^\bullet) = \{\varphi(e_1)\}$;
5. $\forall b_2 \in B_2$
   (a) $N_1(\varphi^{-1}(b_2))$ *is an acyclic net;*
   (b) $\forall b_1 \in {}^\circ N_1(\varphi^{-1}(b_2))$, $\varphi({}^\bullet b_1) \subseteq {}^\bullet b_2$ *and* $({}^\bullet b_2 \neq \emptyset \Rightarrow {}^\bullet b_1 \neq \emptyset)$;
   (c) $\forall b_1 \in N_1(\varphi^{-1}(b_2)){}^\circ$, $\varphi(b_1{}^\bullet) = b_2{}^\bullet$;
   (d) $\forall b_1 \in \varphi^{-1}(b_2) \cap B_1$,
       $(b_1 \notin {}^\circ N_1(\varphi^{-1}(b_2)) \Rightarrow \varphi({}^\bullet b_1) = \{b_2\})$ *and* $(b_1 \notin N_1(\varphi^{-1}(b_2)){}^\circ \Rightarrow \varphi(b_1{}^\bullet) = \{b_2\})$;
   (e) $\forall b_1 \in \varphi^{-1}(b_2) \cap B_1$, *there is a sequential component* N_{SC} *of* N_1 *such that* $b_1 \in B_{SC}$ *and* $\varphi^{-1}({}^\bullet b_2{}^\bullet) \subseteq E_{SC}$.

We require that the map is total and surjective because N_1 refines the abstract model N_2, and any abstract element must be related to its refinement.

In particular, a subset of nodes can be mapped on a single condition $b_2 \in B_2$; in this case, we will call *bubble* the subnet identified by this subset, and denote it by $N_1(\varphi^{-1}(b_2))$; if more than one element is mapped on b_2, we will say that b_2 is *properly refined* by φ.

As we show also in Figs. 4 and 5, in-conditions and out-conditions have different constraints, 5b and 5c respectively. As required by 5c, choices which are internal to a bubble cannot constrain a final marking of that bubble: i.e., each out-condition of the bubble must have the same choices of the condition it refines. Instead, pre-events do not need this strict constraint (5b): hence it is sufficient that pre-events of any in-condition are mapped on a subset of the pre-events of the condition it refines. Moreover, the conditions that are internal to a bubble must have pre-events and post-events which are all mapped to the refined condition b_2, as required by 5d. For example, in this particular case, we know that the choice between e_1 and f_1 of Fig. 4 is made before the bubble, and this is implied also by the requirement 5e on sequential components. Moreover, the conditions that are internal to a bubble must have pre-events and post-events which are all mapped to the refined condition b_2, as required by 5d, see also Fig. 6.

By requirement 5e, events in the neighbourhood of a bubble are not concurrent, and the same holds for their images. Within a bubble, there can be concurrent events; however, post-events are in conflict, and firing one of them

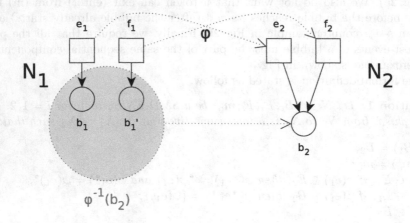

Fig. 4. Pre-events of an in-condition

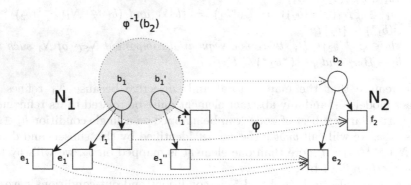

Fig. 5. Post-events of an out-condition

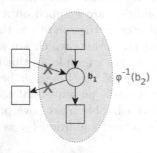

Fig. 6. Constraints on an internal condition

will empty the bubble [6]. Moreover, given that a bubble can be abstracted by a single condition no input event of a bubble is enabled whenever a token is within the bubble [6].

By the combined effect of 5a–5e, in any execution, when a post-event of a bubble fires, in the next marking no local state within the bubble will be marked.

Note that cycles outside the bubbles are preserved and reflected by the morphism: this is given by the finiteness of a Petri Net and by the constraints on the environment of a node.

It is possible to show that the family of SMD-EN Systems together with α-morphisms forms a category [6].

In [1,6] structural and behavioral properties preserved or reflected by α-morphisms has been studied. In particular, sequential components are reflected in the sense that the inverse image of a sequential component is covered by sequential components and α-morphisms preserve reachable markings.

Moreover, stronger properties hold under additional constraints. In order to present them, we have to consider the following construction. Given an α-morphism $\varphi : N_1 \to N_2$, and a condition $b_2 \in B_2$ with its refinement, we define two new auxiliary SMD-EN Systems. The first one, denoted $S_1(b_2)$, contains the following elements: a copy of the subnet which is the refinement of b_2, i.e.: the bubble; its pre- and post-events in E_1 and two new conditions, denoted b_1^{in} and b_1^{out}. b_1^{in} is pre-condition of all the pre-events, and b_1^{out} is post-condition of all the post-events. The initial marking of $S_1(b_2)$ will be $\{b_1^{in}\}$ or, if there are no pre-events, the initial marking of the bubble in N_1. The second system, denoted $S_2(b_2)$, contains b_2, its pre- and post-events and two new conditions: b_2^{in}, which is pre-condition of all the pre-events, and b_2^{out}, which is post-condition of all the post-events. The initial marking of $S_2(b_2)$ will be $\{b_2^{in}\}$ or, if there are no pre-events, the initial marking of b_2. Define φ^S as a map from $S_1(b_2)$ to $S_2(b_2)$, which restricts φ to the elements of $S_1(b_2)$, and extends it with $\varphi^S(b_1^{in}) = b_2^{in}$ and $\varphi^S(b_1^{out}) = b_2^{out}$. Note that $S_1(b_2)$ and $S_2(b_2)$ are SMD-EN Systems and that φ^S is an α-morphism. Let $Unf(S_1(b_2))$ be the unfolding of $S_1(b_2)$, with folding function $u : Unf(S_1(b_2)) \to S_1(b_2)$.

Consider the following additional constraints:

c1 the initial marking of each bubble is at the start of the bubble itself; formally, for each $b_2 \in B_2$ one of the following conditions hold:
 – $\varphi^{-1}(b_2) \cap m_0^1 = \emptyset$ or
 – if ${}^\bullet b_2 \neq \emptyset$ then there is $e_1 \in \varphi^{-1}({}^\bullet b_2)$ such that $\varphi^{-1}(b_2) \cap m_0^1 = e_1{}^\bullet$ or
 – if ${}^\bullet b_2 = \emptyset$ then $\varphi^{-1}(b_2) \cap m_0^1 = {}^\circ\varphi^{-1}(b_2)$;

c2 any condition is refined by a subnet such that, when a final marking is reached, this one enables events which correspond to the post-events of the refined condition, i.e.: $\varphi^S \circ u$ is an α-morphism from $Unf(S_1(b_2))$ (in which we put a token in the in-condition of the net) to $S_2(b_2)$;

c3 different bubbles do not "interfere" with each other, where we say that two bubbles interfere with each other when their images share at least a neighbour.

Note that the third constraint is not restrictive since the refinement of two interfering conditions can be done in two different steps.

Under **c1**, **c2**, and **c3**, the following properties can be proved [6]:

p1 reachable markings of N_2 are reflected:
   for all $m_2 \in [m_0^2\rangle$, there is $m_1 \in [m_0^1\rangle$ such that $\varphi(m_1) = m_2$;
p2 N_1 and N_2 are weakly bisimilar:
   by using φ, define two labelling functions, l_1 and l_2, such that E_2 are all observable, i.e.: l_2 is the identity function, and l_1 is defined as follows: $\forall e \in E_1 : l_1(e) = \varphi(e)$ if $\varphi(e) \in E_2$, $l_1(e) = \tau$ if $\varphi(e) \in B_2$.
   Then (N_1, l_1) and (N_2, l_2) are weakly bisimilar $(N_1, l_1) \approx (N_2, l_2)$.

As a result of property **p1**, modeling a system by refinement has an important advantage in model checking. Since reachable markings of N_2 is reflected by φ, model checking for some properties can be done on N_2 instead of N_1. Having an α-morphism from N_1 to N_2, if the additional constraints defined above hold, we get weak bisimulation between N_1 and N_2 as stated in property **p2**. One of the results of weak bisimulation is that the two nets preserve some properties like deadlock-freeness. Thus, one can deduce that the refined net N_1 is deadlock-free iff N_2 is deadlock-free.

4   Composition Based on α-morphisms

In this section, we recall the composition of SMD-EN Systems based on α-morphisms as defined in [1], on the basis of an example given in Fig. 7.

The two systems to be composed must be mapped onto a common *interface*, which is another SMD-EN System. The interface can be seen, intuitively, as a protocol of interaction, with which the components must comply, or as a common abstraction; in this second view, each component can refine some parts of the common abstraction. The two α-morphisms, from the components to the interface, determine how the two components refine the local states of the interface, and then which elements are to be identified and which events in the two components have to synchronize.

In order to be composed, two net systems must be *canonical* with respect to the corresponding morphisms towards the interface. We say that a net system is canonical with respect to an α-morphism if each bubble contains a condition, called *representation*, that corresponds to the abstraction of that bubble. Examples of representations are $r_{N_1}(b_1)$ and $r_{N_2}(b_0)$ in Fig. 7. If a system is not canonical, it is always possible to construct its unique (up to isomorphism) canonical version by adding the missing representations, and marking them as their images, or by deleting the multiple ones. Because of the constraints on α-morphisms, and in particular of the ones on sequential components, point 5e of Definition 1, this construction does not modify the behavior of the original system and the corresponding modified morphism is still an α-morphism.

In the example given in Fig. 7 the interface N_I is a simple sequence of two events. The two components, N_1 and N_2, refine two different local states, b_1 and b_0, each one by a subnet, shown on a gray background.

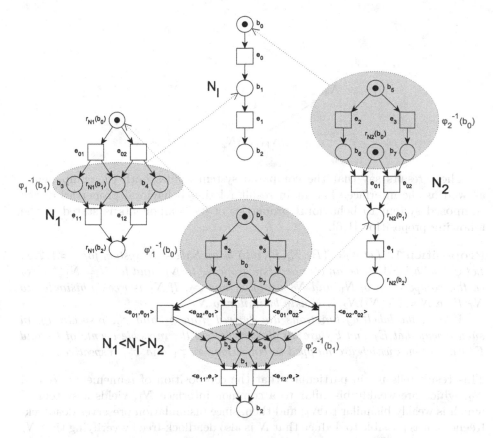

Fig. 7. An example of composition based on α-morphisms

The composed net $N = N_1\langle N_I\rangle N_2$ contains the refinement of each condition of the interface as it is in the two components, but for the representation, plus the condition itself, as we can see for condition b_0 and b_1 of the example. The rest of the net, not refined by the components, is taken as it is, but for the synchronizations of the events in the neighborhood of the refinements/bubbles. Such events must be synchronized so that each possible pair composed by one event of a component and one event of the other component must be created, as we can see for events mapped on events e_0 and e_1 of Fig. 7. Then, also arcs between in- and out-conditions of each bubble and its synchronized pre- and post-events must be created accordingly to the components. The initial marking is the union of the ones in the components. By construction, $N = N_1\langle N_I\rangle N_2$ is an EN System, and it is covered by sequential components [6].

This construction leads to the definition of a map φ_i' from $N = N_1\langle N_I\rangle N_2$ onto N_i, $i = 1, 2$, relating each element local to a component to the corresponding representation and projecting synchronized events. In [6] it is proved that this map is an α-morphism and that the following diagram commutes.

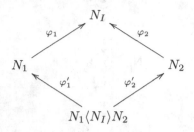

These results say that the composed system refines both the components, as well as the interface. The main result relating behavioral properties of the composed system to behavioral properties of its components is stated in the following proposition [1,6].

Proposition 1. *Let $N_i = (B_i, E_i, F_i, m_0^i)$ be an SMD-EN System for $i = 1, 2, I$. Let φ_i, with $i = 1, 2$, be an α-morphism from N_i to N_I, and let $N = N_1\langle N_I\rangle N_2$ be the composition of N_1 and N_2 using φ_1 and φ_2. If N_1 is weakly bisimilar to N_I then $N = N_1\langle N_I\rangle N_2$ is weakly bisimilar to N_2.*

Where, the labelling functions are derived from φ_1 and φ_2', respectively, in such a way that E_I and E_2 are all observable and the invisible events of E_1 and E are the ones which are mapped to conditions by φ_1 and φ_2', respectively.

This result tells us, in particular, that the composition of refinements N_1 and N_2, which are weakly bisimilar to a common interface N_I, yields a system N which is weakly bisimilar to N_I; and then, since bisimulation preserves deadlock-freeness, it is possible to deduce that N is also deadlock-free by verifying that N_I is deadlock-free. Remember that by **p2** it is possible to check weak bisimilarity between two systems related by an α-morphism by considering their behavior only locally, as required by **c1**, **c2**, and **c3**.

5   Distributed Private Key Generation for id-Based Cryptography

In an id-based cryptographic system, unlike in the other public key cryptographic systems, a publicly known string such as e-mail address, domain name, a physical IP address or a combination of more than one string is used as public key. The idea of id-based cryptography was first proposed by Shamir in [12]. The proposed scheme enables users to communicate securely and to verify signatures without exchanging any private or public key. Consequently, there is no need for a certification authority to verify the association between public keys and users.

Basically, in an id-based cryptographic system there is a private key generator (PKG) which generates private keys for users. A PKG has a key pair which is referred to as *master key pair* consisting of a master private key and a master public key. A PKG generates a private key for a user by first hashing the user's publicly known unique identity string, then signing the hashed id by the master private key. Later, the user can verify its key by using the master public key.

Since the PKG can generate private keys for users, it can sign or decrypt a message for any user or it can make users' private keys public. This is called the key escrow problem. Distributed private key generation (DPKG) is one of the effective solutions to the key escrow problem. In the schemes presented in [3,4], secret sharing methods are used for distributing private key generation among multiple PKGs.

In a DPKG, a number of PKG nodes equally share the responsibility. In our work we followed the identity based distributed private key generation schemes presented in [3,4]. For more details about the algorithms and the terminology it is recommended to refer to these citations.

The components of a DPKG system are divided into two main groups as PKG nodes and clients. PKG nodes are responsible for generating private keys for clients in a distributed manner. There is also an auxiliary component called bulletin board which is responsible for managing the global system variables, collecting the commitments from PKG nodes, calculating the final commitment and broadcasting all commitments.

We can examine the DPKG protocol in three steps: setup, distribution and extraction. Setup is a preparation step to create the system parameters and to get ready for extracting the master key pair distributively and for extracting the private keys. In this step, the bulletin board is given a security parameter and chooses some system variables according to this given security parameter; it then broadcasts public system parameters to be used by the other system components. It also initializes the commitment values to zero in order to set them to the values it will receive from PKG nodes in the distribution step. The final commitment is also set to zero; it will be calculated using the received commitments and will be broadcast later.

In the distribution step, n PKG nodes create a master private key together without using any dealer in such a way that the key cannot be reconstructed without retrieving k shares from these n PKGs. k is the threshold number of PKG nodes needed to collaborate together in order to construct the key. To do this, an improved version of (n, k) Feldman's secret sharing scheme stated in [4] is used. The idea behind secret sharing without a dealer is to make each PKG node create a secret of their own and calculate subshares to distribute among other PKG nodes. At the end, each PKG node will have n subshares including the one it calculated for itself. The sum of these subshares will be the share of the PKG node for the master private key. During the calculation of the subshares each PKG node also creates commitments corresponding to the subshares calculated by them. These commitments are sent to the bulletin board to be used by the PKG nodes for the verification of the received subshares. Note that in this DPKG system none of the PKG nodes knows the master secret key since each of them has only a part of it.

In the extraction step, a client with identity string ID contacts k available nodes from the PKG nodes pool. Each PKG_i signs the hashed identity string of the client with its master private key share and returns a private key piece as $s_i\mathrm{H}(ID)$ over a secure and authenticated channel. After receiving k pieces from k available PKG nodes, the client constructs its private key. The client can verify the key by using bilinear pairings as stated in [4,5].

6   The Model of DPKG

In this section, we present a Petri net model of a simplified DPKG system with three PKG nodes while the threshold number is two. We fixed these numbers for the sake of simplicity but the generated model is more generic and can easily be modified for different threshold and PKG node number as it will be discussed through this section. Our model consists of the following three nets: N_I, N_{PKG} and N_C. N_I is the common interface between N_{PKG} and N_C. It is an abstract model of the whole system which represents the interaction between the main components of the system. This model also includes the abstract behavior of the bulletin board which is basically responsible for managing the global system variables and commitments. N_{PKG} is the net representing the behavior of PKG nodes while N_C is the net representing the behavior of clients in the DPKG system. We aim to compose N_{PKG} and N_C using N_I as the common interface and prove that the composed net $N_{PKG}\langle N_I \rangle N_C$ and the interface N_I preserve and reflect some properties presented in Sect. 3 since there is an α-morphism both from N_{PKG} to N_I and from N_C to N_I.

The net N_I, which represents the interface, is given in Fig. 8. This net is an abstract model of the behavior of all three system components: bulletin board, PKG nodes and clients. The system is idle in the beginning. After event *init* occurs, system components are initialized and all PKG nodes are ready for generating a secret key in a distributed way. The event *init* includes the setup step of the protocol which is explained in Sect. 5. The condition *calculate shares* represents the whole process including calculating subshares and exchanging between PKG nodes in order to calculate their shares for the master private key. During this, each PKG node chooses a secret polynomial. It calculates the commitment corresponding to its secret polynomial and sends it to the bulleting board. It also calculates n subshares using its polynomial where n is the number of PKG nodes in the system. Each PKG node sends the subshare to the related PKG node. After exchanging is completed, each PKG node will have $n-1$ subshares sent by other PKG nodes and one subshare of its own. By using these n subshares each PKG node calculates its share. When the condition *shares calculated* becomes true, it means that all the PKG nodes finished calculating share and each of them is holding a share.

Once PKG nodes have their shares, they can verify their shares using the final commitment value which is already calculated during the abstract event *calculate shares*. If all the shares are correctly verified, the condition *shares verified* becomes true so a client can apply for extracting a private key. In this model, event *apply* includes choosing k available PKG nodes, receiving k pieces and calculating its private key using these pieces. When the condition *key* is

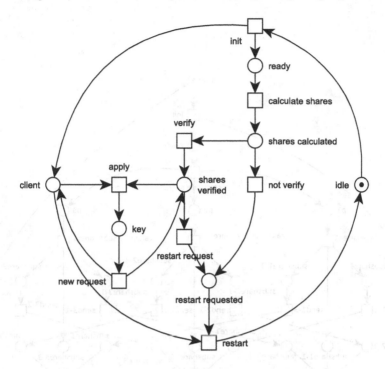

Fig. 8. N_I, the net representing the interface.

true, the client has a key but we do not know if the key is correct or not by look-
ing in this abstract model. In both cases *new request* event can occur then the
system can continue with a restart which repeats the whole distributed private
key generation. In case of a fail during the verification of shares, the system is
forced to a restart without a key extraction.

N_I is a live and reversible net which means that from any reachable marking
one can always get back to the initial state. These two properties are important
because a DPKG system must always be alive to respond to the clients' key
requests and key generation process must be restartable whenever it is needed.
The net N_I is also covered by sequential components which is a requirement in
order to be able to look for an α-morphism. The sequential components covering
the net can be shown as lists of conditions: {*idle, ready, shares calculated, shares
verified, key, restart requested*}, {*idle, client, key*}.

Figure 9 shows the net N_{PKG}. This net refines the interface with respect to
PKG nodes' behavior. All the elements of N_{PKG} are mapped to the element
with the same name in N_I but for the subnet circled by dashed line that is
mapped to a single condition. This subnet forms a bubble which is a refinement
of the condition *shares calculated* in N_I. The bubble shows the calculation and
exchange of subshares between three PKG nodes and calculation of shares by
each PKG node whereas in N_I the occurrence of the whole process is abstracted

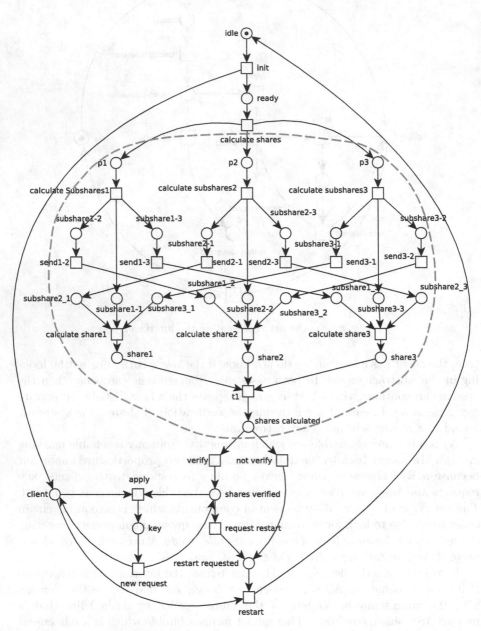

Fig. 9. N_{PKG}, the net representing the PKG nodes.

by one condition. If we model a system with n PKG nodes instead of three nodes, only the bubble will grow, the other elements of the net will remain the same.

N_{PKG} is also live, reversible and covered by sequential components like N_I. It is already shown that the conditions outside the bubble are covered by sequential components. Thus, here we will only show how the bubble is covered by sequential components. After event *calculate shares* the net branches into three paths and after each event *calculate subshares i* for $i = 1, 2, 3$ the net branches again into three paths. This fact results in having nine sequential components inside the bubble. Here we present only some of the sequential components as the lists of conditions that construct the components: {*p1, subshare 1-2, subshare 1_2, share 2, shares calculated*}, {*p1, subshare 1-1, share 1, shares calculated*}, {*p1, subshare 1-3, subshare 1_3, share 3, shares calculated*}. The paths starting with conditions *p2* and *p3* can also be constructed in the same way.

In order to prove that there is an α-morphism from N_{PKG} to N_I we have to show that the requirements in Definition 1 are satisfied. To begin with, the initial states of N_{PKG} and N_I are related. For all the events in N_{PKG} which are mapped to an event in N_I, also the pre-conditions and post-conditions of these events are mapped to the pre- and post-conditions of the related events in N_I. Moreover, for all the events in N_{PKG} that are mapped to a condition in N_I, all the pre- and post-conditions of that event are also mapped to the same condition in N_I. We see that the nets satisfy the first four requirements of α-morphism. To continue with, we can see that the bubble in N_{PKG} is acyclic so 5a is satisfied. As seen in Fig. 9 all the in-elements of the bubble are generated by the only one event entering the bubble which is mapped to the corresponding event in the interface, *calculate shares*. It is also seen that post-events of the out-condition of the bubble are exactly the same post-events of the corresponding condition in the interface. Thus, 5b and 5c are satisfied. 5d is also satisfied because the conditions that are internal to the bubble have pre-events and post-events which are all mapped to the refined condition *shares calculated* in N_I but for in- and out-elements. Finally, as we already listed the sequential components of the net, it is easy to see that for each condition of the bubble there is a sequential component containing that condition and all the pre- and post-events of the bubble, so requirement 5e is satisfied. In this way, we proved that there is an α-morphism from N_{PKG} to N_I.

The net shown in Fig. 10, N_C, is the net representing the behavior of a client. While it includes the whole abstract model, it refines the key extraction process of a client. The bubble shown with a dashed line is the refinement of the condition *key* in the interface N_I. In this refinement, receiving two pieces from chosen PKG nodes, calculating the private key and verification of it, is modeled in more details. In a DPKG system where the threshold number is two, when a client applies for a private key, it receives two pieces from two available PKG nodes. The client can verify the pieces it received. If both pieces are verified then the client can extract its private key by using these pieces and the system reaches a state where extraction is successful. In case at least one of the pieces are not verified then the condition *extraction not successful* becomes true. After

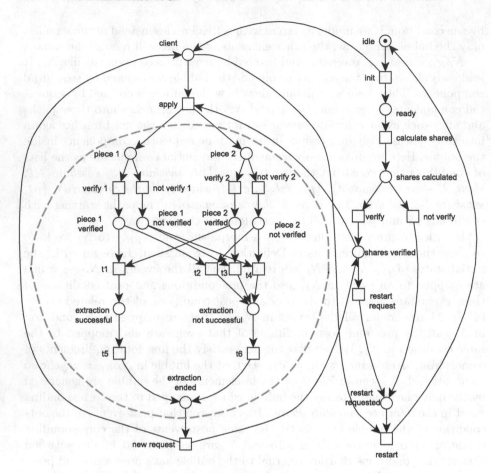

Fig. 10. N_C, the net representing the clients.

both failed or successful extraction, the system reaches a state where *extraction
ended* is true and a new key can be requested by the same client or by any other
client in the system. Again if we improve the model for threshold value k instead
of two, only the bubble will grow but the other elements of the net will remain
the same.

This net is also live, reversible and covered by sequential components. Here
we give the sequential components which are enough to cover the net as lists of
conditions: {*idle, ready, shares calculated, shares verified, piece 1, piece 1 verified, piece 1 not verified, extraction successful, extraction not successful, extraction
ended, restart requested*}, {*idle, ready, shares calculated, shares verified, piece 2,
piece 2 verified, piece 2 not verified, extraction successful, extraction not successful,
extraction ended, restart requested*}, {*client, idle, piece 1, piece 1 verified, piece 1
not verified, extraction successful, extraction not successful, extraction ended*}.

It is very easy to see that the first four requirements of α-morphism are
already satisfied so we can continue with checking the rest of the requirements.

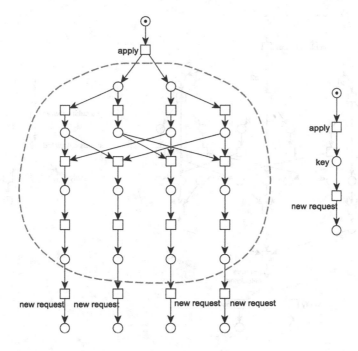

Fig. 11. $Unf(S_C(key))$ and $S_I(key)$

The bubble contains no cycles so 5a of Definition 1 is satisfied. All the in-elements of the bubble are generated by the only one event entering the bubble which is mapped to the corresponding event in the interface, *apply*. There is also only one post-event of out-condition of the bubble which empties the bubble and this event is mapped to the post-event of *key*. With these observation it is easy to see that (with reference to Definition 1) 5b and 5c are satisfied. 5d is also satisfied because the conditions that are internal to the bubble have pre-events and post-events which are all mapped to the refined condition *key* in N_I but for in- and out-elements.

Finally, as we already listed the sequential components of the net, it is easy to see that for each condition of the bubble there is a sequential component containing that condition and all the pre- and post-events of the bubble, so requirement 5e of Definition 1 is satisfied. Considering all the requirements, we can say that there is an α-morphism between N_C and N_I.

Now that we proved that there is an α-morphism both from N_{PKG} to N_I and from N_C and N_I, we can prove that the composed net is weakly bisimilar to the interface by showing that the additional requirements which are stated as **c1**, **c2**, and **c3** in Sect. 3 are satisfied by N_{PKG} and N_C. Proposition 1 states that if both of the components are weakly bisimilar to the interface, then the composed net is also weakly bisimilar to the interface. Thus, here we first show that N_C is weakly bisimilar to the interface N_I. To do this, we follow the construction of the two auxiliary nets given in Sect. 3, i.e., we consider the bubble in N_C and the

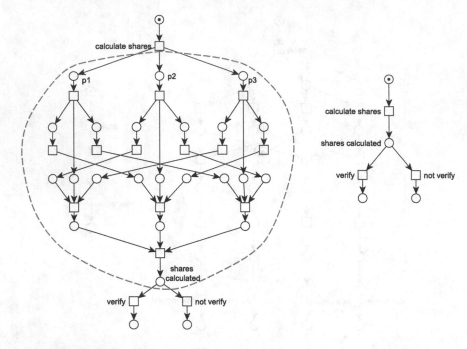

Fig. 12. $Unf(S_{PKG}(shares\,calculated))$ and $S_I(shares\,calculated)$

corresponding condition *key* in N_I and we add their pre- and post-events to the subnets. We also add two more conditions to each subnet: one condition to be a pre-condition to all pre-events and another condition to be a post-condition to all post-events. Let us name these two subnets as $S_C(key)$ and $S_I(key)$. Finally, we build the unfolding of $S_C(key)$, represented as $Unf(S_C(key))$. The resulting nets are shown in Fig. 11.

We follow the same procedure for N_{PKG} and we get two subnets $Unf(S_{PKG}$ $(shares\,calculated))$ and $S_I(shares\,calculated)$ as in Fig. 12. When we examine these subnets, we see that no condition of the bubbles is in the initial marking. Any condition is refined by a subnet such that, when a final marking is reached, this one enables events which correspond to the post-events of the refined condition, and there is an α-morphism both from $Unf(S_C(key))$ to $S_I(key)$ and from $Unf(S_{PKG}(shares\,calculated))$ to $S_I(shares\,calculated)$. Thus, **c1** and **c2** are satisfied. Since there is only one bubble in both N_{PKG} and N_C, **c3** is automatically satisfied. Consequently, we can say that the additional properties **p1** and **p2** hold. The validity of these properties allows us to conclude that N_{PKG} and N_C are weakly bisimilar to N_I and, by considering Proposition 1, also that the composed net $N_{PKG}\langle N_I\rangle N_C$ is weakly bisimilar to N_I. This fact, together with the one that our nets satisfy the requirements of α-morphisms and the other three additional constraints, allows us to infer important behavioural properties of both the components N_{PKG} and N_C and of the composed net $N_{PKG}\langle N_I\rangle N_C$. In particular, being N_I live and reversible, we can directly conclude that also

N_{PKG}, N_C and $N_{PKG}\langle N_I \rangle N_C$ are live and reversible. Moreover, the property **p1** of reflecting reachable markings allows us to solve some reachability problems in the composed net by analyzing corresponding reachability problems in the interface which is advantageous with respect to computational cost. To give an example, we can consider the existence of the following situation in the composed net $N_{PKG}\langle N_I \rangle N_C$: the condition *shares verified* should not be true while there is at least one token in a bubble. Performing a reachability analysis on the composed net is complex in terms of time and space since both the net and the logic formula we have to use to represent the global state to be investigated are big. Instead, the mentioned global state can be easily translated into a global state of the interface, N_I. Since each bubble in the composed net is mapped to a condition in the interface, reachability analysis becomes easier. The previously mentioned critical situation is reflected in the interface as the following: the condition *shares verified* cannot be true while *key* or *shares calculated* is true. Performing a reachability analysis for existence of this situation in N_I is easier than analyzing the composed net. Moreover, we do not even need to build the composed net.

7 Conclusion

We have developed a Petri net model of a protocol for distributed generation of private keys. The model has been obtained by composing two net models on a common interface. The first component models the interactions among PKG nodes, while the second component models clients of the key generator. Both components refine a common interface, representing the interactions among components.

We have then discussed behavioral properties of the model, directly derivable from properties of the components without generating the composed net. In particular, we have shown that some markings are not reachable.

On one hand, we have verified modeling and analysis capacity of the compositional approach proposed in [1] by means of a real world example. We have showed some advantages of α-morphisms in modeling and model checking. On the other side, we have proposed a model of distributed private key generation protocol by using the compositional approach.

We now plan to explore how to extend the approach to other classes of Petri nets, particularly P/T nets and high-level nets. With respect to the model, we plan to improve it giving a less abstract specification in order to propose a formal verification of the protocol and to discuss its weak and strong aspects.

Acknowledgements. This work was partially supported by MIUR and by MIUR - PRIN 2010/2011 grant 'Automi e Linguaggi Formali: Aspetti Matematici e Applicativi', code H41J12000190001.

References

1. Bernardinello, L., Mangioni, E., Pomello, L.: Local state refinement and composition of elementary net systems: an approach based on morphisms. In: Koutny, M., van der Aalst, W.M.P., Yakovlev, A. (eds.) ToPNoC VIII. LNCS, vol. 8100, pp. 48–70. Springer, Heidelberg (2013)
2. Bernardinello, L., Monticelli, E., Pomello, L.: On preserving structural and behavioural properties by composing net systems on interfaces. Fundam. Inform. **80**(1–3), 31–47 (2007)
3. Boneh, D., Franklin, M.K.: Identity-based encryption from the weil pairing. SIAM J. Comput. **32**, 586–615 (2003)
4. Kate, A., Goldberg, I.: Asynchronous distributed private-key generators for identity-based cryptography. IACR Cryptology ePrint Archive 2009, 355 (2009)
5. Kilinc, G., Fovino, I.N., Ferigato, C., Koltuksuz, A.: A model of distributed key generation for industrial control systems. In: 11th Workshop on Discrete Event Systems, Guadalajara, Mexico, vol. 11, pp. 356–363 (2012)
6. Mangioni, E.: Modularity for system modelling and analysis. Ph.D. thesis, Universitá degli Studi di Milano-Bicocca, Dottorato di ricerca in Informatica, ciclo 24 (2013)
7. Milner, R.: Communication and Concurrency. Prentice-Hall Inc., Upper Saddle River (1989)
8. Nielsen, M., Plotkin, G.D., Winskel, G.: Petri nets, event structures and domains, part i. Theor. Comput. Sci. **13**, 85–108 (1981)
9. Nielsen, M., Rozenberg, G., Thiagarajan, P.S.: Elementary transition systems. Theor. Comput. Sci. **96**(1), 3–33 (1992)
10. Pomello, L., Rozenberg, G., Simone, C.: A survey of equivalence notions for net based systems. In: Rozenberg, G. (ed.) APN 1992. LNCS, vol. 609, pp. 410–472. Springer, Heidelberg (1992)
11. Rozenberg, G., Engelfriet, J.: Elementary net systems. In: Reisig, W., Rozenberg, G. (eds.) APN 1998. LNCS, vol. 1491, pp. 12–121. Springer, Heidelberg (1998)
12. Shamir, A.: Identity-based cryptosystems and signature schemes. In: Blakely, G.R., Chaum, D. (eds.) CRYPTO 1984. LNCS, vol. 196, pp. 47–53. Springer, Heidelberg (1985)

Software Engineering with Petri Nets:
A Web Service and Agent Perspective

Tobias Betz, Lawrence Cabac[✉], Michael Duvigneau, Thomas Wagner,
and Matthias Wester-Ebbinghaus

Department of Informatics, Faculty of Mathematics,
Informatics and Natural Sciences, University of Hamburg, Hamburg, Germany
{betz,cabac,duvigne,wagner,wester}@informatik.uni-hamburg.de
http://www.informatik.uni-hamburg.de/TGI

Abstract. The context of this paper is given through a software engineering approach that uses Petri nets as executable code. We apply the particular understanding that Petri nets are not only used to model systems for design purposes but also to implement system components. Following this approach, we develop complex Petri net-based software applications according to the multi-agent paradigm. Agent-internal as well as agent-spanning processes are implemented directly as (high-level) Petri nets. These nets are essential parts of the resulting software application – alongside other parts (operational and declarative ones), which are implemented using traditional ways of programming.

One of our goals is to open our Petri net-based agent framework MULAN/CAPA so that multi-agent applications can communicate and interact with other systems – especially with Web-based applications. With this intention, we present a gateway solution to enable Petri net-based applications to access Web services as well as to offer Web services to other applications: the *WebGateway*. In addition to describing the WebGateway extension itself, we use its presentation to demonstrate the practicability of the Petri net-based software engineering approach in general. We emphasize the benefit of having Petri net models serve as conceptual models that progressively refine the constructed system from simple models to well-defined specifications of the systems. This improves the understanding of the systems.

Keywords: Web services · High-level Petri nets · Multi-agent systems ·
MULAN · RENEW · P*AOSE

1 Introduction

One of the most frequent requirements for modern software applications is to open the access to its offered functionality for other entities in the World Wide Web. In this paper we address the topic of meeting this requirement for Petri-net based software applications. We present a gateway solution for allowing Petri net-based applications to access Web services as well as offering Web services themselves.

© Springer-Verlag Berlin Heidelberg 2014
M. Koutny et al. (Eds.): ToPNoC IX, LNCS 8910, pp. 41–61, 2014.
DOI: 10.1007/978-3-662-45730-6_3

The usefulness of Petri nets for software engineering has been recognized in the context of many paradigms such as object-orientation [1], components and plugins [7,15,22] or agent-orientation [16,20]. In this paper we assume a particular understanding of *Petri net-based software*. In addition to using Petri nets for design-level artifacts and for verification of certain system properties, we utilize Petri nets as our *implementation language*. More precisely, we rely on the high-level Petri net formalism of *Java reference nets* [7,17] that allows to combine multi-level Petri net modeling (according to the *nets-within-nets* concept [26]) with Java programming. The formalism is supported by the RENEW[1] tool. We have developed the multi-agent system (MAS) framework MULAN (see Footnote 1) based on Java reference nets. It provides a powerful middleware for running distributed multi-agent applications on multiple instances of RENEW. In addition, we have developed a Petri net-based agent-oriented software engineering approach (P*AOSE (see Footnote 1)) for the construction of such multi-agent applications.

With the *WebGateway* extension, we introduce the latest addition to the Petri net-based software engineering framework MULAN/CAPA. While the MULAN model is often referred to as the reference architecture, CAPA (Concurrent Agent Platform Architecture) is an extension and implementation of MULAN. CAPA [11] provides convenient ontology-based message processing and an infrastructure for FIPA[2]-compliant agent management and IP-based transport services. The Web-Gateway allows to integrate MULAN applications into Web-based environments via Web services. This *opens* MULAN applications in the sense that MULAN agents can now access resources external to the agent world in a uniform way via Web services instead of having to be equipped with proprietary connectors. In the other direction, MULAN agents can also publish and offer their own services as Web services and thus can likewise be accessed uniformly from anywhere across the Web. Again, we stress our specific understanding of Petri net-based software, which carries over to the integration with Web services. Usually, work on Petri nets and Web services deals with providing semantics to modeling notations that are used within the Web context, such as BPEL[3] and translations [14]. Our approach is to provide a way to offer Web services that are actually *realized by the execution of Petri net models*. The other way around, the *execution of Petri net-based applications can include the access of arbitrary Web services*.

The concrete aim of this paper is twofold. First, the paper introduces the WebGateway itself. Second, the development of the WebGateway framework serves as an example and proof of concept for creating complex, practical and modern software systems with Petri nets – using a *Petri net and agent-based software engineering approach* (P*AOSE [5]). The WebGateway highlights the general and specific benefits that underlie our approach. These benefits include, but are not limited to:

---

[1] For more detailed information about RENEW, MULAN and P*AOSE see [5], http://www.paose.net and http://www.renew.de.

[2] Foundation for Intelligent Physical Agents: http://www.fipa.org.

[3] http://bpel.xml.org/.

1. We follow an engineering approach, in which we move from conceptual models as design artifacts to refined, technical models as software artifacts. This approach of *implementation through specification* [7] allows to iteratively build models/code in a documented and comprehensible way. In addition, core features of a system can be determined in early stages of development and maintained in further refinements.

2. By using *Petri nets as code* we can verify our application code. Of course, this can only happen within certain limits. Both the nets-within-nets nature of our models and the use of Java inscriptions prohibit a comprehensive verification. Nevertheless, we can define abstractions (e.g. P/T net abstractions) of our program code and verify specific properties (e.g. properties of sound workflows). This allows at least partial verification of our application code (which could possibly be supplemented with unit testing mechanisms for reference nets [8]).

3. Software agents are naturally a good fit for Web service environments. With their innate properties they easily overcome obstacles of distribution, asynchronous communication, reasoning/decision mechanics, etc. By bridging the gap between the two worlds of agents and Web services, as we propose in this paper, we open up the functionality offered by Web services to the agent world. At the same time we also open up the aforementioned properties of agents to the Web service world. All in all, both worlds benefit from this integration. This option of integration is not limited to agents and Web services, but can also be applied to other areas, such as workflows (see the discussion in Sect. 6).

The outline of the paper is as follows. In Sect. 2, we present the conceptual model of our WebGateway extension for bringing Petri net-based (agent-oriented) applications and Web services together. Based on this, we present details of the WebGateway implementation in Sect. 3. In combination, these two sections demonstrate the benefits and practicability of our *implementation through specification* approach. In Sect. 4, we demonstrate how the WebGateway and one particular Petri net-based Web service are deployed in the context of our integrated project management environment (IPME) on a day-to-day basis. Section 5 presents a further insight to the implementation in order to demonstrate the refinement process of the model. We discuss the results of the paper in Sect. 6, position them in the context of related work in Sect. 7 before we conclude the paper in Sect. 8.

2 Conceptual Gateway Architecture

The WebGateway extension to the multi-agent framework MULAN/CAPA is realized by a *WebGateway agent*. This agent is coupled to a (Jetty) Web Server and brings the two worlds of the (Web service-based) Internet and multi-agent systems together. In Sect. 3, we address technical details of the WebGateway realization. In this section, we focus on the conceptual architecture. Along the

way, we demonstrate the usefulness of applying a Petri net-based modeling approach. We progressively refine a simple architectural model to a meaningful and
well-defined specification. This specification then represents the basis on which
to actually implement the WebGateway agent's behavior. Due to space limitations, we cannot address the whole functionality of the WebGateway framework,
which includes – among others – registration and look-up of agents and services,
conversion of message formats, the provisioning of basic GUI elements, the automatic setup of the Jetty Web server and a Web interface to inspect and control
the agents. Instead we concentrate on handling Web requests and responses. Further details of the framework's architecture and challenges of the implementation
will be addressed in Sect. 3.

Figure 1 illustrates our starting point. In order to provide communication
in such a heterogeneous setup consisting of Web and multi-agent system parts,
the communication has to be facilitated. The WebGateway provides the translation as an adapter between the two worlds of communication. It provides two
interfaces for this purpose: one for Web-based communication and one for FIPA-
compliant communication. The interfaces are depicted in Fig. 1 as white rectangles. The Internet is shown as a cloud and the MULAN reference model (cf. [16])
stands as an exemplary multi-agent system.

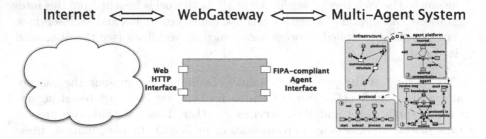

Fig. 1. WebGateway context.

In the following we will consecutively refine the WebGateway as a Petri net
model. Figure 2 shows the first step in this refinement. The WebGateway's main
functionality of translating messages from one domain to the other is represented
as two transitions that are included in the transformation component. The two
interfaces are now depicted as transitions[4]. Messages may enter through the
interface transitions with outgoing arcs, are received on the buffer places and
ready for transformation processing.

Translation is an important and already technically challenging part (cf. [4])
but not the only task of the WebGateway. In addition, it has to make sure
that responses are matched to requests across the heterogeneous setup. In our

---

[4] The notion of transitions being interfaces fits nicely with an object-oriented paradigm, if one presumes that these (on one side open) transitions are one port of
synchronous channels.

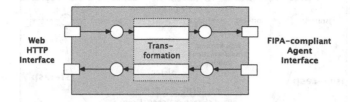

Fig. 2. Simple WebGateway architecture model

approach the WebGateway keeps a copy of a request message in order to be able to provide this matching. When the WebGateway processed a response, the information contained in the response is compared to and matched to the stored copies in the WebGateway. Thus responses can be routed to the right recipient. In Fig. 3 an exemplary conversation direction is modeled: a request from the Web to an agent-implemented service. The original request (e.g. from a Web browser) is a JSON message (JavaScript Object Notation). The WebGateway translates this message to FIPA-SL (Semantic Language), which can be understood by agents in the multi-agent system. A copy of the message is kept within the gateway, which allows the gateway to route the response message to the requester after the answer has been translated back from FIPA-SL to JSON. Please note that JSON stands for just one possibility of a Web message's content. Content types such as XML or HTML form data can be translated in a similar fashion.

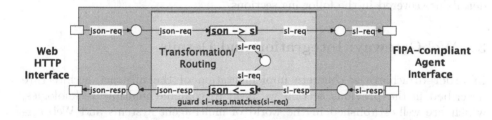

Fig. 3. WebGateway architecture model for handling Web-client requests

While Fig. 3 covers one exemplary interaction type, namely a request sent by a Web-based client to an agent-based service, the WebGateway also provides the possibility that a Web service request is initiated from the agent's side. In this case an SL encoded request will be translated to (for instance) JSON, a copy of this message will be kept for later routing and the answer from a Web application will be translated from JSON to SL in order to deliver it to the requesting agent. Both initiating directions are supported by the WebGateway and use the same interface as depicted in Fig. 4.

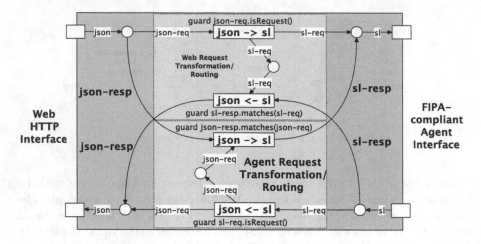

Fig. 4. WebGateway architecture for two-way service request handling

In addition to the request interactions covered so far, the WebGateway also supports a unidirectional communication (*inform* interaction), which is not discussed here.

While this conceptual Petri net model of the WebGateway architecture shows the basic (internal) behavior of the WebGateway, it neither specifies the interactions between WebGateway and Web applications or agents nor does it present a realistic level of detail for the implementation of the WebGateway agent. These details are covered in the following sections.

3   WebGateway: Integration and Details

In order to achieve a concrete implementation of the abstract architecture described in the previous section we need to combine multiple technologies, which are well-established in the world of multi-agent systems and Web services. In this section, we describe how those technologies are combined for the implementation of the WebGateway in order to obtain the desired integration of both application domains. For this we present two parts of the adapter functionality of the WebGateway. The first is concerned with the message routing and translation as well as service registration. It focuses on the Web interface side, which – from the perspective of the multi-agent system – is the external interface. The realization of this interface, which requires the integration of the required technologies, is presented in Sect. 3.1. The second part focuses on the WebGateway as a part of the agent system and its communication with other agents. Hence, Sect. 3.2 introduces the communication protocol nets[5] provided by the WebGateway extension.

---

[5] In the context of MULAN/CAPA protocol nets (also abbreviated as simply *protocols*) refer to agent behavior nets, which are executed by the individual agents.

3.1   Integration of the Required Technologies

An initial requirement is that the WebGateway must be able to interact with communication partners of both worlds. Because of this, the WebGateway provides two communication interfaces as shown in Fig. 5. We have included the conceptual architecture model from the previous section in order to illustrate its relation to the actual WebGateway implementation.

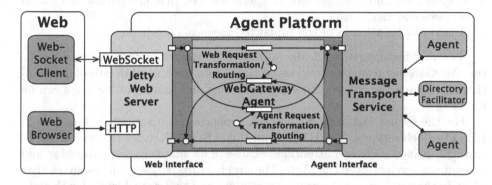

Fig. 5. Integration of the WebGateway in the multi-agent system

As the WebGateway is realized as an agent itself, the agent interface for communication with other agents is inherently part of the underlying multi-agent system framework (MULAN/CAPA in our case). Consequently, the *ordinary* FIPA-compliant agent communication infrastructure of our framework enables communication with other agents both on the same platform and on remote platforms. This part can be considered as the WebGateway's *internal communication interface*.

In addition, the WebGateway agent needs a Web interface that serves the communication with Web services and Web clients. It is realized using a Web server (Jetty[6]). This is where we have extended our framework. For each MULAN/CAPA host, one Web server is launched. A MULAN/CAPA host may include multiple agent platforms, but typically we have a one-to-one correspondence between a host and a platform. For each platform, a WebGateway agent is launched and connects automatically to the platform's Web server. This can be considered as the WebGateway's *external communication interface*. The Web server enables communication between the WebGateway agent and Web services/clients using the well established HTTP protocol (Hypertext Transfer Protocol[7]) as well as the HTML5 WebSocket protocol[8]. In contrast to HTTP, a WebSocket connection allows to exchange messages asynchronously between client and server. This

---

[6] http://www.eclipse.org/jetty.
[7] http://www.w3.org/Protocols.
[8] http://dev.w3.org/html5/websockets/.

allows more flexibility for browser-based Web applications and fits quite well with the agent paradigm as it traditionally relies on asynchronous interactions.

Besides mediating communication *technically*, there are further challenges in order for the WebGateway to really provide a transparent and bidirectional communication between the agent and the Web service world. We identify the following required key features.

1. Routing and management of messages between the different interfaces.
2. Registration and management of agent services that are published as Web services and vice versa.
3. A two-way translation of the supported message encodings.

The first feature is specifically addressed by the conceptual architecture for the WebGateway from the previous section. More (technical) details of our solution concerning the cross-technological tracking and routing of messages can be found in [4].

For the second feature, our approach supports – and actually is limited to – RESTful Web services. The **RE**presentational **S**tate **T**ransfer (REST) architecture [12] gained increased attention because of its simplicity for publishing and consuming services over the Web. The architecture is based on resources that identify the participants of service interactions and that are addressed with globally unique URIs[9]. Such a resource can be manipulated over a uniform interface with a fixed set of operations (GET, POST, PUT, DELETE, etc.) that are traditionally part of the underlying HTTP networking protocol. Resources are also decoupled from their representations so that their content can be accessed in a variety of formats e.g. HTML, JSON[10], XML or even JPEG images. For our purposes, we treat artifacts from the multi-agent world (hosts, platforms, agents, agent services) as REST resources in the Web world, i.e. the resources' representations can be accessed through a URL. The structure of the URL is based on the hierarchical structure of the agent system. The technical counterparts for these *agent-based REST resources* on the Web server side are implemented as Java Servlets[11]. These are responsible for providing the resource representations and also act as connection endpoints for HTTP and WebSocket connections, forwarding all incoming messages to the responsible WebGateway agent. In [4], we provide more details on addressing agent-based REST resources and on how to provide suitable presentations.

The last feature was also briefly addressed in the previous section (translation between FIPA-SL and JSON/XML/HTML form data). We will not cover this topic here, but again refer to [4].

3.2   The WebGateway as a MULAN/CAPA Agent

So far we have mainly focused on Web technologies that are necessary for realizing the WebGateway according to the conceptual architecture presented in

---

[9] Uniform Resource Identifier.

[10] JavaScript Object Notation (JSON).

[11] http://www.oracle.com/technetwork/java/index-jsp-135475.html.

the previous section. However, we have already stressed the fact that the Web-Gateway is actually realized as an *agent* in our MULAN/CAPA framework. We have presented the development approach (P*AOSE) for MULAN/CAPA multi-agent systems together with corresponding tools on other occasions (cf. [5,6]). Basically, a MULAN/CAPA agent is designed in terms of three aspects: the agent knowledge, the agent-internal processes and the agent-spanning processes. These aspects eventually manifest in three types of software artifacts for agent implementation: a *knowledge base, decision components* (DCs) for managing agent-internal processes and *protocol nets* for managing interactions with other agents. Basically, the conceptual architecture described in Sect. 2 provides the foundation, on which the agent's decision components are designed. In the previous subsection, we have covered the technologies that are needed to finalize the conceptual architecture in order to arrive at an actual implementation.

One central aspect of agent design is its interactions with other system parts. Interactions between the WebGateway and Web applications take place via HTTP/WebSockets. For interactions between the WebGateway and other agents we have to provide equally well-defined protocols. Basically, the WebGateway agent offers five protocol nets for this purpose:

– WebGateway_registerAgent for registering agent services as Web services.
– WebGateway_sendrequest for forwarding request from Web applications to application agents
– WebGateway_receiverequest for forwarding request from application agents to Web applications
– WebGateway_sendinform and WebGateway_receiveinform for sending inform messages in both directions

We cannot cover all of these interactions in this paper, instead we will focus on one of them as an example. Figure 6 shows an AUML diagram for the sendrequest interaction involving the WebGateway. AUML (Agent UML, see [6,9]) Interaction Protocol diagrams are derived from Sequence Diagrams. They allow the folding of several sequences into one scenario by providing modeling elements for alternatives or concurrency – similar to UML2 Interaction Diagrams. Here, we regard the sample case where a Web application requests the export functionality of an application agent and the WebGateway agent acts as the mediator. Each of the principle agents is represented in Fig. 6 as an individual vertical lane containing the agent's actions and different alternatives depending on the conditions. Horizontal arrows represent messages sent between the agents. We address the export application scenario more deeply in the next section.

In the P*AOSE approach, we use these AUML diagrams to (semi-) automatically generate the interaction parts for each party as Petri nets (cf. [9]). These resulting *protocol nets* are then directly used for the implementation of agent interactions. It is important to note that the WebGateway_sendrequest protocol net is generic. Here, it is shown in the context of the export example. But it is designed to be applicable for arbitrary requests sent from a Web application

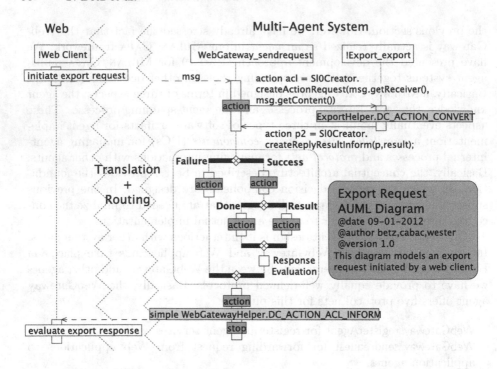

Fig. 6. A model of the export request interaction initiated by a Web client.

to an application agent. For instance, we have developed a Web component-based GUI framework for browser applications that relies on exchanging Web component events between browsers and agents (so called *Agentlets*).

For each new way of making use of the WebRequest_sendrequest protocol net, the two interaction sides have to *fit* together. This means that the composition of the WebRequest_sendrequest protocol net and its counterpart protocol net has to (at least) result in a sound protocol[12].

4   Application of the WebGateway/Export Example

As a real world example we present an application that utilizes the WebGateway's functionality to provide a Web service. The *Export Service* takes a representation of a RENEW diagram (e.g. a Petri net) in the form of a serialized RENEW drawing or as PNML and returns an image representation of the model[13].

---

[12] Although the soundness property is not well-defined for protocol nets, we conceive this property in analogy to soundness of workflow nets.

[13] In fact the service takes any file type that can be read by RENEW, e.g. RENEW nets (.rnw), JHotDraw drawings (.draw), PNML, several diagram types used within P*AOSE (.aip,.arm) and also Lola net files (.net). The RENEW import/export system is also extensible, so any envisioned file type in the context of Petri nets and UML modeling can be easily implemented.

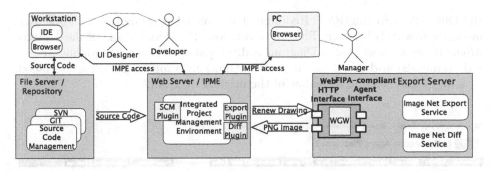

Fig. 7. A schematic architecture for the export Web service/Redmine plugin.

The *Diff Service* takes two representations of models and returns a graphical diff [10] of the two models.

People can access these Web services directly through a Web page interface. But the main application for the Web services is currently a different one. In the context of software engineering, in which we use our models, a tight integration of available tools ensures the efficiency and therefore the acceptance of the available tools among developers. Thus we have integrated the two Web services in our preferred integrated project management environment (IPME, see [3]).

Figure 7 shows a schematic model of the setup of our IPME. The IPME – in this case: *Redmine*[14] – runs on a standard Web server shown in the center of the model. It includes several plugins for the access of the source code management system (SCM, possibly located on another server) and the Export/Diff Web services (again located on another server). Developers can, for example, interact with the source code repositories to introduce new versions of artifacts, to examine the commit history or to examine differences of the selected versions. Managers as well as developers can use the IPME's planning and documentation features. In addition, the IPME also integrates the SCM's source code repository, which can be comfortably examined in a Web browser. One main part of the functionality provided by the IPME is that developers and project managers can browse quickly through the source code and choose to display the differences between versions of the source code directly in the Web browser. However, the default browsing and diffing functionality of IPMEs works exclusively on text-based source code, while large parts of our code are Petri net-based. A textual representation of diagrams – for example in PNML – is not very significant for human readers. Moreover, a text-based diff of versions of the diagram's text representations is completely useless. Thus, the Export and Diff plugins take the text representations for diagrams from the SCM, hand them to the Export and Diff Web services and integrate the returned images smoothly into the Web page-based display for the developer. Figure 8 shows a screenshot of the integration of

---

[14] http://www.redmine.org/.

the Diff Service in the IPME Redmine. The screenshot shows the Redmine user interface in a Web browser. The diff of revisions 12214 and 12424 of the *Matrix-ModelMaker* Coarse Design Diagram is displayed. Differences are highlighted in red (removals) and green (additions)[15]. All other graphical elements are faded to a foggy gray leaving a shadow of the original diagram.

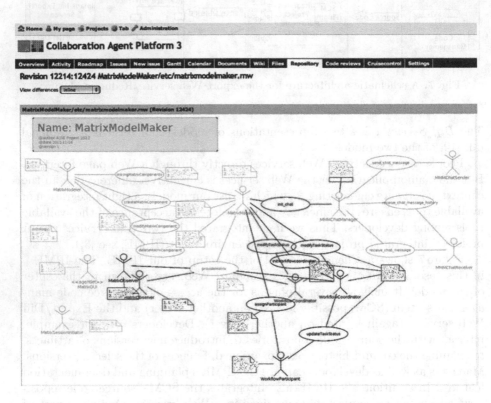

Fig. 8. Screenshot of a diff image integrated in Redmine: Coarse Design Diagram for the MatrixModelMaker application (anonymized).

Consequently, within our development environment the Web services are used by the IPMEs[16] and are thus provided to the developers in an integrated way. A server instance of the RENEW simulator executes the MULAN/CAPA framework with its WebGateway extension as well as an Export Agent, which provides the *Export* and *Diff* Web services for potential clients. A publicly accessible Export/Diff Web page and a demonstration page of the Redmine integration can be accessed from the P*AOSE Web Site[17].

---

[15] In black & white printing the location of the manipulated parts are still recognizable, although it becomes impossible to distinguish removals from additions.

[16] We provide plugins for Redmine and Trac (http://trac.edgewall.org/).

[17] http://www.paose.net/.

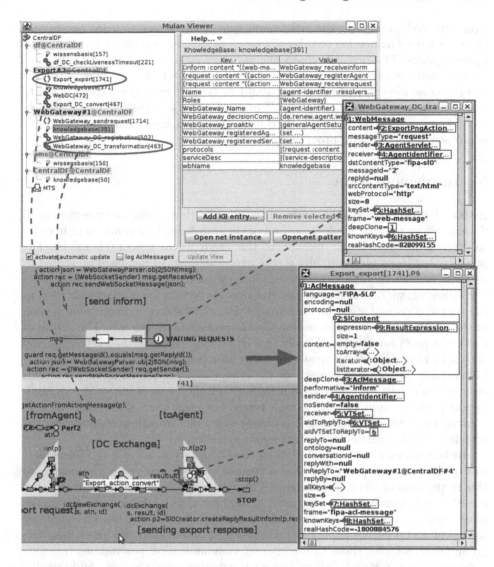

Fig. 9. A screenshot of the agent application while running the export interaction.

Figure 9 shows a screenshot of the presented multi-agent application showing an export interaction. The MulanViewer on the left shows the multi-agent system's status in terms of all started agents, their decision components, knowledge bases and currently executed protocol nets. In the lower left, parts of the involved nets are shown: these are – from top to bottom – the *transformation* decision component of the WebGateway and the *export* protocol net of the Export agent. The *sendrequest* protocol net of the WebGateway is not shown but listed in the MulanViewer's tree view. During this interaction the WebGateway *sends* the request to the Export agent after the request has been *received* from the Web client. On the right hand side of the screenshot are two frames showing a deep inspection of tokens, which are located as indicated on the high-lighted places. The first one shows the *request* message in FIPA-SL, waiting to be matched with the response for routing purposes (cf. Sect. 2). The second is the response message, which is just about to be sent from the Export agent to the WebGateway[18]. The availability[19] of the Export and Diff Web services provided by a running instance of a Petri net application shows that our framework is already beyond a pure proof of concept.

5   Implementation

Although executable models tend to grow to a size that cannot be presented in all details, we present the implementation of the transformation component in order to discuss the specification refinement that leads to the executable model. The process that leads incrementally to the executable model has been presented as *implementation through specification* [7]. In the executable model, presented in the following, we do not discuss inscriptions nor certain technical details such as the preparation and selection of messages. Figure 10 shows an executable version of the WebGateway Transformation Component as an overview[20]. The details of the main parts are presented again in Fig. 11. Compared to the abstract model shown in Fig. 4 this model shows several refinements. First of all the interfaces – indicated by the dashed boxes – of the component have been duplicated. This results from the fact that our implementation allows for additional communication protocols and two connection types. For each kind of message (*request, inform, synchronous, asynchronous*) there exists one transition representing the interface for this particular form of communication.

In the abstract model we described the possibility to serve a typical request protocol. Thus, one party can send a request message and receive an answer to this in the form of an inform message. This protocol may be triggered from either the Web server interface or the agent system interface. Additionally, the implementation also allows for a simple inform message that has not been triggered by a request and does not expect any follow-ups. Consequently, we have three outgoing transitions for these three different communication possibilities (request, inform as answer, simple inform) on each outgoing interface side. Additionally, we included the possibility to connect as a Web service in two possible ways. The first is the well-known HTTP connection, the second, which is a WebSocket connection, allows for asynchronous communication through a bidirectional permanent connection link.

---

[18] Although the messages could also be inspected in String representation, the UML representation is much clearer and more concise.

[19] The service is publicly available since 2011 (see http://www.paose.net).

[20] The Petri net is presented as a whole, in order to show the final result of the refinement process. Most of the details, such as declarations are only of minor importance. The main details are presented in a magnified version in Fig. 11 for convenient inspection.

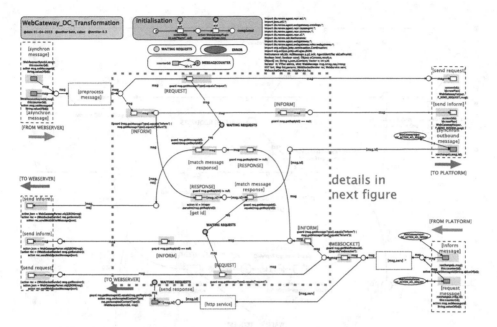

Fig. 10. Implementation of the WebGateway Transformation Component.

In the center of the net – displayed in more detail in Fig. 11 – one can prominently conceive the buffer places (labeled *Waiting Requests*) that hold the messages for matching answers to request in order to determine the receiver. The buffer places are filled during the processing of the requests, which is done within the first branch leading to one transition of the outgoing interface. During the processing of the answer the waiting message is removed from the buffer place and the answer is propagated to the second transition of the outgoing interface. The last interface transition serves for the simple inform messages. We have hidden several parts of the original net – indicated by large transitions. These transitions hide message processing and routing as well as the processing of the HTTP answers.

6   Discussion

The presented example and the publicly available Web services and Web site demonstrate that the presented application is more than just a proof of concept. Especially the availability of the Export and Diff services as Web services has proven their usefulness in the straight-forward and seamless inclusion within several used instances of IPMEs (internal as well as public). We have also briefly mentioned the realization of Web-based GUIs where Web events related to the GUI components are transmitted between a browser and application agents (Agentlets). While this application of the WebGateway is still under development and still in an experimental stage, we have successfully made use

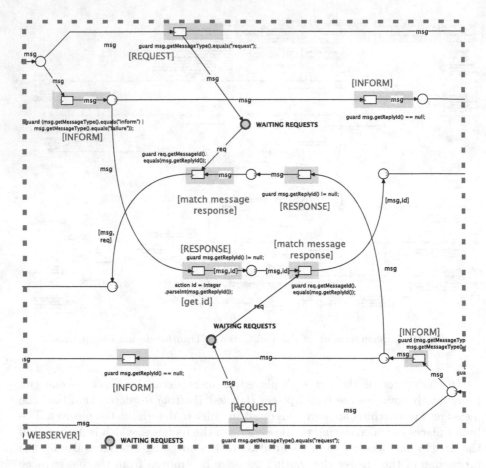

Fig. 11. Fragment of the WebGateway Transformation Component.

of it in academic projects where students develop browser-based applications for collaboration support.

The choice of RESTful Web services in combination with WebSockets brings more flexibility to our gateway than strict WSU[21] stack-based gateways can provide. Currently, we use rather simple service descriptions, which might hinder the automation of service workflows. A possible improvement in this area could be the integration of WADL[22], which plays a similar role for RESTful Web service as WSDL for SOAP Web services.

The role Petri nets play in our approach is quite interesting. Within the WebGateway we achieved the integration of agents and Web services by using Petri nets as a common basis and connection tool. By providing a net model, with which Web services can communicate and interact, it was possible to join both

---

[21] WSDL, SOAP, UDDI (WSU).

[22] Web Application Description Language (WADL): http://java.net/projects/wadl.

paradigms. This kind of integration is not limited to agents and Web services. In fact, in related research we present an integration of agents and workflows in a similar way [27]. The aim of that research is to open up the advantages of workflow modeling and execution to agents and vice versa. The influence of the research carried out in the context of the WebGateway is not only a functional aspect (i.e. incorporating Web services into workflows) but a conceptual question as well.

The WebGateway clearly demonstrates some of the advantages of our Petri net-based software engineering approach. For example, the consecutively refined Petri net models of the WebGateway's Transformation Component, starting from the very simple architecture shown in Fig. 2 and ending in the complex implementation shown in Fig. 10, show the same component in different stages of development. Resemblance of analogous net structures and conceptual coherence are recognizable in each refinement stage. Through the gradual refinement of specification, the development process becomes comprehensible. Here the advantage of using (executable) Petri nets becomes apparent. Throughout all stages of development – all the way from the most abstract specification to the concrete implementation – no change of modeling/implementation language is required and all transitions from one stage to the following adhere to well-defined refinement practices. In consequence, the process of development remains gap-less throughout the whole *implementation through specification* process.

7 Related Work

Service-oriented architectures, especially those in combination with Web applications, are currently a popular field in the research community. Hence, the integration of Web services into multi-agent systems is a well-researched topic with many interesting solutions. Greenwood et al. [13] present an approach, which has influenced our introduced architectural design. They introduce a *Web Service Integration Gateway Service* (WSGIS), which acts as a broker between the service participants and provides translation and routing mechanisms. Shafiq et al. [25] offers a slightly different solution that addresses the interconnection of FIPA-compliant multi-agent systems and Web services. Their approach relies on a middleware software that handles the communication of the service participants without any modification on the respective communication systems. Melliti et al. [19] describe a framework for the interoperability of multi-agent systems based on Web services. Within their interoperability architecture each computer hosting agents has deployed an interoperability module (IM). This module is responsible for publicizing an agent's capabilities as a Web service and for researching and invoking other published capabilities. In contrast to these approaches, which are based on Web services that use the standard WSU stack, the approach of Soto [18] makes use of the advantages of Web services that comply with the RESTful architecture [23]. He provides a *Web Service Message Transport Service* (WSMTS) for JADE platforms that is capable of handling FIPA-SL messages in XML representation. These messages are extended with additional information that ensure an end-to-end communication with only one single message encoding. In this case, agents are able to register themselves with a specific address to publish their services as a REST service.

A still problematic issue, concerning the use and composition of RESTful services, is the change of state of a resource and the corresponding update of clients. Especially Web clients have to constantly send *GET* requests to check if the state has changed, which will result in heavy traffic and unnecessarily high load of JavaScript. For a bidirectional communication, as used for instance in a User Interface Framework, Aghaee et al. [2, Sect. 5.2] recommend the use of W3C WebSockets[23]. The WebSocket API provides a mechanism to send data in various representations (JSON, XML, etc.) to clients when the resource has changed.

Petri nets in a general software engineering context have long been a topic of research (e.g. [24]). Moldt et al. [21] propose an approach concerning the modeling of Web services using high-level Petri nets. The authors introduce a four-layer architecture that focuses on modeling the internal behavior of a Web service and provide a proposal for lifecycle management and interconnection of Web services.

With the approach presented in this paper we provide a prerequisite that enables us to verify the soundness of internal Web service processes by examination of agent interactions. In order to examine the composition of Web services we have to extend our approach to the external Web service interactions and their interfaces. Wolf [28] and his team at the University of Rostock present a related approach. They provide formal models based on Petri nets to describe service interfaces and tools[24] that support the discovery and synthesis of matching service partners.

8   Conclusion and Future Works

In this paper, we presented a gateway architecture that enables the interconnection of FIPA-compliant multi-agent systems and RESTful Web services. More specifically, it creates a bridge between Petri net-based (MULAN) agents and arbitrary Web service providers or clients. Its suitability for daily use has been proven by coupling image conversion and comparison services (provided by MULAN agents) with an integrated project management environment (running as a classic Web server, using these services). Besides its useful functionality, the gateway as an artifact exemplifies the benefits of engineering Petri net-based software. The gateway architecture, its message routing core and its multi-agent interface are completely modeled and implemented in Java reference nets. We presented the design of the core gateway functionality as coarse Petri net models, the integration of concrete functionality into these Petri nets – thus turning them into application code – and the validation of certain application properties by using well-known Petri net analysis techniques.

---

[23] http://dev.w3.org/html5/websockets.
[24] Service-Technology: http://service-technology.org/tools/.

On the practical side, the gateway broadens the range of applications for FIPA-compliant agents (and especially MULAN agents). Their functionality becomes available for any Web service client, and they can refer to functionality provided by any other Web service. The interaction with Web services is restricted to the request-response pattern or just unidirectional information distribution and thus not as feature-rich as the speech act-based communication in the multi-agent world. Nevertheless, these simple interaction patterns form the basis of any complex interaction and can thus be considered as sufficient for everyday use.

One of the most prominent features of agents is their inherent adaptivity and intelligence. While outside of the scope of this paper, this characteristic of agents can be used to the advantage of Web service execution and orchestration. Through the WebGateway the agents can control and manage Web services. If the agents possess adaptive or intelligent capabilities, these capabilities can be transferred to the Web services, which are controlled by these agents. In other words, the WebGateway has created the basis on which the orchestration of Web services can be managed through agent systems.

On the Petri net-based software engineering side, the tools and methods of the P*AOSE approach are evolving while we use them for the design and implementation of applications such as the WebGateway. A major focus is currently put on validation and testing of the application's Petri net-based code artifacts. Having essential parts of the software system being implemented with Petri nets allows to carry out (partial) verification of our application code by means of standard formal methods from the field of Petri net theory. Especially distributed system development can profit from the formal foundation offered by Petri net languages. The further use of the P*AOSE approach in future student projects and the continuous advancement of the agent-based collaboration platform will help to improve the gateway functionality and software engineering techniques step by step.

In conclusion, the WebGateway extension has demonstrated that our approach of Petri net and agent-based software engineering is viable in practical and complex scenarios. While adhering to this approach, we are able to offer the individual possibilities of Web services and agents to one another. Individually these domains possess strong and well-examined capabilities. These established capabilities can now be used in a common setting for the benefit of both domains.

Acknowledgment. We would like to thank the TGI group of the Department of Informatics, University of Hamburg and especially Dr. Daniel Moldt for the support, constructive criticism and fruitful discussions.

References

1. Agha, G., De Cindio, F., Rozenberg, G. (eds.): APN 2001. LNCS, vol. 2001. Springer, Heidelberg (2001)
2. Aghaee, S., Pautasso, C.: Mashup development with HTML5. In: Proceedings of the 3rd and 4th International Workshop on Web APIs and Services Mashups, Mashups '09/'10, pp. 10:1–10:8. ACM, New York (2010). http://doi.acm.org/10.1145/1944999.1945009

3. Betz, T., Cabac, L., Güttler, M.: Improving the development tool chain in the context of Petri net-based software development. In: Duvigneau, M., Moldt, D., Hiraishi, K. (eds.) Proceedings of the Petri Nets and Software Engineering, International Workshop PNSE'11. CEUR Workshop Proceedings, Newcastle upon Tyne, UK, June 2011, vol. 723, pp. 167–178. CEUR-WS.org (2011). http://CEUR-WS.org/Vol-723

4. Betz, T., Cabac, L., Wester-Ebbinghaus, M.: Gateway architecture for Web-based agent services. In: Klügl, F., Ossowski, S. (eds.) MATES 2011. LNCS, vol. 6973, pp. 165–172. Springer, Heidelberg (2011). http://dx.doi.org/10.1007/978-3-642-24603-6_17

5. Cabac, L.: Modeling Petri Net-Based Multi-Agent Applications, Agent Technology - Theory and Applications, vol. 5. Logos Verlag, Berlin (2010)

6. Cabac, L., Dörges, T., Duvigneau, M., Moldt, D., Reese, C., Wester-Ebbinghaus, M.: Agent models for concurrent software systems. In: Bergmann, R., Lindemann, G., Kirn, S., Pĕchouček, M. (eds.) MATES 2008. LNCS (LNAI), vol. 5244, pp. 37–48. Springer, Heidelberg (2008)

7. Cabac, L., Duvigneau, M., Moldt, D., Rölke, H.: Modeling dynamic architectures using nets-within-nets. In: Ciardo, G., Darondeau, P. (eds.) ICATPN 2005. LNCS, vol. 3536, pp. 148–167. Springer, Heidelberg (2005). http://dx.doi.org/10.1007/11494744_10

8. Cabac, L., Duvigneau, M., Moldt, D., Wester-Ebbinghaus, M.: Towards unit testing for Java reference nets. In: Bergenthum, R., Desel, J. (eds.) Algorithmen und Werkzeuge für Petrinetze. 18. Workshop AWPN 2011, Hagen, September 2011, Tagungsband, pp. 1–6 (2011)

9. Cabac, L., Moldt, D., Rölke, H.: A proposal for structuring Petri net-based agent interaction protocols. In: van der Aalst, W.M.P., Best, E. (eds.) ICATPN 2003. LNCS, vol. 2679, pp. 102–120. Springer, Heidelberg (2003)

10. Cabac, L., Schlüter, J.: ImageNetDiff: a visual aid to support the discovery of differences in Petri nets. In: 15. Workshop Algorithmen und Werkzeuge für Petrinetze, AWPN'08. CEUR Workshop Proceedings, vol. 380, pp. 93–98. Universität Rostock (2008). http://CEUR-WS.org/Vol-380/paper15.pdf

11. Duvigneau, M., Moldt, D., Rölke, H.: Concurrent architecture for a multi-agent platform. In: Giunchiglia, F., Odell, J., Weiß, G. (eds.) Proceedings of the 3rd International Workshop on Agent-Oriented Software Engineering, AOSE 2002, Bologna, pp. 147–159. ACM Press (2002)

12. Fielding, R.T., Taylor, R.N.: Principled design of the modern Web architecture. ACM Trans. Internet Technol. 2, 115–150 (2002). http://doi.acm.org/10.1145/514183.514185

13. Greenwood, D., Calisti, M.: Engineering Web service - agent integration. In: 2004 IEEE International Conference on Systems, Man and Cybernetics, vol. 2, pp. 1918–1925 (2004)

14. Hinz, S., Schmidt, K., Stahl, C.: Transforming BPEL to Petri nets. In: van der Aalst, W.M.P., Benatallah, B., Casati, F., Curbera, F. (eds.) BPM 2005. LNCS, vol. 3649, pp. 220–235. Springer, Heidelberg (2005)

15. Kindler, E., Rubin, V., Wagner, R.: Component tools: integrating Petri nets with other formal methods. In: Donatelli, S., Thiagarajan, P.S. (eds.) ICATPN 2006. LNCS, vol. 4024, pp. 37–56. Springer, Heidelberg (2006)

16. Köhler, M., Moldt, D., Rölke, H.: Modelling the structure and behaviour of Petri net agents. In: Colom, J.-M., Koutny, M. (eds.) ICATPN 2001. LNCS, vol. 2075, pp. 224–241. Springer, Heidelberg (2001). http://dx.doi.org/10.1007/3-540-45740-2_14

17. Kummer, O., Wienberg, F., Duvigneau, M., Schumacher, J., Köhler, M., Moldt, D., Rölke, H., Valk, R.: An extensible editor and simulation engine for Petri nets: RENEW. In: Cortadella, J., Reisig, W. (eds.) ICATPN 2004. LNCS, vol. 3099, pp. 484–493. Springer, Heidelberg (2004). http://dx.doi.org/10.1007/978-3-540-27793-4_29

18. León Soto, E.: Agent communication using Web services, a new FIPA message transport service for jade. In: Petta, P., Müller, J.P., Klusch, M., Georgeff, M. (eds.) MATES 2007. LNCS (LNAI), vol. 4687, pp. 73–84. Springer, Heidelberg (2007). http://dx.doi.org/10.1007/978-3-540-74949-3_7

19. Melliti, T., Haddad, S., Suna, A.: Web-masi: multi-agent systems interoperability using a web services based approach. In: International Conference on Intelligent Agent Technology, IEEE/WIC/ACM, pp. 739–742. IEEE Computer Society, Washington, DC (2005)

20. Miyamoto, T., Kumagai, S.: An agent net approach to autonomous distributed systems. In: Proceedings of 1996 IEEE Systems, Man, and Cybernetics, Beijing, China, 14–17 October 1996, pp. 3204–3209 (1996)

21. Moldt, D., Offermann, S., Ortmann, J.: A Petri net-based architecture for Web services. In: Cavedon, L., Kowalczyk, R., Maamar, Z., Martin, D., Müller, I. (eds.) Proceedings of the Workshop on Service-Oriented Computing and Agent-Based Engineering, SOCABE 2005, Utrecht, Netherland, 26 July 2005, pp. 33–40 (2005)

22. Padberg, J., Ehrig, H.: Petri net modules in the transformation-based component framework. J. Logic Algebraic Program. **97**(1–2), 198–225 (2006)

23. Pautasso, C., Zimmermann, O., Leymann, F.: Restful web services vs. "big" web services: making the right architectural decision. In: Proceeding of the 17th International Conference on World Wide Web, WWW '08, pp. 805–814. ACM, New York (2008). http://doi.acm.org/10.1145/1367497.1367606

24. Reisig, W.: Petri nets in software engineering. In: Brauer, W., Reisig, W., Rozenberg, G. (eds.) Petri Nets: Applications and Relationships to Other Models of Concurrency. LNCS, vol. 255, pp. 62–96. Springer, Heidelberg (1987). http://dx.doi.org/10.1007/3-540-17906-2_22

25. Shafiq, M.O., Ding, Y., Fensel, D.: Bridging multi agent systems and Web services: towards interoperability between software agents and semantic Web services. In: 10th IEEE International Enterprise Distributed Object Computing Conference, EDOC '06, pp. 85–96 (2006)

26. Valk, R.: Object Petri nets - Using the nets-within-nets paradigm. In: Desel, J., Reisig, W., Rozenberg, G. (eds.) ACPN 2003. LNCS, vol. 3098, pp. 819–848. Springer, Heidelberg (2004). http://dx.doi.org/10.1007/978-3-540-27755-2_23

27. Wagner, T., Quenum, J., Moldt, D., Reese, C.: Providing an agent flavored integration for workflow management. In: Jensen, K., Donatelli, S., Kleijn, J. (eds.) ToPNoC V. LNCS, vol. 6900, pp. 243–264. Springer, Heidelberg (2012)

28. Wolf, K.: Does my service have partners? In: Jensen, K., van der Aalst, W.M.P. (eds.) ToPNoC II. LNCS, vol. 5460, pp. 152–171. Springer, Heidelberg (2009). (special Issue on Concurrency in Process-Aware Information Systems)

Modeling Organizational Structures and Agent Knowledge for Mulan Applications

Lawrence Cabac$^{(\boxtimes)}$, David Mosteller, and Matthias Wester-Ebbinghaus

Department of Informatics, Faculty of Mathematics,
Informatics and Natural Sciences, University of Hamburg, Hamburg, Germany
{cabac,mosteller,wester}@informatik.uni-hamburg.de
http://www.informatik.uni-hamburg.de/TGI

Abstract. In software engineering the initial setup of a system, as well as the self-adaptation processes within a system are challenging tasks. We address these challenges by providing explications of organizational structures through modeling. In this paper we present a service-oriented perspective on the organizational structure of MAS and we present modeling techniques and tools for supporting this perspective. We pursue a model-driven approach and a tight integration between various models on the one hand and between the models and the generated code on the other hand. In particular, we use ontologies to define a meta-model for organizational structures in a way that we can easily generate the initial content of agent knowledge bases in the form of FIPA semantic language (SL) fragments, depending on the positions the agents occupy in the context of the organizational structure. This allows the agents to reason and to communicate about their organizational embedding, which is a prerequisite for self-adaptation in multi-agent systems.

Keywords: RENEW · MULAN · P*AOSE · Petri nets · Multi-agent systems · Model-driven development · Organizational structures

1 Introduction

The modeling of the fundamental organizational structure is one of the central tasks during the development of a multi-agent system (MAS) [9]. While agents are considered autonomous in their actions, they are also supposed to fulfill certain functions in relation to the purpose of the overall multi-agent application (MAA). A wide spectrum of approaches for organizing multi-agent systems exists [15] and some of them are quite sophisticated in drawing inspiration from organizing principles of social systems (including multiple organizational modeling dimensions like social structures, tasks, social interactions, norms etc., cf. [1,8]). We argue that at the core of most of these approaches lies the determination of an organizational structure in terms of agent functions and agent dependencies based on functional dependencies. This concerns the questions, *which agents* are required/allowed to do *what* (responsibilities/abilities) and *to whom* they can refer for help in certain cases (support/delegation). Basically, this

M. Koutny et al. (Eds.): ToPNoC IX, LNCS 8910, pp. 62–82, 2014.
DOI: 10.1007/978-3-662-45730-6_4

is a service-oriented perspective on agent relationships. Agents offer functional services to other agents and in turn require the services of other agents in order to fulfill some of their own functionality.

We apply this functional and service-oriented perspective for the design of the basic organizational structure of a MAS in our P*AOSE approach (**P**etri net-based **A**gent- and **O**rganization-oriented **S**oftware **E**ngineering, http://www. paose.net). It provides a general basis for MAS organization that can be extended if necessary.[1] We have presented our P*AOSE approach on previous occasions and we have particularly elaborated on the model-driven nature of P*AOSE in [6]. Our multi-agent platform MULAN/CAPA [16,22] tightly combines model and code as it is based on a fusion of high-level Petri nets and Java. This allows us to model/implement all processes as directly executable Petri nets. In addition, we use UML-style modeling techniques for development, where we need a more declarative perspective than is offered by Petri nets. The section on the P*AOSE development process (Sect. 3.1) goes into detail about our working context.

In this paper, we specifically refer to the part of P*AOSE that is concerned with modeling organizational structures in terms of agent roles and service dependencies between roles. This part relies on ontology modeling as we explicate the concepts used for organizational structures as an ontology. In adaptable or self-organizing systems, the organizational structure is not only designed initially by the developers, it is also addressed by the intrinsic components of the system. Since the concepts behind the organizational structure are defined through the agents' ontology, the agents achieve the ability to reason and communicate about their own organizational structure through the same concepts, using the same ontology. The modeling approach benefits from the ontological basis, since the designed models can be easily translated into multiple initial knowledge bases for multiple agents (depending on the agents' positions in the organizational structure). The modeler benefits from immediate validation of the model provided by a syntax check, which also results from the ontological basis. The content of the knowledge bases is generated in FIPA semantic language (http://www.fipa.org), which provides the technical basis for agents to reason about and to communicate about their organizational embedding. This is a prerequisite for self-adaptation in multi-agent systems. Compared with our previous work presented in [6, 7], we present a considerable rework including new tools. Our revision basically takes care of a better and tighter integration between the tools used as well as between the models and the generated code.

Our aim is to provide a lightweight modeling technique that allows defining agent role hierarchies, service dependencies (between agent roles) and additional content of the initial agent knowledge bases. We are striving for a maximal overview of relationships between agent roles (dependencies and hierarchies), while allowing a modular modeling approach and retaining the independence

---

[1] For example, we have developed the SONAR model [17,18] for multi-agent teamwork support, where we use a more elaborated model of functional service dependencies between agents based on task delegation structures and a behavior-based notion of service refinement.

of artifacts (initial knowledge bases). Furthermore, we aim at a tighter integration of agent knowledge representation and agent-internal communication; i.e. we want to express initial agent knowledge through the native agent language mechanisms. Our vision is enabling agents to be self-aware of their organizational embedding to coordinate the self-organized adaptation process within the system.

In Sect. 2 we provide an overview of role and service (dependency) modeling in the MAS field and motivate our own approach. In Sect. 3, we present our concrete models and the supporting tools. We place our contribution in the context of our development process P*AOSE and introduce the agent framework MULAN/CAPA. We also describe how the tools fit into the model-driven nature of our P*AOSE approach. Section 4 gives an example of our tools in use, demonstrated in a concrete application scenario. We close with a short summary and some aspects of future research and development that builds upon the results presented in this paper in Sect. 5.

2   Organizational Structures of Multi-agent Systems

In this section we elaborate on our conceptual approach to modeling organizational structures in terms of agent roles and service dependencies. We motivate the use of the two core concepts of *roles* and *services* in the context of related work.

2.1   Modeling Agent Roles and Service Dependencies

The establishment of organizational structures in multi-agent systems has always been an important part of agent research. One can argue that it is an important part of software design in general (although the architecture metaphor is more established than the organization metaphor). However, in the case of MAS this topic becomes even more imperative. Artificial social agents are regarded as very sophisticated software components with complex knowledge and reasoning mechanisms that often only offer a limited visibility. Consequently, high-level system perspectives are necessary, in which one can abstract from agent-internal details and still comprehend the system on a more abstract level.

The concept of a role has been used extensively in this context and has been established as one of the core concepts of agent-oriented software design [19]. Rights and responsibilities are associated with roles independently from the specific agents that will occupy the roles. Consequently, this leads to a certain degree of predictability and controllability of global MAS behavior without knowing anything about the agents' internals. Examples of bringing the concept of roles to use (cf. Ref. [1]) is to enable as well as constrain agent behavior in terms of (1) which roles belong together to a common group context (allowing acquaintance and communication between group members), (2) defining which roles are expected to be associated with which goals, tasks and necessary capabilities and (3) which roles are supposed to take part in which conversations in which way.

Basically, all these efforts boil down to the abstract question what an agent, occupying a specific role, is supposed to do just because of taking on that role. We are mainly interested in an explication of a functional perspective on roles and role relationships. Of special interest is the specification of the functionality of roles in the context of the wider multi-agent application and the dependencies that exist between different role occupants. Thus, we apply a service-oriented perspective on agent roles. A service in this context consists of a functionality that is provided by one agent (provider) for another agent (user/requester). Usually, the provided service has some kind of value for the user. In order to establish the service relationship the provider has to publish the service by providing a service description to a service look-up and the user has to look-up the service provider. In order to execute the service the agents have to participate in an interaction according to their roles: one agent in the role of the requester and another agent in the role of the provider. In the models we want to express which agent roles provide or require the services. We are aiming at a rather minimalistic model of agent roles and their relationships in terms of service dependencies. These can be enriched with more sophisticated concepts if needed (e.g. goal/task hierarchies, conversation guidelines).

Table 1. Specification of the roles within a simple chat scenario.

Role Schema:	*Receiver*
Description	*A role that permits an agent to receive and display messages.*
Protocols and Activities	*chat*
	provides service: ChatMessageReception
Responsibilities	
Liveness	*incoming chat messages are received*
Safety	*received message equals displayed message*

Role Schema:	*Sender*
Description	*A role that enables an agent to provide the possibility for a user to enter messages and send them to Receivers.*
Protocols and Activities	*chat*
	uses service: ChatMessageReception
Responsibilities	
Liveness	*sends messages to receivers*
Safety	*entered message equals sent message*

Table 1 shows a specification of the roles as schemas for the running example, which is used in the following sections. The introduced model is a simple setting of agents participating in chat communication. An agent occupying the *Sender* role uses the ChatMessageReception service description to find and address potential chat partners. An agent, who is intended to receive chat messages, takes the *Receiver* role and, in order to fulfill this role, he is committed to provide/implement the service ChatMessageReception. The specification focuses on the definition of the roles, thus providing an introverted perspective for the (initial) agent knowledge. However, dependencies remain implicit and hidden in the configuration of each single component, i.e. the used and provided service. In the following sections we elaborate and develop a general perspective on the overall organizational structure of the components as well as their cooperation and dependencies. This view often remains implicit when taking other approaches as a basis for system design.

2.2   Related Work

Not only in agent-oriented approaches to software development the modeling of component dependencies is one of the major challenges. One main problem (also applying to some of the approaches for role-based specifications mentioned above) is that dependencies are often hidden underneath quite complex specifications. Ensel and Keller summarize Gopal [13] in the following way: "However, the main problem today lies in the fact that dependencies between services and applications are not made explicit, thus making root cause and impact analysis particularly difficult" [10, p. 148]. Therefore our motivation is to gain the ability to explicitly model dependencies for MAS and our choice is to model component dependencies (agent dependencies) in terms of roles and service dependencies. The actual dependencies between running agents then result from the roles they occupy.

In the context of the different approaches to software development there exist various ways of handling component dependencies. Some of them are restricted to managing service dependencies by utilizing declarative service descriptions, i.e. using XML [10, p. 148], [24]. From our point of view the more promising approach consists in making use of diagram-based methods.

The most obvious benefit lies in the incomparably better visualization of diagram-supported models over declarative service descriptions. This was identified as a central issue, taking up the above mentioned citation by Ensel and Keller again. On the one hand, the diagram is the means to make the dependencies explicit [3] instead of an implicit declaration located in the configuration files of the (distributed) components as it is for example the case in OSGi service descriptions [24]. An explicit representation of the dependencies is of special value during the design phase for a developer/administrator. On the other hand, the capabilities of model transformation are given in both possibilities to describe dependencies as model-based and as declarative descriptions. A similar approach was taken in [26] for Web Services and BDI-Agents. Service dependencies are specified in the model domain and tool support is realized as a Rational Software Modeler extension. "Dependencies between the various components are modeled at the PIM-level and two-way model transformations help us to ensure interoperability at the technical level and consistency at the PIM-level" [26, p. 114]. There are other efforts, which mainly address specification of dependencies between agents and Web Services (e.g. [14]), whereas our work is focused on agent relations.

Most software developing methodologies contain a technique for modeling some kind of dependencies between their components. The Tropos methodology distinguishes four kinds of dependencies between agents, from hard dependencies (resource) to soft ones (soft-goal). Silva and Castro [23] display how Tropos dependency relations can be expressed in UML for real time systems. Ferber et al. [11] show how the organizational structure of an agent-based system can be modeled using the AGR technique. One of the proposed diagrams, the organizational structure diagram, shows roles, interactions and the relations between roles and interactions. This diagram is comparable to the Roles/Dependencies diagram.

In Gaia Zambonelli et al. [25] focus on the organizational modeling of agent systems. One of the important models is the service model. Our Roles/Dependencies diagram can be regarded as an implementation of the Gaia service model. However, Gaia does not recognize hierarchical roles. Padgham and Winikoff [21] explicitly model acquaintances in Prometheus. But from these models they do not derive any agent (role) dependencies. Roles are not modeled in Prometheus; instead the focus lies on agents. The system model in Prometheus gives a good overview of the system comparable with the overview of the Roles/Dependencies diagram. It is much more detailed but does not explicitly show any dependencies, except for the interaction protocols or messages that connect agents. The structure of the system model reflects the one of the acquaintances model.

In the following, we introduce our approach for a minimalistic (but extensible) comprehension of organizational structures of MAS in terms of role descriptions and role dependencies based on service relationships. Our previous work covered details on the conceptual side of modeling the basic organizational structure of MAS, introducing modeling techniques [4, 5, 7] and tools [6]. In our current work we improve the methods and tools by putting an even stronger focus on the model-driven nature of our approach. We pursue a tighter integration of the provided tools and a minimized gap between the models and the code generated from the models. One specific benefit of our approach lies in the fact that the meta-model for organizational structures is expressed in the agents' language – i.e. as an agent ontology. Thus, the agents are able to communicate and reason about their own organizational structures. Furthermore our model-driven approach facilitates the application in a different context. Since our method is based on model-driven techniques, we can support the portability to other application domains by implementing exchange formats for our models. This is part of our future work and we will return to this later on in Sect. 4.2.

3   Role/Dependency Tool Support for Model-Driven Development in PAOSE

In the following we point out how the integration of the conceptional basis we introduced in the previous section is established in our MULAN framework and the P*AOSE development process. These two entities define the context of our work. They are presented in the following section. We introduce two types of diagrams, namely for ontology modeling and for roles/dependencies modeling. They support the discussed features in a clear and intuitive way, making use of well-known constructs from UML. We also present our tool solution to support our model-driven development approach. All our P*AOSE tools are realized as plugins for the high-level Petri net tool RENEW[2]. They extend RENEW with modeling techniques that are not necessarily based on Petri nets.

3.1   The P*AOSE Development Process

This section puts the subsequent work into the context of the P*AOSE approach, which aims at the development of MULAN applications. The approach focuses on aspects of distribution, concurrency and model-driven development. The framework MULAN offers the basic artifacts and structuring for the application. Its four-layered architecture features as basic artifacts the communication infrastructure, the agent platforms, the agents and the agent internals (protocols, decision components and knowledge bases). With the exception of the communication infrastructure, all artifacts are implemented as Java Reference nets. CAPA extends the MULAN architecture with FIPA-compliant communication features, providing inter-platform (IP-based) agent communication. Also the MULAN applications (MAA) are – similar to the MULAN/CAPA framework – implemented in Java Reference nets and Java. They are executed, together with the MULAN/CAPA framework, in the RENEW virtual machine. While the implementation in Java Reference nets introduces concurrency for MULAN applications, the CAPA extension enables the agents to run in distributed environments.

The organization of MAS can be explicitly modeled using model-driven techniques [6], as described in the following sections. However, in addition to the organizational structure of the MAA, we apply the agent-oriented view onto the organizational structure of the development team through the metaphor of the *multi-agent system of developers* [2]. The metaphor provides the perspective that human participants of the development team form an organization, similar to agents in an MAA, and their collaborative efforts constitute the development process, similar to the MAA process. During development the responsibilities for the diverse tasks are distributed among the developers, which allows for concurrent and distributed collaboration as well as explicit identification of dependencies between the team participants. In the previous sections we motivated a service-oriented composition of MAS based on roles and service dependencies. Here we argue that developers dependencies result from the organizational structure and the application's dependencies. These dependencies are also reflected in the P*AOSE development process, which consists in iterative repetitions of specific fundamental steps of design and implementation, as shown in Fig. 1. The figure depicts a simplified Petri-net process of the P*AOSE design cycle.

---

[2] RENEW (http://www.renew.de) also provides the virtual machine that executes MULAN applications.

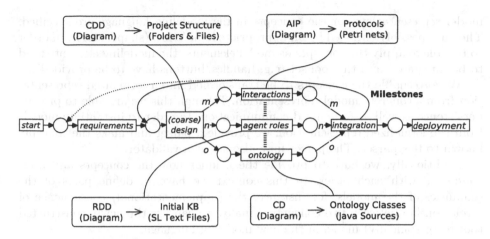

Fig. 1. The P*AOSE development process and techniques. Modified from [3, p. 133].

A project starts with the requirements analysis resulting in a coarse design of the overall structure of the MAA. The coarse design identifies essential roles and interactions of the organization. It is used to generate the initial structure (development artifacts) of a project. The main step of an iteration consists of three tasks of modeling and implementation. These are the modeling of interactions, agent roles and ontologies, as well as generating sources from the models and refining the implementation. The integration of the resulting artifacts completes an iteration. In the diagram annotations refer to modeling techniques, which are utilized to carry out a corresponding task and the artifacts, which are generated from the design models. Taking up the aforementioned view on the organization of a development team, the completion of an iteration requires the synchronized, collaborative effort of the participants.

In the context of this work we introduce a technique and a tool for the modeling of agent roles. To this end, we utilize the ontology model used in P*AOSE as a meta-model. In this sense the following sections describe the conceptual approach and how our integrated approach essentially applies ontology concepts for the design of a new modeling technique and a corresponding tool – in this case the modeling of organizational structures of MAA.

3.2 Conceptual Approach

Conceptually, the approach we are taking resembles a typical model-driven approach. We aim at the design of a modeling language as well as the implementation of appropriate tool support.

We start by defining a meta-model for the (abstract) syntax of the modeling language. The meta-model defines all available concepts and relations. From the meta-model's concept hierarchy we are able to generate a class hierarchy.

Then we use the derived classes to construct a modeling tool. In order to be able to adequately use the concepts within the modeling language, the model representations for the concepts in the modeling language are specified. They are possibly enriched by an appropriate look & feel (shape, style). In order to be able to apply the concepts as model elements, the modeling elements need to be integrated into the tool set (e.g. handles/buttons have to be provided).

We also enable the concepts to be transformed into a formalized representation from a concrete model representation. Through this we are able to provide persistence as well as formalized communication. In order to instantiate models from the formalized representation, we provide a parser and make the concepts known to this parser. The parser may also act as a validator.

Additionally, we have to provide the manner how the concepts are interconnected with each other. In this context we have to define parts of the semantics of the models, for instance, the (implementational) consequence of a relationship between two concepts. Finally, we can use the newly constructed tool to (graphically) model in the new modeling language.

In the following section we integrate the described model-driven approach with the P*AOSE development approach. We employ the tools and techniques from the P*AOSE approach in order to execute several of the above described development steps.

3.3   Integrated Approach

We support the development of modeling languages in the model-driven approach (sketched above) through the integration of models, generated code, serialized representations and tools, which are already used in the P*AOSE approach. This leads to a threefold integrative approach that is illustrated in Fig. 2 and that we discuss in the following. The described architecture, we denominate as the three-part basic model of agent knowledge, can be understood as a variant of the semantic triangle known from linguistic theory.

Integration encompasses three parts: (1) an ontology including multiple concepts, (2) the code generated from the ontology and (3) the serialized representations of concept instances in FIPA Semantic Language (SL) format [12].

Ontologies are modeled using a lightweight technique called *Concept Diagram*[3]. These agent ontologies constitute the meta-models in the conceptual approach described above. The concepts defined in the ontology are transformed into Java classes, one class for each concept. Instances of these classes (ontology objects) can be extracted into SL-formatted text. Through an SL parser the serialized SL text representations can be used to instantiate Java ontology objects in the reverse direction. Instantiation and serialization are both provided by the generator and parser of the MULAN framework and employed within the model-driven approach. Consequently, we utilize three tools for these three tasks: (1) the *ConceptDiagram-Modeler*, (2) the *OntologyGenerator* and (3) the *SL parser*.

This basic integrative approach described so far has several benefits. The development process takes on a model-driven approach, which allows for the

---

[3] An example of a Concept Diagram will be discussed in the context of defining a knowledge base format in Sect. 3.4.

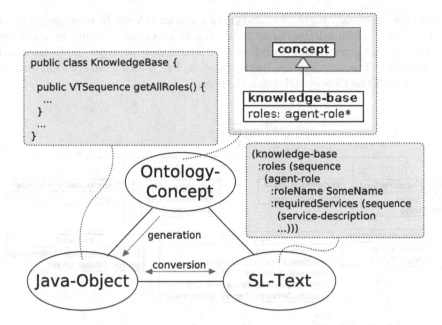

```
public class KnowledgeBase {

public VTSequence getAllRoles() {
...
}
...
}
```

concept

knowledge-base
roles: agent-role*

Ontology-Concept

(knowledge-base
 :roles (sequence
  (agent-role
   :roleName SomeName
   :requiredServices (sequence
    (service-description
    ...)))

generation

conversion

Java-Object

SL-Text

Fig. 2. The three-part basic model of agent knowledge.

specification of ontological concepts in a graphical notation. Concept Diagrams are very similar to the widely used UML Class Diagrams. They are quite intuitively comprehensible and easy to manage. Manipulation of attributes can be carried out directly in the diagram. Additionally, by making use of code generation and the bi-directional conversion between Java objects and SL text representations for concept instances, the integration of the different representations is very tight, i.e. transformation is transparent to a user. By using SL for the text representations of ontology objects we employ an agent-comprehensible format, as MULAN agents use SL text representations for message encoding. This facilitates the usage of our ontologies in FIPA compliant MAS and also supports the application to other ontology-based systems. In addition, our experience has indicated that SL text is also better human-readable in comparison to an equivalent XML representation and shows a lower overhead.

In the following, we show how we apply this method in the case of modeling service dependencies and agent knowledge.

3.4 Concept Diagrams for Role and Knowledge Base Concepts

The previous section provides a general overview of our model-driven approach based on the integration of multiple representations. Now we describe how the three basic parts (ontology, Java code, SL text representation) are applied in the case of modeling as well as establishing organizational structures in multi-agent applications (MAA). The model-driven approach starts with the specification of an ontology encompassing organizational concepts (roles, services, protocols) and concepts necessary for the generation of agent knowledge from organizational structure models (knowledge bases as aggregations of role definitions resulting from a mapping between agents and roles, in which multiple roles can be assigned to each agent). The ontology we use is shown in Fig. 3 as a Concept Diagram. It is created with the ConceptDiagramModeler.

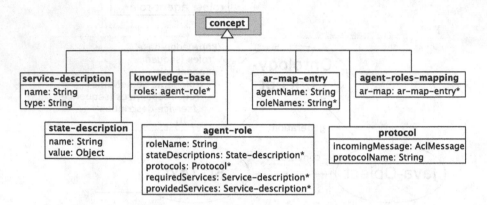

Fig. 3. A Concept Diagram for agent knowledge base concepts.

The Concept Diagram serves in a twofold way. First, it defines all the content types of the agent communication in an application. Second, it serves as a meta-model for the tools that handle the modeled contents.

From here on, we rely on further tool support for code generation and conversion between the different representations of concepts and concept instances. We use the OntologyGenerator (based on Velocity, http://velocity.apache.org) and the SL parser provided by the MULAN framework. Ontology modeling in terms of Concept Diagrams and code generation from these models is already a part of the P*AOSE development process (cf. [3, p. 173]). Thus, the approach described here for handling organizational structures and agent knowledge fits neatly into the context of our wider work.

Basically, Fig. 3 can be regarded as capturing the ontology for knowledge bases of MULAN agents (the schema of a knowledge base). It illustrates the modeling technique of Concept Diagrams in terms of inheritance and the use of concepts for the definition of other concepts (this could also be modeled via associations between different concepts).

Besides capturing the ontology for knowledge bases, the ontology is also used by the AgentRoleModeler tool presented in the next subsection. Java ontology classes that are generated by the OntologyGenerator tool are specializations of generic ValueTuple (VT) and KeyValueTuple (KVT) classes. VT and KVT structures are the root interfaces of an implementation of the FIPA SL.

As mentioned above, by using an SL parser, ontology objects can be instantiated from their SL string representations. This is a feature that lies at the heart of creating *agent instances* from knowledge base patterns (because knowledge-base

is a concept in the diagram from Fig. 3 and thus each knowledge base as a whole
has an SL representation). Ontology classes provide *getters*, *setters* and convenience methods for operations on the data structures. The Ontology-Generator
tool is integrated into the build environment of the MULAN framework and the
SL parser can be used on the fly in a running MULAN MAA. All in all, this
supports our ambition of realizing a tight integration of different models, tools
and code.

Using the knowledge base ontology shown in Fig. 3 the following section
explains how we model roles and dependencies in multi-agent applications.

3.5   Roles/Dependencies Diagrams

Roles and role dependencies are modeled with the AgentRoleModeler tool. The
corresponding Roles/Dependencies Diagrams combine notations from Class Diagrams and Communication Diagrams. The tool is embedded in our model-driven
development approach. The content of Roles/Dependencies Diagrams (Fig. 5) is
based on the concepts that were already defined in the ontology from Fig. 3.
Hence, the AgentRoleModeler tool allows for the generation of knowledge base
descriptions in FIPA SL from Roles/Dependencies Diagrams using the knowledge base ontology from Fig. 3 as a meta-model. Thus, the concepts from the
Concept Diagram reappear as stereotypes in the Roles/Dependencies Diagram.
The knowledge base descriptions resulting from a Roles/Dependencies Diagram
are used as patterns for the initialization of agent instances in the MULAN multi-
agent framework.

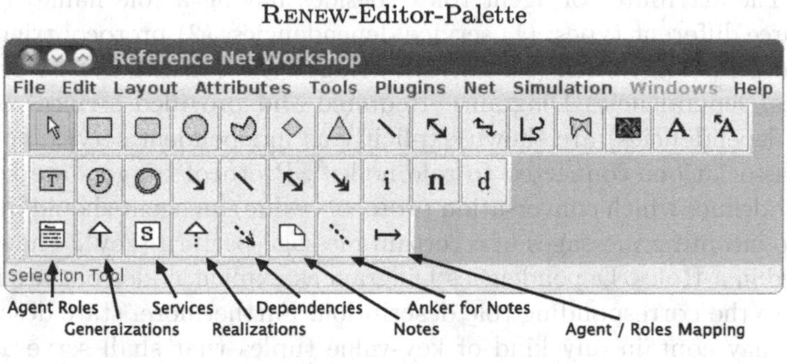

RENEW-Editor-Palette

Fig. 4. The RENEW-Editor-Palette.

The AgentRoleModeler is a drawing plugin for RENEW and adds a custom
palette for drawing elements of Roles/Dependencies Diagrams as shown in Fig. 4
(the AgentRoleModeler palette is shown at the bottom, under RENEW's standard palettes). The graphical representation of Roles/Dependencies Diagram elements is displayed in Fig. 5. The nodes of Roles/Dependencies Diagrams (roles
and services) contain the text in FIPA SL format, specifying the corresponding

attributes of the element. For a compact representation all drawing elements can be collapsed to a smaller view. This provides a very compact and high-level view of an organizational structure in terms of roles and role dependencies based on service dependencies. Expanding the drawing elements allows manipulation of their attributes.

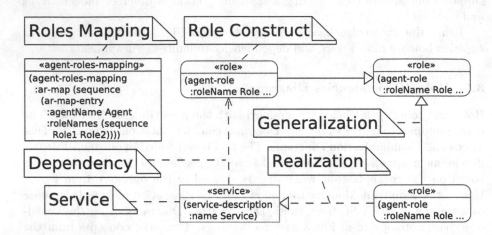

Fig. 5. Constructs of a Roles/Dependencies Diagram.

Following Fig. 3, the knowledge base of a MULAN agent contains an arbitrary number of agent role descriptions, depending on which roles the agent occupies. The attributes of agent roles (besides having a role name) are basically of three different types: (1) service dependencies, (2) protocol triggers and (3) state descriptions. Such (initial) knowledge base content can be generated from Roles/Dependencies Diagrams. Required and provided services of a role (i.e. hard dependencies) are shown explicitly as independent service nodes and offer/use associations connected to role nodes[4]. Protocol triggers are key-value tuples that define, which conversation protocol (value) an agent should initiate in reaction to incoming messages of a certain message pattern (key). They are not represented in a Roles/Dependencies Diagram as explicit nodes but are inserted directly into the corresponding role description. Furthermore, state descriptions for a role may contain any kind of key-value tuples that shall serve as initial knowledge for role occupants. In addition to this flat specification of role dependencies, it is also possible to define inheritance relationships between roles. This introduces hierarchical relationships.

A Roles/Dependencies Diagram contains exactly one node that defines an *agent-role mapping*. Basically, this node serves to define *agent types* in terms of what roles a specific agent type should encompass. For each such agent type, a pattern in FIPA SL can be generated that serves as the basis for the initial knowledge of instantiated agents of that type.

---

[4] Refer to [7] for a discussion of our view on hard and soft dependencies.

4   Application

Aforementioned, we motivate the modeling of organizational structures in MAS. Our approach to modeling organizations is grounded on an ontological content definition, namely the three-part basic model of agent knowledge. We introduced the three-part basic model in Sect. 3. We showed how the concrete realization of a tool for modeling organizations utilizes the ontological content definition. In this spirit the previous section introduced the notation of the Roles/Dependencies diagram and the AgentRoleModeler tool. We will now use the technique of a Roles/Dependencies diagram to model a sample application. The organizational structure is brought into the MAS by the means of generic knowledge base patterns. In the following example we demonstrate our method of extracting initial agent knowledge and structural information from the graphical model and show how they are brought into the running system. We illustrate the modeling of organizational structures and agent knowledge in a sample application in the next section. Then we discuss the presented approach as well as some possible further developments.

4.1   Chat Example

The AgentRoleModeler tool was developed in the context of a bachelor's thesis [20] at the University of Hamburg. After its completion it was used in several student projects for agent-oriented software development. In one of these projects about 20 team members worked on implementing applications for an agent-based collaboration platform. The following example from Fig. 6 is taken from this project. It displays the scenario of a chat application, in which agents occur in the roles of chat senders and receivers.

Figure 6 shows an instance of a Roles/Dependencies diagram. The model consists in the concepts that were already used in the previous section, introduced in Sect. 3.3 and illustrated in Fig. 5. The Sender/Receiver-Scenario is an example we regularly use to demonstrate the MULAN-Framework in student projects. It consists in two roles, a Sender and a Receiver (cf. Table 1). Both roles inherit attributes from the generic CapaAgent role, thus they are specializations of this role. We will go into more detail about this later. The Sender is in possession of a decision component named SenderDC, which enables him to sporadically participate in conversations. He is dependent on a service (ChatMessageReception) allowing him to find and address chat partners. The Receiver is a role, which provides such a service, as can be seen by the realization relation between the Receiver role and the ChatMessageReception service. Upon receiving a chat message, the Receiver role reacts by initiating a chat protocol. The role specification formalizes reactive behavior as a protocol trigger, which can be seen on the lower right part of the above figure. A protocol trigger maps a type of message, identified by a message pattern, to a protocol. Every time a message of the defined type is received, the protocol will be triggered. The chat protocol passes chat messages to a decision component of the Receiver (ReceiverDC) allowing him to process the message. He can carry out internal reasoning about

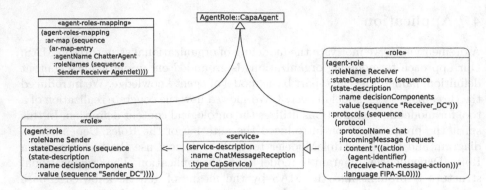

Fig. 6. ARM of WebChat.

the conversation and decide on his further actions, such as creating a response or initiating a new conversation. The diagram constructs described up to this point make up the Roles/Dependencies model. Additionally, Fig. 6 shows the agent-roles mapping construct in the upper left corner of the diagram, which formalizes an agent specification. It determines the initial roles for all agents. In this case, the agent-roles mapping maps both roles to one type of agent, the ChatterAgent. The reason is that a ChatterAgent should naturally have the ability to do both, send and receive chat messages.

The example displays our notion of functional abilities and responsibilities in terms of service dependencies. This specification of roles and services in form of the Roles/Dependencies diagram can be used to generate initial knowledge base contents for the agent instances dedicated to fulfill the corresponding roles. The following example focuses on the succeeding step of extracting the information required to initialize agent instances from the model.

Figure 7 shows a fragment of the Roles/Dependencies diagram that basically refers to one of the roles from the example above. The blue-bordered role figure (round corners) displays the attributes for the role name, protocol triggers and state descriptions. On the right hand side one can see a snippet of the FIPA SL code generated from the Roles/Dependencies diagram. Here, the service provided by the Receiver role (ChatMessageReception) is also included directly in the FIPA SL text. It can also be seen that the FIPA SL fragment contains more than one state description. The additional state descriptions are inherited from the CapaAgent super role.

The roles and their mutual service dependencies are compiled into knowledge base patterns. The knowledge base patterns are in FIPA SL text, so they can directly be used to initialize agent instances, as they are specified in the language (ontology) of MULAN-agents. The example shows how this information is extracted from the model. It also shows how the model can express hierarchies of roles in terms of role specializations, enabling inheritance of attributes. Besides using the specialization relation between role constructs inside one single diagram, the mechanism implemented in the AgentRoleModeler tool also

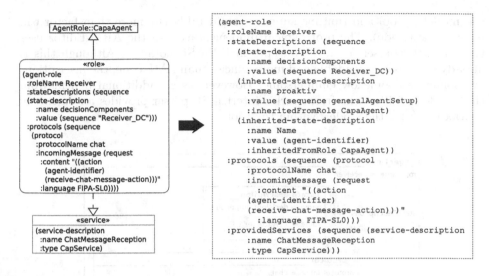

Fig. 7. Role attributes and FIPA SL code generation.

allows using inheritance across diagrams. This is also shown in the above figure. The CapaAgent role is accessed from the Roles/Dependencies diagram named AgentRole. The displayed notation containing double colons denotes this. With the support for expressing specializations with the AgentRoleModeler tool it is possible to build graphical models containing hierarchies and compile them into knowledge base patterns, which allows us to project the overall organizational structure onto the MAA.

The approach for modeling basic organizational structures of MAS in terms of roles and role relationships fits neatly into the general model-driven nature of our P*AOSE approach. In particular, it helps to generate initial agent knowledge bases.

4.2 Discussion

The presented minimalistic approach of modeling organizational structures with Roles/Dependencies Diagrams offers several advantages. One of the most prominent advantages is that the modeling language and the modeling tool are based on the concepts that are provided by the agent-internal language specifications. Thus, the same concepts can be used to provide the meta-model for the modeling language and for reasoning and communication about the organizational structures within the adaptable system by the internal components. With the presented language we are able to model dependencies and hierarchies of agent roles while retaining the possibility to divide the model into reasonable, independent parts. Thus, we achieve to model an overview of relationships, while still being able to distribute role definitions in extendable modules of the overall system model. By using the agent framework's infrastructure and the ontology-based (meta-model-based) approach we were able to reduce the code base for the modeling tool and runtime support considerably (by more than factor 6 in lines of Java code). The prototypical implementation of the ARM-Editor uses the internal representation of concepts in FIPA-SL notation. Although this is already much better readable and more concise than XML code, the inscriptions are sometimes somehow cumbersome. However, as an additional benefit from the ontological basis the framework's internal SL parser provides an on-the-fly syntax check for the models within the tool.

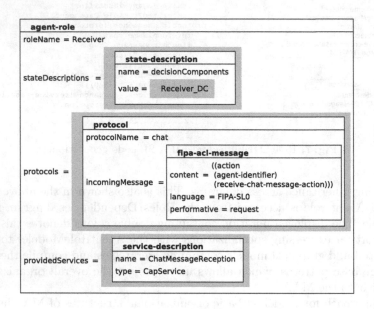

Fig. 8. Alternative representation of SL content.

In the context of our current research we elaborate on generalizing the approach that was presented in this paper to a further step. The idea is not only to apply the model-driven approach for code generation, conversion and transformation of models, but to generate special purpose tools from ontology diagrams as well. A step in this direction is generalizing the AgentRoleModeler tool to a generic SLEditor tool. The UI of a current prototype is shown in Fig. 8. It displays the previously introduced role description of a Receiver from the Sender/Receiver application in a nested graphical figure. The outer frame is that of the agent-role. The highlighted constructs (in gray) indicate *ValueTuples*. This representation allows for displaying any nested structure of *KeyValueTuples* and *ValueTuples*. It can be seen as an alternative view to the plain text representation in Semantic Language. Further efforts are being made to utilize an ontology – modeled with the technique of a Concept Diagram – as a meta-model to generate specialized structures and at the same time generate the modeling tools by using the generic SLEditor. We are occasionally confronted with criticism against grounding our work on an *outdated* infrastructure, because we still rely on the FIPA Semantic Language for the specification of MAA. We address this subject with our development plan on extending the SLEditor. With the generic SLEditor tool we can support the modeling of MAA using other languages for content specification, such as XML, which would enable interoperability with external tools. This can be achieved by extending the ontology to support XML to express knowledge contents.

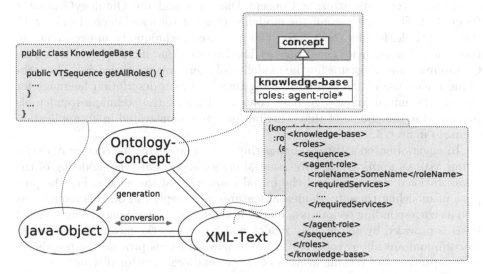

Fig. 9. The three-part basic model of agent knowledge, extended to support XML for content specification.

Taking up the Fig. 2 from Sect. 3.3 the three-part basic model of agent knowledge is extended to display an XML ontology of an agent role. The Fig. 9 reveals what is required to enable this feature: an XML schema definition specifying the format of our ontologies and the methods for conversion of representations between XML-Text and Java-Objects. They are at this time not integrated in MULAN, but there exist standard tools that support XML conversion.

5   Conclusion

In the context of the P*AOSE approach we utilize the technique of Concept Diagrams and the OntologyGenerator tool to specify ontology concepts in order to design multi-agent applications. In this paper both, technique and tool, are introduced together with another technique that is used to model agent roles and their dependencies, the Roles/Dependencies Diagram. Furthermore we present the AgentRoleModeler, a supporting tool – (also) implemented as plugin for the Renew IDE – that offers the lightweight modeling of Roles/Dependencies Diagrams.

In Sect. 2 we elaborate on organizational concepts in MAS research and motivate our approach to modeling organizational structures. The main part of our contribution is preceded by an introduction to the P*AOSE development process and the MULAN framework (Sect. 3.1), which constitute the context of our work. Our approach to modeling roles and dependencies is introduced in three steps. First, we introduce our conceptual approach (Sect. 3.2) and the three-part basic model of the integrated approach (Sect. 3.3). Second, we illustrate the modeling of ontology concepts utilizing Concept Diagrams and the OntologyGenerator (Sect. 3.4). Third, we present the modeling of agent roles and dependencies with the AgentRoleModeler (Sect. 3.5). The presented technique is an occurrence of the Roles/Dependencies Diagram – a Class Diagram that includes notations from Communication Diagrams for the modeling of agent role dependencies. The technique makes use of the Semantic Language (SL) as a description language for the agents' initial knowledge base contents. Finally, the techniques and tools presented in the course of this contribution are demonstrated in an application scenario in Sect. 4.

In agent-oriented software engineering and especially in the context of developing MULAN applications two essential design aspects are the modeling of the organizational structures and the initial knowledge of the agents. For the purpose of modeling these fundamental features a conceptional basis is required as well as corresponding techniques, methods and tools. The presented conceptional basis is provided by an ontology model, which provides the means for the agents to communicate about roles and dependencies and thus provide the possibility for adaptation and reconfiguration of the agents' organizational structure.

Acknowledgment. We would like to thank the TGI group of the Department of Informatics, University of Hamburg and especially Dr. Daniel Moldt for the support, constructive criticism and fruitful discussions.

References

1. Boissier, O., Hübner, J.F., Sichman, J.S.: Organization oriented programming: From closed to open organizations. In: O'Hare, G.M.P., Ricci, A., O'Grady, M.J., Dikenelli, O. (eds.) ESAW 2006. LNCS (LNAI), vol. 4457, pp. 86–105. Springer, Heidelberg (2007)
2. Cabac, L.: Multi-agent system: A guiding metaphor for the organization of software development projects. In: Petta, P., Müller, J.P., Klusch, M., Georgeff, M. (eds.) MATES 2007. LNCS (LNAI), vol. 4687, pp. 1–12. Springer, Heidelberg (2007)
3. Cabac, L.: Modeling Petri Net-Based Multi-Agent Applications, Agent Technology - Theory and Applications, vol. 5. Logos Verlag, Berlin (2010). http://logos-verlag.de/cgi-local/buch?isbn=2673
4. Cabac, L., Dirkner, R., Moldt, D.: Modeling with service dependency diagrams. In: Moldt, D., Ultes-Nitsche, U., Augusto, J.C. (eds.) Proceedings of the 6th International Workshop on Modelling, Simulation, Verification and Validation of Enterprise Information Systems, MSVVEIS-2008. conjunction with ICEIS 2008. Barcelona, Spain, June 2008, pp. 109–118. INSTICC PRESS, Portugal (2008)

5. Cabac, L., Dirkner, R., Rölke, H.: Modelling service dependencies for the analysis and design of multi-agent applications. In: Moldt, D. (ed.) Proceedings of the Fourth International Workshop on Modelling of Objects, Components, and Agents. MOCA'06. pp. 291–298. No. FBI-HH-B-272/06 in Report of the Department of Informatics, University of Hamburg, Department of Informatics, Vogt-Kölln Str. 30, D-22527 Hamburg, Germany (2006)
6. Cabac, L., Dörges, T., Duvigneau, M., Moldt, D., Reese, C., Wester-Ebbinghaus, M.: Agent models for concurrent software systems. In: Bergmann, R., Lindemann, G., Kirn, S., Pěchouček, M. (eds.) MATES 2008. LNCS (LNAI), vol. 5244, pp. 37–48. Springer, Heidelberg (2008)
7. Cabac, L., Moldt, D.: Support for modeling roles and dependencies in multi-agent systems. In: Köhler-Bußmeier, M., Moldt, D., Boissier, O. (eds.) Organizational Modelling, International Workshop, OrgMod'09. Proceedings. pp. 15–33. Technical Reports Université Paris 13, Université Paris 13, 99, avenue Jean-Baptiste Clément, 93 430 Villetaneuse (2009). http://www.informatik.uni-hamburg.de/TGI/events/orgmod09/#proceedings
8. Coutinho, L., Sichmann, J., Boissier, O.: Modelling dimensions for agent organizations. In: Dignum, V. (ed.) Handbook of Research on Multi-Agent Systems: Semantics and Dynamics of Organizational Models, pp. 18–50. Information Science Reference (2009)
9. Dignum, V.: The role of organization in agent systems. In: Dignum, V. (ed.) Handbook of Research on Multi-Agent Systems: Semantics and Dynamics of Organizational Models, pp. 1–16. Information Science Reference (2009)
10. Ensel, C., Keller, A.: An approach for managing service dependencies with xml and the resource description framework. J. Netw. Syst. Manage. 10, 147–170 (2002). http://dx.doi.org/10.1023/A:1015902715532
11. Ferber, J., Gutknecht, O., Michel, F.: From agents to organizations: An organizational view of multi-agent systems. In: Giorgini, P., Müller, J.P., Odell, J.J. (eds.) AOSE 2003. LNCS, vol. 2935, pp. 214–230. Springer, Heidelberg (2004)
12. Foundation for Intelligent Physical Agents (FIPA): FIPA SL Content Language Specification (2002). http://www.fipa.org/specs/fipa00008/index.html
13. Gopal, R.: Layered model for supporting fault isolation and recovery. In: Network Operations and Management Symposium, 2000, NOMS 2000, 2000 IEEE/IFIP, pp. 729–742. IEEE (2000)
14. Hahn, C., Jacobi, S., Raber, D.: Enhancing the interoperability between multiagent systems and service-oriented architectures through a model-driven approach. In: 2010 IEEE/WIC/ACM International Conference on Web Intelligence and Intelligent Agent Technology (WI-IAT), vol. 2, pp. 415–422. IEEE (2010)
15. Horling, B., Lesser, V.: A survey of multi-agent organizational paradigms. Knowl. Eng. Rev. 19(4), 281–316 (2005)
16. Köhler, M., Moldt, D., Rölke, H.: Modelling the structure and behaviour of Petri net agents. In: Colom, J.-M., Koutny, M. (eds.) ICATPN 2001. LNCS, vol. 2075, p. 224. Springer, Heidelberg (2001)
17. Köhler-Bußmeier, M., Wester-Ebbinghaus, M., Moldt, D.: A formal model for organisational structures behind process-aware information systems. In: Jensen, K., van der Aalst, W.M.P. (eds.) Transactions on Petri Nets and Other Models of Concurrency II. LNCS, vol. 5460, pp. 98–114. Springer, Heidelberg (2009)
18. Köhler-Bußmeier, M., Wester-Ebbinghaus, M., Moldt, D.: Generating executable multi-agent system prototypes from SONAR specifications. In: De Vos, M., Fornara, N., Pitt, J.V., Vouros, G. (eds.) COIN 2010. LNCS, vol. 6541, pp. 21–38. Springer, Heidelberg (2011)

19. Mao, X., Yu, E.: Organizational and social concepts in agent oriented software engineering. In: Odell, J.J., Giorgini, P., Müller, J.P. (eds.) AOSE 2004. LNCS, vol. 3382, pp. 1–15. Springer, Heidelberg (2005)
20. Mosteller, D.: Entwicklung eines Werkzeugs zur Modellierung der initialen Wissensbasen und Rollen-Abhängigkeiten in Multiagentenanwendungen im Kontext von PAOSE/MULAN. Bachelor's Thesis, University of Hamburg, Department of Informatics (2010)
21. Padgham, L., Winikoff, M.: Developing Intelligent Agent Systems : A Practical Guide. Wiley Series in Agent Technology, p. 225. Wiley, Chichester (2004). ISBN:0-470-86120-7
22. Rölke, H.: Modellierung von Agenten und Multiagentensystemen - Grundlagen und Anwendungen, Agent Technology - Theory and Applications, vol. 2. Logos Verlag, Berlin (2004). http://logos-verlag.de/cgi-local/buch?isbn=0768
23. Silva, C.T.L.L., Castro, J.: Modeling organizational architectural styles in UML: The Tropos case. In: Pastor, O., Díaz, J.S. (eds.) Anais do WER02 - Workshop em Engenharia de Requisitos, pp. 162–176 (2002)
24. Tavares, A.L., Valente, M.T.: A gentle introduction to OSGi. SIGSOFT Softw. Eng. Notes **33**, 8:1–8:5 (2008). http://doi.acm.org/10.1145/1402521.1402526
25. Zambonelli, F., Jennings, N., Wooldridge, M.: Developing multiagent systems: The Gaia methodology. ACM Trans. Softw. Eng. Methodol. **12**(3), 317–370 (2003)
26. Zinnikus, I., Benguria, G., Elvesæter, B., Fischer, K., Vayssière, J.: A model driven approach to agent-based service-oriented architectures. In: Fischer, K., Timm, I.J., André, E., Zhong, N. (eds.) MATES 2006. LNCS (LNAI), vol. 4196, pp. 110–122. Springer, Heidelberg (2006). http://dx.doi.org/10.1007/11872283_10

A Canonical Contraction for Safe Petri Nets

Thomas Chatain[(✉)] and Stefan Haar

INRIA & LSV (CNRS & ENS Cachan),
61, Avenue du Président Wilson, 94235 Cachan Cedex, France
{chatain,haar}@lsv.ens-cachan.fr

Abstract. Under maximal semantics, the occurrence of an event a in a concurrent run of an occurrence net may imply the occurrence of other events, not causally related to a, in the same run. In recent works, we have formalized this phenomenon as the *reveals* relation, and used it to obtain a contraction of sets of events called *facets* in the context of occurrence nets. Here, we extend this idea to propose a canonical contraction of general safe Petri nets into pieces of partial-order behaviour which can be seen as "macro-transitions" since all their events must occur together in maximal semantics. On occurrence nets, our construction coincides with the facets abstraction.Our contraction preserves the maximal semantics in the sense that the maximal processes of the contracted net are in bijection with those of the original net.

1 Introduction and Motivation

The properties of the long-run, *maximal* behaviour of discrete event systems induce correlations between occurrences, i.e. relations of the type "if a fires, then b will fire sooner or later – unless it already has". This could be exploited in *predicting* (in the sense e.g. of failure prognosis, see [8]) events that inevitably will occur: Consider the sequential system shown in Fig. 1(a). It is given here as a Petri net for convenience, but easily translated into an equivalent finite automaton of six states, eight transitions and initial state 0. When in state 0, the system can perform either a, e, or h. Whatever the choice of the first transition, however, in each case the *second* choice is imposed: after a no other transition than b is possible, after e only f, and after h only i.

It is known that structural transformations can facilitate verification of some system properties, as witnessed by e.g. Berthelot [3], Desel and Merceron [5], and other works. Here, we focus on other properties, those that depend only on the language of the *maximal* runs of the system, such as liveness properties, or particular other properties such as *diagnosability* or *predictability*, see [9,10]. In such a perspective, the system can be thought of as *contracted*: any stretch of consecutive transitions that occur always together in a maximal behavior provided that any *one* of them occurs, is fused into a single *macro-transition* that inherits pre- and post-places from the first and (if it exists) last transitions. In Fig. 1(b): each of the new transitions is labeled with the transition chain that it represents. Note that the infinite word hi^ω is obtained via a single macro-transition without post-place, since the word has no last transition. Of course,

© Springer-Verlag Berlin Heidelberg 2014
M. Koutny et al. (Eds.): ToPNoC IX, LNCS 8910, pp. 83–98, 2014.
DOI: 10.1007/978-3-662-45730-6_5

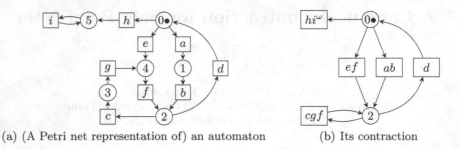

(a) (A Petri net representation of) an automaton   (b) Its contraction

Fig. 1. Contracting automata by removing non-branching states (here 1, 3, 4 and 5)

not all *temporal* properties of the system are preserved, since not all *finite* words survive the contraction: $abcg$ is a word produced by a run in Fig. 1(a), but not in Fig. 1(b) which has no intermediate word between (ab) and $(ab)(cgf)$. However, one sees quickly that the *maximal* words – which coincide with the *infinite* words – of the original system of Fig. 1(a) are in bijection with the infinite words of the contracted system in Fig. 1(b). This contraction represents a reduction of the original system onto its essential behavior.

When *concurrent* behavior in partial order semantics is considered, the language of words is replaced by a collection of partial orders representing the non-sequential runs. The theory of the reveals relation and of reduced occurrence nets is given in [1,2,6,7]. Figure 3(a) (whose formal discussion is postponed to Sect. 2) illustrates the facets of an occurrence net; the contraction of its facets yields the reduced occurrence net in Fig. 3(b). The present work is based on a combination of the ideas shown, on the one hand, in the automata contraction such as in the example of Fig. 1, and on the other hand of the facet contraction in the context of occurrence nets. We will identify *macro-transitions* in safe Petri nets that allow contraction with preservation of *maximal* semantics, and thus to give a contracted normal form for any given safe Petri net. If the definition is applied to occurrence nets, we obtain exactly the facets according to [1,2,6,7]. The relation between unfolding and reduction will be clarified below, in particular Theorems 4 and 5, as well as Fig. 6. At the same time, the reduced net has never more, and generally much fewer, transitions than the original net.

Related work. Best and Randell [4] considered atomicity of subnets in occurrence graphs, focusing on non-interference in the temporal behavior and identifying atomic and hence contractable blocks of behavior. The structures obtained can be embedded into non-branching occurrence nets, allowing the approach to be compared with ours. However, while the construction of facets appears geometrically similar, the approach of [1,2,6,7] focuses on the question of *logical occurrence* regardless of the order in which events occur.

Occurrence nets are linked to safe Petri nets in the sense that the partial order unfolding semantics of such Petri nets yields occurrence nets, as defined above. The converse is true for occurrence nets corresponding to regular trace

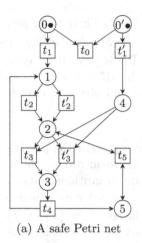

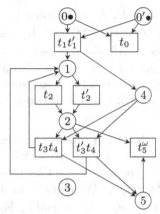

(a) A safe Petri net

(b) Its canonical contraction. (Place 3 is not used any more and could be forgotten.)

Fig. 2. Overview of the canonical contraction of a safe Petri net

languages: Following Zielonka [12], any regular trace language $\mathcal{L}$ is accepted by an asynchronous automaton $A_{\mathcal{L}}$; moreover, $A_{\mathcal{L}}$ can be synthesized directly from $\mathcal{L}$. As there are natural translations from asynchronous automata into safe Petri nets, the approach extends immediately into a procedure that takes as input an occurrence net ON and synthesizes a safe Petri net N whose unfolding semantics yields again ON (up to isomorphism). The present paper aims *not* at mimicking this synthesis but rather provides a contraction on the generating safe Petri net itself.

Organization of the paper. We begin by recalling the basic definitions on unfoldings, and results from [1,2,6,7] concerning facets in occurrence nets, based on the *reveals*-relation, in Sect. 2. Section 3 contains the core of the present work, with the study of *macro-transitions* that generalize facets from occurrence nets to safe Petri nets. In Sect. 4, we identify the canonical reduced version for a given safe net. The relation between the operations of reduction and of unfolding is studied in Sect. 5. Finally, Sect. 6 concludes.

2   Reveals Relation and Facets in Occurrence Nets

Petri Nets, Occurrence Nets and Unfoldings. This part collects several basic definitions used below. In this paper, only safe Petri nets are considered.

Definition 1 (Petri Net). *A* Petri net (PN)*, or simply* net*, is a tuple* (P, T, F, M^0) *where* P *and* T *are sets of* places *and* transitions *respectively,* $F \subseteq (P \times T) \cup (T \times P)$ *is a* flow relation*, and* $M^0 \subseteq P$ *is an* initial marking*.*

For any node $x \in P \cup T$, we call *pre-set* of x the set $^\bullet x = \{y \in P \cup T \mid (y, x) \in F\}$ and *post-set* of x the set $x^\bullet = \{y \in P \cup T \mid (x, y) \in F\}$. A *marking* of a net is a subset M of P. A transition t is *enabled* at M iff ${}^\bullet t \subseteq M$. Then t can *fire*, leading to $M' = (M \setminus {}^\bullet t) \cup t^\bullet$. In that case, we write $M \xrightarrow{t} M'$. A marking M is *reachable* if $M^0 \longrightarrow^* M$, where $\longrightarrow \overset{def}{=} \bigcup_{t \in T} \xrightarrow{t}$. A PN is *safe* iff for each reachable marking M, for each transition t enabled at M, $(t^\bullet \cap M) \subseteq {}^\bullet t$. As usual, in figures, transitions are represented as rectangles and places as circles. If $p \in M$, a black token is drawn in p (see Fig. 2(a)).

Partial-Order Semantics *Occurrence nets* are used to represent the partial-order behaviour of Petri nets. We need a few definitions to introduce them. Denote by $\lessdot$ the *direct causality* relation defined as: for any transitions s and t, $s \lessdot t \overset{def}{\Leftrightarrow} s^\bullet \cap {}^\bullet t \neq \emptyset$. We write $<$ for its transitive closure and $\leq$ for its reflexive transitive closure, called *causality*. For any transition t, the set $\lceil t \rceil \overset{def}{=} \{s \mid s \leq t\}$ is the *causal past* of t, and for $T' \subseteq T$, the causal past of T' is defined as $\lceil T' \rceil \overset{def}{=} \bigcup_{t \in T'} \lceil t \rceil$. Two distinct transitions s and t are in *direct conflict*, denoted by $s \#_d t$, iff ${}^\bullet s \cap {}^\bullet t \neq \emptyset$. Two transitions s and t are in *conflict*, denoted by $s \# t$, iff $\exists s' \in \lceil s \rceil, t' \in \lceil t \rceil : s' \#_d t'$, and the *conflict set* of t is defined as $\#[t] \overset{def}{=} \{s \mid s \# t\}$. Finally, two transitions s and t are *concurrent*, denoted by $s \text{ co } t$, iff $\neg(s \# t) \wedge \neg(s \leq t) \wedge \neg(t \leq s)$.

Definition 2 (Occurrence net). *An* occurrence net *(ON) is a Petri net (B, E, F, C^0) where elements of B and E are called* conditions *and* events, *respectively, and such that:*

1. $\forall b \in C^0 \quad {}^\bullet b = \emptyset$,
2. $\forall b \in B \setminus C^0 \quad |{}^\bullet b| = 1$ *(no backward branching)*,
3. $\forall e \in E \quad \neg(e < e)$ *($\leq$ is a partial order)*,
4. $\forall e \in E \quad \neg(e \# e)$ *(no self-conflict)*,
5. $\forall e \in E \quad |\lceil e \rceil| < \infty$ *(finite causal pasts)*.

We say that event e *consumes* the conditions ${}^\bullet e$ and *creates* the conditions $e^\bullet$.

Figure 3(a) gives an example of ON.

Occurrence nets are branching structures which have several possible executions in general. Each execution appears under the form of a *configuration*.

Definition 3 (Configurations and Maximal Configurations). *A* configuration *of an ON is a conflict-free and causally closed set of events, i.e. $\omega \subseteq E$ is a configuration iff $\forall e \in \omega$, $(\#[e] \cap \omega = \emptyset) \wedge (\lceil e \rceil \subseteq \omega)$. A configuration is* maximal *iff it is maximal w.r.t. $\subseteq$. We write Ω_{gen} for the set of all configurations and Ω_{max} for the set of maximal configurations.*

Notice that not every infinite configuration is maximal: in an ON with several concurrent branches, a configuration containing only one branch is not maximal, even if the branch is infinite.

Executions of safe Petri nets will be represented as *non-branching processes*, using occurrence nets related to the original Petri net by a *net homomorphism*.

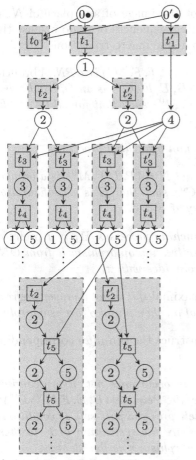

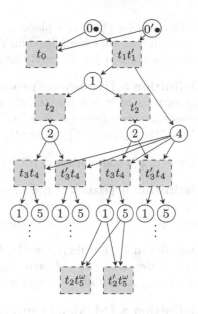

(a) A prefix of the unfolding of the Petri net of Figure 2(a). Dashed boxes indicate facets.

(b) The corresponding reduced ON. The condensed labels of facets indicate the events that they contain; e.g. the facet labeled t_1t_1' is the one depicted in Figure 4(b).

Fig. 3. An ON and its reduction through the facet abstraction.

Definition 4 (Net homomorphism). *A net homomorphism from $N = (P, T, F, M^0)$ to $N' = (P', T', F', M'^0)$ is a pair of maps $\pi = (\pi_P, \pi_T)$, where $\pi_P : P \to P'$ and $\pi_T : T \to T'$, such that:*

- *for all $t \in T$, $\pi_{P|\bullet t}$ (the restriction of π_P to $\bullet t$) is a bijection between $\bullet t$ and $\bullet\pi_T(t)$, and $\pi_{P|t\bullet}$ is a bijection between $t^\bullet$ and $\pi_T(t)^\bullet$;*
- *and $\pi_{P|M^0}$ maps injectively M^0 to (a subset of) M'^0.*

We will often write simply π instead of π_P or π_T.

Net homomorphisms preserve the semantics of nets in the sense that they map every firing sequence of N to a firing sequence of N', and $\pi_{P|M^0}$ needs not be a bijection for that. If a place p' of N' is not the image of any place of N, it simply means that the images in N' of the firing sequences of N do not use the token initially in p'. We need this subtlety to define macro-transitions later.

Definition 5 (Branching process). *Let $N = (P, T, F, M^0)$ be a PN. A branching process of N is a pair (O, π), where $O = (B, E, F', C^0)$ is an ON and π is a homomorphism from (B, E, F', C^0) to (P, T, F, M^0) such that for all $t, t' \in E$, $(\,^\bullet t = \,^\bullet t' \wedge \pi(t) = \pi(t')) \Rightarrow t = t'$.*

When E is a configuration, (O, π) is called a *non-branching process*.

Definition 6 (Run). *A run of a safe Petri net $N = (P, T, F, M^0)$ is a branching process (O, π) of N with $O = (B, E, F', C^0)$ such that E is a configuration and $\pi(C^0) = M^0$. The run is called* nonempty *if $E \neq \emptyset$.*

Definition 7 (Prefix). *For Π_1, Π_2 two branching processes, Π_1 is a prefix of Π_2, written $\Pi_1 \sqsubseteq \Pi_2$, if there exists an injective homomorphism h from ON_1 into ON_2, such that the composition $\pi_2 \circ h$ coincides with π_1.*

Definition 8 (Maximal run). *A run ρ is* maximal *if it is not a proper prefix of any run, i.e. for every run ρ', if ρ is a prefix of ρ', then ρ and ρ' are isomorphic.*

We define a function μ which allows us to construct the run $\mu(\omega)$ corresponding to a configuration ω of an ON.

Definition 9 (μ). *Let $O = (B, E, F, C^0)$ be an occurrence net. Every conflict-free set of events $E' \subseteq E$ defines a run $\mu(E')$ of the Petri net $(B, E, F, \,^\bullet E' \backslash E'^\bullet)^1$. The occurrence net $\mu(E')$ has E' as events, their pre- and post-sets as conditions, and $\,^\bullet E' \backslash E'^\bullet$ as initial conditions. The arcs are the restriction of F to these events and conditions, and the folding homomorphism π is the identity.*

Definition 10 (Unfolding). *Let N be a PN. By Theorem 23 of [11], there exists a unique (up to an isomorphism) $\sqsubseteq$-maximal branching process, called the* unfolding *of N and denoted $U(N)$; by abuse of language, we will also call unfolding of N the ON obtained by the unfolding.*

Reveals Relation and Facets Abstraction. The structure of an ON defines three relations over its events: *causality*, *conflict* and *concurrency*. But these structural relations do not express all logical dependencies between the occurrence of events in maximal configurations. A central fact is that concurrency is not always a logical independency: it is possible that the occurrence of an event implies, under the perspective of *maximal* runs, the occurrence of another one, which is structurally concurrent. This happens with events labeled t_1 and t_1' in Fig. 3(a): we observe that t_1 is in conflict with t_0 and that any maximal configuration contains either t_0 or t_1'. Therefore, if t_1 occurs in a maximal configuration,

---

[1] Notice that $(B, E, F, \,^\bullet E' \backslash E'^\bullet)$ is not an occurrence net in general: it satisfies items 3, 4 and 5 of Definition 2, but items 1 and 2 may not hold.

then t_0 does not occur and eventually t'_1 necessarily occurs. Yet t_1 and t'_1 are concurrent.

Another case is illustrated by events labeled t_3 and t_4 on the left of the same figure: because t_3 is a causal predecessor of t_4, the occurrence of t_4 implies the occurrence of t_3; but in any maximal configuration, the occurrence of t_3 also implies the occurrence of t_4, because t_4 is the only possible continuation to t_3 and nothing can prevent it. Then t_3 and t_4 are actually made logically equivalent by the maximal progress assumption.

Definition 11 (Reveals relation [1,2,6,7]). *We say that event e reveals event f, and write $e \triangleright f$, iff $\forall \omega \in \Omega_{max}, (e \in \omega \Rightarrow f \in \omega)$.*

Definition 12 (Facets Abstraction in Occurrence Nets [6]). *Let $\sim$ be the equivalence relation defined by $\forall\, e, f \in E : \ e \sim f \stackrel{def}{\iff} (e \triangleright f) \wedge (f \triangleright e)$. Then a facet of an ON is an equivalence class of $\sim$.*

In Fig. 3(a), the facets are highlighted in grey. If ψ is a facet, then for any maximal configuration $\omega \in \Omega_{max}$ and for any event e such that $e \in \psi$, $e \in \omega$ iff $\psi \subseteq \omega$. In this sense, facets can be seen as atomic sets of events (under the maximal semantics). Denote the set of O's facets as $\Psi(O)$.

For any facet and for any configuration, either *all* events in the facet are in the configuration or *no* event in the facet is in the configuration. Therefore, facets can be seen as events.

Definition 13 (Reduced occurrence net). *A reduced ON is an ON (B, E, F, C^0) such that $\forall e_1, e_2 \in e, \quad e_1 \sim e_2 \iff e_1 = e_2$.*

As shown in [1,6], every occurrence net $O = (B, E, F, C^0)$ has a uniquely defined *reduction* ON $\overline{O}$ whose events are the facets of O and whose conditions those from B that are post-conditions of a maximal event of some facet:

Definition 14 (Reduction of an occurrence net). *The reduction of occurrence net $O = (B, E, F, C^0)$ is the occurrence net $\overline{O} = (\overline{B}, \Psi(O), \overline{F}, C^0)$, where*

$$\overline{B} = C^0 \cup \{b \in B : \ \exists\, \psi \in \Psi(O), \ e \in \psi : \ (e, b) \in F \wedge b^\bullet \cap \psi = \emptyset\} \tag{1}$$

$$\overline{F} = \ \{(b, \psi) : \ b \in \overline{B} \wedge \exists\, e \in \psi : \ (b, e) \in F\} \tag{2}$$
$$\cup \{(\psi, b) : \ b \in \overline{B} \wedge \exists\, e \in \psi : \ (e, b) \in F\}$$

Figure 3 shows the facets of an occurrence net and its reduction.

3 Generalizing Facets to Safe Petri Nets

We propose to identify pieces of partial-order behaviour of a safe Petri net, under the form of *macro-transitions* which group events that always occur together when at least one of them occur in any maximal run of the original net. There will be a fundamental difference in the approach here with respect to the work in [1,2,6,7]: there, the set of events to be contracted (the *facets*) were obtained as the strongly connected components of a transitive binary *reveals*-relation, where a reveals b iff any run containing a also contains b. Here, such a relation is not available on the level of transitions. Our approach is thus to identify directly sets of transitions such that, if any one of them fires, all others fire sooner or later.

Definition 15 (Macro-transition). *Let $N = (P, T, F, M^0)$ be a PN. A macro-transition of N is a run $\phi = (O, \pi)$ of $(P, T, F, \pi(C^0))$ (the net N initialized with any marking $\pi(C^0)$, thus denoted as the image of the initial conditions C^0 of O) such that for any reachable marking M of N with $\pi(C^0) \subseteq M$ and for any maximal run ρ of (P, T, F, M) (the net N starting at M), if there exists a nonempty prefix ϕ' of ϕ which is also a prefix of ρ, then the entire ϕ is a prefix of ρ.*

Figures 4 and 5 show examples and counter-examples of macro-transitions of the Petri net of Fig. 2(a).

- ϕ_1 is trivially a macro-transition.
- In ϕ_2 we have two events: an occurrence of t_1 and one of t_1'. The initial conditions of ϕ_2 are mapped to places 0 and $0'$ of N. The only reachable marking of N which contains $\{0, 0'\}$ is $\{0, 0'\}$ itself; in $\{0, 0'\}$, if one of the two transitions fire, the other one will necessarily fire in any maximal run.
- Consider now ϕ_3: again the only reachable marking of N which contains $\{1, 5\}$ is $\{1, 5\}$ itself. From it, if t_2 fires, it is necessarily followed by an infinite sequence of firings of t_5. ϕ_3 is exactly a prefix of it.

  We also find counter-examples here:

- ϕ_4 is not a macro-transition as it is not a run: t_0 and t_1 are in conflict.
- ϕ_5 is not a macro-transition because an occurrence of t_1 is not necessarily followed by an occurrence of t_2.
- Concerning ϕ_6, it is exactly a prefix of every maximal run from $\{1, 0'\}$ starting by an occurrence of t_2, but not of every run starting by an occurrence of t_1' (because t_2' can fire instead of t_2).

  The two following properties are immediate consequences of the definition.

Property 1. Any single transition $t \in T$ induces a macro-transition defined as the (unique, up to isomorphism) non-branching process which contains a single event mapped to t and whose initial conditions are mapped to ${}^\bullet t$. For example, the facet induced by t_1 in the net of Fig. 2(a) is the one depicted in Fig. 4(a).

Property 2. Let ϕ be a macro-transition of a Petri net N. Then any prefix of ϕ with the same initial conditions as ϕ is also a macro-transition of N.

Definition 16 (Φ-contracted net). *Given a set Φ of macro-transitions of a Petri net $N = (P, T, F, M^0)$, we construct the Φ-contracted net $N_{/\Phi}$ by replacing the transitions of N by the macro-transitions. The contracted net is formally defined as the net $N_{/\Phi} = (P, \Phi, F_\Phi, M^0)$ where the macro-transitions are interpreted as transitions and with the flow relation F_Φ defined such that, for every $\phi = (O, \pi) \in \Phi$, ${}^\bullet\phi$ is the image by π of the initial conditions of O, and $\phi^\bullet$ is the image by π of the conditions of O that are not consumed by any event of O.*

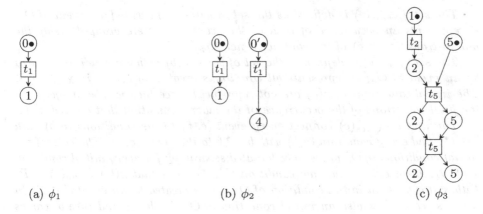

(a) ϕ_1 (b) ϕ_2 (c) ϕ_3

Fig. 4. Examples of macro-transitions of the Petri net of Fig. 2(a)

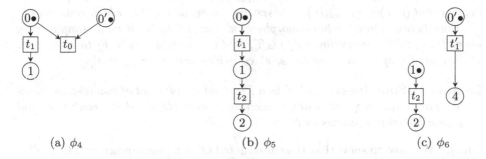

(a) ϕ_4 (b) ϕ_5 (c) ϕ_6

Fig. 5. Counter-examples of macro-transitions of the Petri net of Fig. 2(a)

To express the soundness of this contraction, we define a function χ which maps any branching process (O, π) of the contracted net $N_{/\Phi}$ to a branching process of N. Intuitively, χ simply expands every event e of O into a set of events corresponding to the content of the macro-transition $\pi(e)$. For example, the reduced unfolding of Fig. 3(b), viewed as a branching process of the contraction of the unfolding U of Fig. 3(a), is mapped by χ to U.

Definition 17 (χ). *Let $N = (P, T, F, M^0)$ be a Petri net, Φ a set of macro-transitions of N and $\rho = (O, \pi)$ a branching process of the contracted net $N_{/\Phi}$, with $O = (B, E, F, C^0)$. We define the branching process $\chi(\rho)$ of N as $\chi(\rho) = (O', \pi')$ with $O' = (C^0 \cup \chi_{cond}(E), \chi_{events}(E), \chi_{arcs}(E), C^0)$ where $\chi_{events}, \chi_{cond}$ and χ_{arcs} associate to every event $e \in E$ a set of events $\chi_{events}(e)$, a set of conditions $\chi_{cond}(e)$ and a set of arcs $\chi_{arcs}(e)$, all specified below. Note that e is an occurrence of transition $\pi(e)$ of $N_{/\Phi}$, which is also a macro-transition of N and thus has the form (O_e, π_e) with O_e an occurrence net and π_e a net homomorphism from O_e to $(P, T, F, \pi(C_e^0))$, where C_e^0 are the initial conditions of O_e.*

· The set $\chi_{events}(e)$ is defined as the set of pairs (e, f) with f an event of O_e; it represents an occurrence of each of the events that were grouped inside the macro-transition $\pi(e)$ of the contracted net $N_{/\Phi}$.

The set $\chi_{cond}(e)$ is defined as the set of pairs (e, b) with b a condition created by an event of O_e; it represents all conditions created by events in $\chi_{events}(e)$. The initial conditions of $\pi(e)$ are not reproduced since they will be merged with the final conditions of the occurrence of the macro-transition that created them.

The arcs in $\chi_{arcs}(e)$ connect every event (e, f) to the conditions (e, b) with $b \in f^\bullet$, and every condition (e, b) with $b \in {}^\bullet f$ to the event (e, f). The case of the initial conditions of O_e needs to be handled separately: for every initial condition b of O_e, there exists a unique condition $b' \in {}^\bullet e$ such that $\pi(b') = \pi_e(b) \in P$. Either this b' is an initial condition of O or it is created by an event $e' \in E$. In the first case, b' is also an initial condition of O'; in the second case b' comes from a final condition of $\pi(e')$, which appears in $\chi_{cond}(e')$ under the form of a pair (e', b''). Thun an arc is added in $\chi_{arcs}(e)$ to connect either b or (e', b'') to every event $(e, f) \in \chi_{events}(e)$ representing an event f of O_e which consumes b.

Finally, we define the homomorphism π' from O' to N. It maps simply every event (e, f) to the transition $\pi_e(f) \in T$, and every condition (e, b) to $\pi_e(b) \in P$. On the set C_0 of initial conditions, π' coincides with $\pi : \pi_{|C_0} \equiv \pi'_{|C_0}$.

Lemma 1 (Soundness). *Let N be a Petri net and Φ a set of macro-transitions of N. The function χ maps any branching process (O, π) of the contracted net $N_{/\Phi}$ to a branching process of N.*

Proof. We have to show that the constructed O' is an occurrence net. Causality in O' is a partial order because causality in O is, as well as causality in each macro-transition. Take now an event e of O' and assume that e is in self conflict: this conflict originates at two events in the causal past of e. Either these two events come from the same occurrence of a macro-transition, which contradicts the fact the the macro-transition is conflict-free; or they come from different occurrences of macro-transitions (i.e. different events of O), and then this implies that the event of O from which e comes, is in self-conflict in O.

The rest is direct.   □

Definition 18 (Completeness). *A set Φ of macro-transitions of a Petri net $N = (P, T, F, M^0)$ is complete if for every reachable marking M of the contracted net $N_{/\Phi} = (P, \Phi, F', M^0)$ and every transition $t \in T$ firable from M, the run of (P, T, F, M) composed of all the events revealed by the initial occurrence of t in the unfolding of (P, T, F, M), is the image by χ of a run of (P, Φ, F', M).*

Lemma 2. *Let N be a Petri net and Φ a complete set of macro-transitions of N. Then every maximal run ρ of N is (isomorphic to) the image by χ of a maximal run ρ' of $N_{/\Phi}$.*

Proof. To construct the ρ', start from the process with no events and initial conditions corresponding to the initial marking of N (which is also the initial marking of $N_{/\Phi}$). Then, as long as there are events in ρ which are not in $\chi(\rho')$, take one which is minimal w.r.t. causality and call it e. (Among the possible choices, e should be of minimal depth[2] so that every event of ρ is eventually in $\chi(\rho')$.) The transition t of N which is the image of e by the homomorphism of ρ, can fire from the marking M reached after ρ' (which is also the marking reached after $\chi(\rho')$). By the completeness hypothesis, there exists a run of (P, Φ, F', M) whose image by χ yields all the events revealed by the firing of t from M. Then ρ' can be augmented by this run. Our e of ρ is now one of the new events in $\chi(\rho')$; and the other new events are also in ρ because they are revealed by the occurrence of t from M and ρ is maximal.

Notice that at each step, $\chi(\rho')$ is a prefix of ρ. The iteration may not terminate but, since ρ' always grows, we consider its limit (containing all the events that are eventually added). By construction this limit is the desired process. □

Definition 19 (Non-Redundancy). *A set Φ of macro-transitions of a Petri net $N = (P, T, F, M^0)$ is called* non-redundant *if for every transition $t \in T$, at most one macro-transition $\phi \in \Phi$ starts by[3] t.*

Theorem 1 (Facets as Macro-Transitions). *Let $O = (B, E, F, C^0)$ be an occurrence net and $\psi \subseteq E$ a facet of O. Then $\mu(\psi)$ is a macro-transition of O. Moreover the image by μ of all the facets of O is a complete non-redundant set of macro-transitions of O.*

Proof. Consider a reachable set of conditions $C \supseteq {}^\bullet\psi$, and let ω be a maximal run of (B, E, F, C) starting by a nonempty prefix of $\mu(\psi)$. Then ω starts by $\mu(\{e\})$ with e an initial event of ψ. By Definition 12, e reveals all the events in ψ. This implies that ω starts by the entire $\mu(\psi)$.

For completeness, remark that for every run ρ of the contracted ON, the set of events in $\chi(\rho)$ is a union of facets of O. After such a run, every maximal run corresponds again to a union of facets.

Non-redundancy holds because the facets are a partition of the events. □

4   Canonical Contraction

Before defining our canonical contraction, we study the markings that are reachable after a run of a contracted net.

For every configuration O, we call *cut* of O the set of conditions which are created and not consumed along O. When O is the ON in a finite run (O, π) of a net N, the homomorphism π maps the cut of O to a reachable marking of N. And conversely every reachable marking of N is the image of the final conditions of a finite run.

But in this paper we focus on maximal runs, which are in general infinite. And the image of a cut of an infinite run may be only a *subset* of a reachable

---

[2] The depth of an event e is the size of the longest path from an initial condition to e.
[3] By "ϕ starts by t", we mean that there exists an event in ϕ which is mapped to t and consumes only initial conditions of ϕ.

marking of N. An example is the maximal run of the net of Fig. 1(a) containing an occurrence of h and an infinite chain of i's. All the conditions are consumed, and the cut is empty. Yet the empty marking is not reachable after any finite run.

Then we call *asymptotically reachable* (or *a-reachable* for short) in N any marking that is the image of the cut of a (possibly infinite) run of N.

Lemma 3 (A-Reachability in a Contracted Net). *Let N be a Petri net and Φ a set of macro-transitions of N. Any marking a-reachable in $N_{/\Phi}$ is also a-reachable in N.*

Proof. This is an immediate consequence of Lemma 1.   □

Notice however that in general not every marking a-reachable in N is a-reachable in $N_{/\Phi}$. And this is actually what allows us to skip some intermediate markings and give a more compact representation of the behaviour of the net.

In this sense we can say that a complete contracted net $N_{/\Phi}$ is more compact than another $N_{/\Phi'}$ if all markings a-reachable in $N_{/\Phi}$ are also a-reachable in $N_{/\Phi'}$. We will show now that there exists a complete non-redundant contracted net which is optimal w.r.t. this criterion: i.e. all markings a-reachable in this contracted net are a-reachable in any complete non-redundant contracted net.

Definition 20 ($\mathcal{M}_N$ and $\mathcal{R}_N$). *We define inductively a set $\mathcal{M}_N$ of markings of M and a set $\mathcal{R}_N$ of runs as the smallest sets satisfying:*

– *$M^0 \in \mathcal{M}_N$;*
– *for every $M \in \mathcal{M}_N$, for every transition t firable from M, $\mu(E) \in \mathcal{R}_N$, where E is the set of events revealed by the initial occurrence of t in $U((P,T,F,M))$ (note that by its definition, E is conflict-free);*
– *for every $M \in \mathcal{M}_N$, for every $\rho \in \mathcal{R}_N$ such that ${}^\bullet\rho \subseteq M$, the marking $(M \setminus {}^\bullet\rho) \cup \rho^\bullet$ reached after firing ρ from M, belongs to $\mathcal{M}_N$;*
– *for every $\rho_1, \rho_2 \in \mathcal{R}_N$, the largest common prefix of ρ_1 and ρ_2 is in $\mathcal{R}_N$.*

Theorem 2. *Let $N = (P, T, F, M^0)$ be a Petri net and Φ a non-redundant complete set of macro-transitions. All markings of $\mathcal{M}_N$ are a-reachable in $N_{/\Phi}$.*

Proof. Let $N_{/\Phi} = (P, \Phi, F', M^0)$. The theorem is a direct consequence of the following lemma: for every marking M a-reachable in N every run $\rho \in \mathcal{R}_N$ firable from M satisfies the property that ρ is the image by χ a run ρ' of (P, Φ, F', M). This lemma is proved by induction, following the construction of $\mathcal{R}_N$: at each step of the construction, we prove that if all the runs in the current $\mathcal{R}_N$ satisfy the property, then the new runs added to $\mathcal{R}_N$ also satisfy it. Initialization of the induction is trivial since $\mathcal{R}_N$ is initially empty.

By completeness of Φ, the property is satisfied by all the runs of the form $\mu(E)$ with E the set of events revealed by the initial occurrence of a transition t in $U((P, T, F, M))$. For every run ρ constructed as the largest common prefix of two runs ρ_1 and ρ_2 already in $\mathcal{R}_N$, assume that ρ_1 and ρ_2 satisfy our property and call ρ_1' and ρ_2' the corresponding runs of the contracted net. By non-redundancy of Φ, ρ_1' and ρ_2' must coincide on the largest common prefix ρ of ρ_1 and ρ_2. Then ρ is the image by χ of the largest common prefix of ρ_1' and ρ_2'.   □

Definition 21 (Canonical contraction $\overline{N}$). *We define the* canonical contraction *of a safe Petri net N as the contracted net $\overline{N} \stackrel{def}{=} N_{/\Phi_N}$ where Φ_N is the set of nonempty runs of $\mathcal{R}_N$ which are minimal w.r.t. the prefix relation.*

Theorem 3. *For every safe Petri net N, the set Φ_N of macro-transitions in $\overline{N}$ is complete and non-redundant, and the set of states a-reachable in $\overline{N}$ is precisely $\mathcal{M}_N$. Moreover $|\Phi_N| \leq |T|$.*

Proof. Completeness is ensured by the insertion in $\mathcal{R}_N$ of all the runs of the form $\mu(E)$ with E the set of events revealed by the initial occurrence of a transition t in $U((P, T, F, M))$. For redundancy, assume two runs ρ_1 and ρ_2 of $\mathcal{R}_N$ both start by an occurrence of t. Then their common prefix ρ is nonempty and is in $\mathcal{R}_N$. Then ρ_1 and ρ_2 are not minimal in $\mathcal{R}_N$ w.r.t. the prefix relation, and they are not in Φ_N. By construction all the states a-reachable in $\overline{N}$ are in $\mathcal{M}_N$. Finally the inequality $|\Phi_N| \leq |T|$ is a direct consequence of the non-redundancy of Φ_N. $\square$

Illustration. Let us construct the canonical contraction of the net N of Fig. 2(a). $\mathcal{M}_N$ contains the initial marking $\{0, 0'\}$. From this marking t_0, t_1 and t_1' are firable. Since t_1 and t_1' reveal each other, $\mathcal{R}_N$ contains the runs t_0 and $t_1 t_1'$, and $\mathcal{M}_N$ contains the reached markings $\{\}$ and $\{1, 4\}$. From $\{1, 4\}$, t_2 and t_2' can fire; they reveal nothing, so they are added as such to $\mathcal{R}_N$. The marking $\{2, 4\}$ is now reachable; it is added to $\mathcal{M}_N$. From $\{2, 4\}$, t_3 and t_3' can fire, and in both cases an occurrence of t_4 necessarily follows. Hence $t_3 t_4$ and $t_3' t_4$ are added to $\mathcal{R}_N$. We can now reach $\{1, 5\}$ and fire t_2 or t_2' again. But, from $\{1, 5\}$ firing t_2 (or t_2') reveals an infinite sequence of occurrences of t_5. For this $t_2 t_5^\omega$ and $t_2' t_5^\omega$ are added to $\mathcal{R}_N$. But, since t_2 and t_2' already appear "alone" – i.e. as singleton transitions – in $\mathcal{R}_N$, marking $\{2, 5\}$ obtained after firing them from $\{1, 5\}$ must also be added to $\mathcal{M}_N$. And from it, t_5^ω can fire and is added to $\mathcal{R}_N$. Now, Φ_N is constructed by extracting the runs of $\mathcal{R}_N$ that are minimal w.r.t. the prefix relation. Here we get all of them, except $t_2 t_5^\omega$ and $t_2' t_5^\omega$. The resulting contracted net is shown in Fig. 2(b).

Contraction and Automata. It is clear that applying our contraction to the Petri net representation N of an automaton (i.e. a Petri where every transition has exactly one input- and one output-place) removes the deterministic states (or places), i.e. those from which there is no choice. Concretely, these places will not appear in the set $\mathcal{M}_N$. The macro-transitions are the paths between non-deterministic states with only deterministic intermediate states.

5   Reductions and Unfoldings

When *concurrent* behavior in partial order semantics is considered, our contraction is related to the facets reduction [6].

Theorem 4 (Reduction as contraction of ONs). *For every occurrence net O, the canonical contraction of O is isomorphic to its facet reduction.*

Proof. By Definition 20, all runs in $\mathcal{R}_O$ correspond to unions of facets of O. Now, let $\rho \in \mathcal{R}_O$ be a run containing more than one facet. By definition of facets, the reveals relation on facets is antisymmetric. Then one of O's initial facets, say ψ_1, does not reveal the other, say ψ_2. Take an initial event e of ψ_1 and a marking $M \in \mathcal{M}_O$ from which ρ can fire; e is firable from M in O. Therefore $\mathcal{R}_O$ contains the run ρ' containing the events revealed by e from M. This run contains ψ_1 but not ψ_2. By definition, $\mathcal{R}_O$ contains the largest common prefix

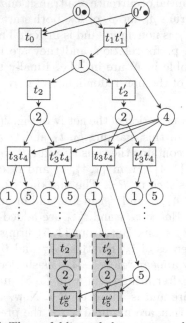

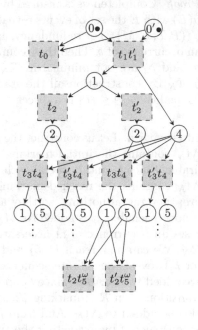

(a) The unfolding of the contracted Petri net of Figure 2(b). Remark that the unfolding is not reduced: the last occurrence of t_2 and the following t_5^ω are in the same facet (similarly for t_2' and the following t_5^ω).

(b) Its reduction (or contraction) is isomorphic to the reduction of the unfolding of N already represented in Figure 3(b).

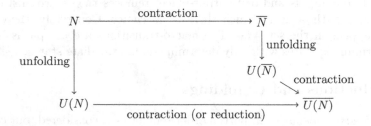

Fig. 6. Unfolding and contraction.

of ρ and ρ'. Hence ρ is not minimal in $\mathcal{R}_O$ w.r.t. the prefix relation, and is not in Φ_O. □

As illustrated in Fig. 6, the operation of reduction does not entirely commute with unfolding. That is, in general, the unfolding $U(\overline{N})$ of reduced Petri net $\overline{N}$ is coarser, as an occurrence net, than the reduction $\overline{U(N)}$ of the original net N's unfolding. In the example of Fig. 6, the facets labeled $t_2 t_5^\omega$ and $t_2' t_5^\omega$ in $\overline{U(N)}$ are both split into two events of $U(\overline{N})$.

However, one retrieves the reduction of $U(N)$ from $U(\overline{N})$ as follows.

Theorem 5. *For every net N, applying the occurrence net facet reduction to $U(\overline{N})$ yields $\overline{U(N)}$ up to isomorphism.*

Proof. By definition of macro-transitions, for every event e of $U(\overline{N})$, all the events of $U(N)$ which are in $\chi_{events}(e)$, reveal each other. Then $\chi_{events}(e)$ is included in a facet ψ of $U(N)$. And for two events e_1 and e_2 of $U(\overline{N})$, an event in $\chi_{events}(e_1)$ reveals (in $U(N)$) an event in $\chi_{events}(e_2)$ iff e_1 reveals e_2 in $U(\overline{N})$. Therefore the facets reduction of $U(\overline{N})$ regroups e_1 and e_2 into the same facet iff the events in $\chi_{events}(e_1)$ and those in $\chi_{events}(e_2)$ are in the same facet. □

6   Conclusion

We have presented a method for identifying and contracting *macro-transitions* in safe Petri nets. The procedure includes and justifies our previous work in [1,2,6,7] focusing on *facets* in occurrence nets.The result is a unique contracted 1-safe Petri net with no more macro-transitions than transitions in the original net. The construction provides a unique *canonical* version for any given 1-safe Petri net, whose maximal behaviour offers a condensed view of the maximal behaviour of the original net. By computing offline the canonical version, verification procedures for any property that depends only on the maximal run behavior can be run on the smaller contracted net instead. This is for instance the case of all the properties that can be reduced to fireability of a transition. Computing the contraction (with finite representations of the macro-transitions) is in general costly (computing the reveals relation on the unfolding of a finite Petri net is PSPACE-complete [7]), but in practice many syntactic sufficient conditions can be used to identify macro-transitions. For instance, a run in which every intermediate condition corresponds to a place of the Petri net which has only one output transition, is a macro-transition. Also, in practice, models are usually built hierarchically by transition refinement; this gives natural candidates for macro-transitions. Hence our contraction appears as an optimal, canonical contraction, to which other contractions based on macro-transitions can be compared.

References

1. Balaguer, S., Chatain, T., Haar, S.: Building tight occurrence nets from reveals relations. In: Proceedings of the 11th International Conference on Application of Concurrency to System Design, pp. 44–53. IEEE Computer Society Press (2011)

2. Balaguer, S., Chatain, T., Haar, S.: Building occurrence nets from reveals relations. Fundam. Inform. **123**(3), 245–272 (2013)
3. Berthelot, G.: Checking properties of nets using transformation. In: Rozenberg, G. (ed.) APN 1985. LNCS, vol. 222, pp. 19–40. Springer, Heidelberg (1986)
4. Best, E., Randell, B.: A formal model of atomicity in asynchronous systems. Acta Inform. **16**(1), 93–124 (1981)
5. Desel, J., Merceron, A.: Vicinity respecting homomorphisms for abstracting system requirements. In: Proceedings of International Workshop on Abstractions for Petri Nets and Other Models of Concurrency (APNOC) (2009)
6. Haar, S.: Types of asynchronous diagnosability and the reveals-relation in occurrence nets. IEEE Trans. Autom. Control **55**(10), 2310–2320 (2010)
7. Haar, S., Kern, C., Schwoon, S.: Computing the reveals relation in occurrence nets. In: Proceedings of GandALF'11. Electronic Proceedings in Theoretical Computer Science, vol. 54, pp. 31–44 (2011)
8. Kumar, R., Takai, S.: Decentralized prognosis of failures in discrete event systems. IEEE Trans. Autom. Control **55**(1), 48–59 (2010)
9. Madalinski, A., Khomenko, V.: Diagnosability verification with parallel LTL-X model checking based on Petri net unfoldings. In: Control and Fault-Tolerant Systems (SysTol'2010), pp. 398–403. IEEE Computing Society Press (2010)
10. Madalinski, A., Khomenko, V.: Predictability verification with parallel LTL-X model checking based on Petri net unfoldings. In: Proceedings of the 8th IFAC Symposium on Fault Detection, Diagnosis and Safety of Technical Processes (SAFEPROCESS'2012), pp. 1232–1237 (2012)
11. Nielsen, M., Plotkin, G.D., Winskel, G.: Petri nets, event structures and domains, part I. Theoret. Comput. Sci. **13**, 85–108 (1981)
12. Zielonka, W.: Notes on finite asynchronous automata. RAIRO Theoret. Inform. Appl. **21**, 99–135 (1987)

Symbolic Termination and Confluence Checking for ECA Rules

Xiaoqing Jin[1], Yousra Lembachar[1], and Gianfranco Ciardo[2]([⊠])

[1] Department of Computer Science and Engineering,
University of California, Riverside, USA
{jinx,ylemb001}@cs.ucr.edu
[2] Department of Computer Science, Iowa State University, Ames, USA
ciardo@iastate.edu

Abstract. Event-condition-action (ECA) rules can specify decision processes and are widely used in reactive systems and active database systems. Applying formal verification techniques to guarantee properties of the designed ECA rules is essential to help the error-prone procedure of collecting and translating expert knowledge. However, while the non-deterministic and concurrent semantics of ECA rule execution enhances expressiveness, it also makes analysis and verification more difficult. We propose an approach to analyze the dynamic behavior of a set of ECA rules, by first translating them into an extended Petri net, then studying two fundamental correctness properties: *termination* and *confluence*. Our experimental results show that the symbolic algorithms we present greatly improve scalability.

Keywords: ECA rules · Termination · Confluence · Verification

1   Introduction

Event-condition-action (ECA) [18] rules are expressive enough to describe complex events and reactions. Thus, this event-driven formalism is widely used to specify complex systems [1,3] such as industrial-scale management, and to improve efficiency when coupled with technologies such as embedded systems and sensor networks. Analogously, active DBMSs enhance security and semantic integrity of traditional DBMSs using ECA rules; these are now found in most enterprise DBMSs and academic prototypes thanks to the SQL3 standard [15]. ECA rules are used to specify a system's response to events, and are written in the format "on the occurrence of a set of events, if certain conditions hold, perform these actions". However, for systems with many components and complex behavior, it may be difficult to correctly specify these rules.

Termination, guaranteeing that the system does not remain "busy" internally forever without responding to external events, and *confluence*, ensuring that all interleavings of a set of triggered rules yields the same result, are fundamental correctness properties. While termination has been studied extensively and many

© Springer-Verlag Berlin Heidelberg 2014
M. Koutny et al. (Eds.): ToPNoC IX, LNCS 8910, pp. 99–123, 2014.
DOI: 10.1007/978-3-662-45730-6_6

algorithms have been proposed to verify it, confluence is more challenging due to a potentially large number of rule interleavings [2] and its complex semantics, which cannot be expressed in the temporal logics LTL or CTL [11].

Researchers began studying these properties for active databases in the 90's, by transforming ECA rules into a graph and applying static analysis techniques on it to verify properties [2,4,17,20]. These approaches based on static methods can detect redundancy, inconsistency, incompleteness, and circularity. However, as they may not explore the whole state space, they can easily miss some errors. Also, they can find scenarios that do not actually result in errors because the discovered error states may not be reachable. Moreover, they have poor support in providing concrete counterexamples and analyzing ECA rules with priorities. Reference [2] looks for cycles in the rule-triggering graph to disprove termination, but the cycle-triggering conditions may be unsatisfiable. Reference [4] improves this work with an activation graph describing when rules are activated; while its analysis detects termination where previous work failed, it may still report false positives when rules have priorities. Reference [5] proposes an algebraic approach emphasizing the condition portion of rules, but does not consider priorities either. Other researchers [17,20] chose to translate ECA rules into a Petri Net (PN), whose nondeterministic interleaving execution semantics naturally models unforeseen interactions between rule executions. However, as they analyze the ECA rules through structural PN techniques based on the incidence matrix, false positives are again possible.

Model checking tools such as SMV [21] and SPIN [7] have also been proposed. While closer to our work, these dynamic approaches manually transform ECA rules into an input script, assume a priori bounds for all variables, do not support priorities, and require the initial system states to be known; our approach does not have these limitations. Reference [12] analyzes both termination and confluence by transforming ECA rules into Datalog rules through a "transformation diagram"; this supports rule priority and execution semantics, but requires the graph to be commutative and restricts event composition. Most of these works show limited results, and none of them properly addresses confluence; we present detailed experimental results for both termination and confluence. UML Statecharts [23] provide visual diagrams to describe the dynamic behavior of reactive systems and can be used to verify these properties. However, event dispatching and execution semantics are not as flexible as for PNs [19].

Our approach transforms a set of ECA rules into a PN, then dynamically verifies termination and confluence and, if errors are found, provides concrete counterexamples to help debugging. It uses our tool SMART, which supports PNs with priorities to easily model ECA rules with priorities. Moreover, a single PN can naturally describe both the ECA rules as well as their nondeterministic concurrent environment and, while our *multiway decision diagram* (MDD) [14] based symbolic model-checking algorithms [24] require a finite state space, they do not require to know a priori the variable bounds (i.e., the maximum number of tokens that each place may contain). Finally, our framework is not restricted to termination and confluence, but can be easily extended to verify a broader set of properties.

The rest of the paper is organized as follows: Sect. 2 briefly recalls Petri nets, symbolic algorithms, and CTL model checking; Sect. 3 introduces our syntax for ECA rules; Sect. 4 describes the transformation of ECA rules into a Petri net; Sect. 5 presents algorithms for termination and confluence; Sect. 6 shows experimental results; Sect. 7 concludes.

2 Preliminaries

This section provides the formal definition of the specific class of Petri nets used in our approach, as well as a brief background on key symbolic data structures and algorithms for their analysis. We use the symbols $\mathbb{N}$ and $\mathbb{B}$ to denote the natural numbers and the set $\{0, 1\}$, respectively.

2.1 Self-Modifying Petri Nets with Priorities and Inhibitor Arcs

A *self-modifying Petri net* [22] (PN) with *priorities* and *inhibitor arcs* is described by a tuple $(\mathcal{P}, \mathcal{T}, \pi, \mathbf{D}^-, \mathbf{D}^+, \mathbf{D}^\circ, \mathbf{s}^{init})$, where:

- $\mathcal{P}$ is a finite set of *places*, drawn as circles, and $\mathcal{T}$ is a finite set of *transitions*, drawn as rectangles, satisfying $\mathcal{P} \cap \mathcal{T} = \emptyset$ and $\mathcal{P} \cup \mathcal{T} \neq \emptyset$.
- $\pi : \mathcal{T} \to \mathbb{N}$ assigns a *priority* to each transition.
- $\mathbf{D}^- : \mathcal{P} \times \mathcal{T} \times \mathbb{N}^{\mathcal{P}} \to \mathbb{N}$, $\mathbf{D}^+ : \mathcal{P} \times \mathcal{T} \times \mathbb{N}^{\mathcal{P}} \to \mathbb{N}$, and $\mathbf{D}^\circ : \mathcal{P} \times \mathcal{T} \times \mathbb{N}^{\mathcal{P}} \to \mathbb{N} \cup \{\infty\}$ are the *marking-dependent* cardinalities of the *input*, *output*, and *inhibitor* arcs.
- $\mathbf{s}^{init} \in \mathbb{N}^{\mathcal{P}}$ is the *initial marking*, the number of *tokens* initially in each place.

Transition t has *concession* in marking $\mathbf{m} \in \mathbb{N}^{\mathcal{P}}$ if, for each $p \in \mathcal{P}$, the input arc cardinality is satisfied, i.e., $\mathbf{m}_p \geq \mathbf{D}^-(p, t, \mathbf{m})$, and the inhibitor arc cardinality is not, i.e., $\mathbf{m}_p < \mathbf{D}^\circ(p, t, \mathbf{m})$. If t has concession in $\mathbf{m}$ and no other transition t' with priority $\pi(t') > \pi(t)$ has concession, then t is *enabled* in $\mathbf{m}$ and can *fire* and lead to marking $\mathbf{m}'$, where $\mathbf{m}'_p = \mathbf{m}_p - \mathbf{D}^-(p, t, \mathbf{m}) + \mathbf{D}^+(p, t, \mathbf{m})$, for all places p (arc cardinalities are evaluated in the current marking $\mathbf{m}$ to determine the enabling of t and the new marking $\mathbf{m}'$). In our figures, $tk(p)$ indicates the number of tokens in p for the current marking, a thick input arc from p to t represents an arc with cardinality $tk(p)$, i.e., a *reset* arc. We omit arcs with cardinality 1, input or output arcs with cardinality 0, and inhibitor arcs with cardinality ∞.

The PN defines a discrete-state model $(\mathcal{S}_{pot}, \mathcal{S}_{init}, \mathcal{A}, \{\mathcal{N}_t : t \in \mathcal{A}\})$. The *potential state space* is $\mathcal{S}_{pot} = \mathbb{N}^{\mathcal{P}}$ (we assume that the reachable set of markings is finite or, equivalently, that the number of tokens in each place is bounded, but we do not require to know the bound a priori). $\mathcal{S}_{init} \subseteq \mathcal{S}_{pot}$ is the set of *initial states*, $\{\mathbf{s}^{init}\}$ in our case (assuming an arbitrary finite initial set of markings is not a problem). The set of (asynchronous) model *events* is $\mathcal{A} = \mathcal{T}$. The *next-state function* for transition t is $\mathcal{N}_t$, such that $\mathcal{N}_t(\mathbf{m}) = \{\mathbf{m}'\}$ if transition t is enabled in marking $\mathbf{m}$, where $\mathbf{m}'$ is as defined above, and $\mathcal{N}_t(\mathbf{m}) = \emptyset$ otherwise. Thus, the next-state function for a particular PN transition is deterministic, although the overall behavior remains nondeterministic due to the choice of which transition should fire when multiple transitions are enabled.

2.2   Multiway Decision Diagrams and the Saturation Algorithm

Traditional symbolic algorithms for state-space generation or temporal-logic model checking use *binary decision diagrams* (BDDs) [6] to encode sets of (or relations on) states and compute sets of interest as the fixpoint of *breadth-first* iterations. Our approach uses instead *multiway decision diagrams* (MDDs) [14], which are more natural when encoding variables with unknown range (e.g., the number of tokens in a place), and, more fundamentally, computes fixpoints using *saturation* [9], which tends to be very efficient for largely asynchronous systems. We introduce these two concepts, see our recent survey [10] for more details.

Consider a sequence of *domain variables* $(v_L, \ldots, v_1)$ with an order "$\succ$" defined on them, such that $l > k$ implies $v_l \succ v_k$, and where v_k has finite domain $\mathcal{X}_k = \{0,1,\ldots,n_k -1\}$ for some $n_k > 0$. An *(ordered) multiway decision diagram* (MDD) over $(v_L, \ldots, v_1)$ is an acyclic directed edge-labeled graph where:

- The only *terminal* nodes can be **0** and **1**, and are associated with the *range* variable $\mathbf{0}.var = \mathbf{1}.var = v_0$, satisfying $v_k \succ v_0$ for any domain variable v_k.
- A *nonterminal* node p is associated with a domain variable $p.var$.
- For each $i \in \mathcal{X}_k$, a nonterminal node p associated with v_k has an outgoing edge labeled with i and pointing to a child $p[i]$, where $p.var \succ p[i].var$.

If $p.var = v_k$, node p encodes function $f_p : \mathcal{X}_L \times \cdots \times \mathcal{X}_1 \to \mathbb{B}$, recursively given by $f_p(i_L, \ldots, i_1) = p$, if $k = 0$, and $f_p(i_L, \ldots, i_1) = f_{p[i_k]}(i_L, \ldots, i_1)$, otherwise (we write f_p as a function of L variables even when $k < L$, to stress that *any* variable v_h not explicitly appearing on a path from p to a terminal node is a "don't care" for f_p, regardless of whether $h < k$ or $h > k$).

Canonical MDDs, which have no *duplicate nodes* (if $p.var = q.var = v_k$ and, for each $i \in \mathcal{X}_k$, $p[i] = q[i]$, then $p = q$) and are in *quasi-reduced form* (if $p.var = v_k$, then $p[i].var = v_{k-1}$ and $k = L$ if p is a root) or in *fully-reduced form* (if $p.var = v_k$, then there are indices $i, j \in \mathcal{X}_k$, s.t. $p[i] \neq p[j]$), are quite efficient and compact: if functions f and g are encoded with canonical MDDs, *satisfiability* (is $f \neq 0$?) and *equivalence* (is $f = g$?), are answered in $O(1)$ time, while the MDD encoding the result of elementwise operations such as *conjunction* ($f \wedge g$) is built in time and space proportional to the product of the number of nodes in f and g.

Of course, in symbolic system analysis, the domain $\mathcal{X}_{pot} = \mathcal{X}_L \times \cdots \times \mathcal{X}_1$ is the *potential state space* (states that the system *may* reach during its evolution), and an MDD root p encodes the set $\mathcal{X} = \{(i_L, \ldots, i_1) : f_p(i_L, \ldots, i_1) = 1\} \subseteq \mathcal{X}_{pot}$. Figure 1, adapted from [10], gives an example of a potential state space and the set of states $\mathcal{X}$ encoded by a quasi-reduced or a fully-reduced MDD. A relation $\mathcal{T}$ over states can also be encoded by MDDs, using two *interleaved* copies of the domain variables, so that a path $(i_L, i'_L, \ldots, i_1, i'_1)$ in such MDD signifies $((i_L, \ldots, i_1), (i'_L, \ldots, i'_1)) \in \mathcal{T}$. If $\mathcal{T}$ represents the *transition relation*, this would mean that the system can move from $(i_L, \ldots, i_1)$ to $(i'_L, \ldots, i'_1)$ in one step.

Many sets of interest are fixpoints. For example, the reachable state space $\mathcal{X}_{rch}$ is the smallest fixpoint of $\mathcal{X} = \mathcal{X}_{init} \cup \mathcal{X} \cup \mathcal{T}(\mathcal{X})$, where $\mathcal{X}_{init}$ is the set of initial states and $\mathcal{T}(\mathcal{X})$ is the image of $\mathcal{X}$ through the transition relation $\mathcal{T}$.

Potential state space $\mathcal{X}_{pot}$:
$\{0,1,2,3\} \times \{0,1,2\} \times \{0,1\} \times \{0,1,2\}$

Set $\mathcal{X}$ encoded by either MDD:
$\{0210, 1000, 1010, 1100, 1110,$
$1210, 2000, 2010, 2100, 2110,$
$2210, 3010, 3110, 3200, 3201,$
$3202, 3210, 3211, 3212\}$

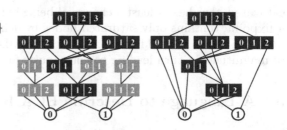

Fig. 1. A set of states encoded as a quasi-reduced (left) or fully-reduced (right) MDD.

Fixpoints also play a key role in CTL [11]. A CTL state formula is inductively defined as: $\phi := \top \mid a \mid \neg\phi \mid \phi_1 \wedge \phi_2 \mid \mathbf{A}\,\varphi \mid \mathbf{E}\,\varphi$, where $\top$ indicates the "true" proposition that holds in every state, a is an atomic proposition that may hold in each particular state, and φ is a path formula of the form $\varphi := \mathbf{X}\phi \mid \phi_1 \mathbf{U} \phi_2$, where ϕ, ϕ_1, and ϕ_2 are state formulas. Intuitively, s satisfies $\mathbf{A}\,\varphi$ if φ holds on all paths starting at s, while it satisfies $\mathbf{E}\,\varphi$ if φ holds on at least one path starting at s; for path formulas, $\mathbf{X}\phi$ holds on a path σ if the next state on σ satisfies ϕ, while it satisfies $\phi_1 \mathbf{U} \phi_2$ if there is a state s on σ that satisfies ϕ_2 and all the states before s on σ satisfy ϕ_1. In CTL, the set of states $\mathcal{X}_{\mathbf{E}a\mathbf{U}b} = \{i : \exists d > 0, \exists i^{(1)} \to i^{(2)} \to \cdots \to i^{(d)} \wedge i = i^{(1)} \wedge i^{(d)} \in \mathcal{B} \wedge \forall c, 1 \leq c < d, i^{(c)} \in \mathcal{A}\}$ is the *smallest* fixpoint of $\mathcal{X} = \mathcal{B} \cup (\mathcal{A} \cap \mathcal{T}^{-1}(\mathcal{X}))$, where $\mathcal{T}^{-1}$ is the *backward* transition relation and $\mathcal{A}$ and $\mathcal{B}$ are the states satisfying a or b, respectively, while $\mathcal{X}_{\mathbf{E}\mathbf{G}a} = \{i : \forall d > 0, \exists i^{(1)} \to i^{(2)} \to \cdots \to i^{(d)} \wedge i = i^{(1)} \wedge \forall c, 1 \leq c \leq d, i^{(c)} \in \mathcal{A}\}$ is the *largest* fixpoint of $\mathcal{X} = \mathcal{A} \cap \mathcal{T}^{-1}(\mathcal{X})$.

Consider now, for example, the fixpoint equation for state-space generation. Its obvious symbolic implementation initializes $\mathcal{X}$ to $\mathcal{X}_{init}$, iteratively computes $\mathcal{T}(\mathcal{X})$, and adds the resulting set of states to $\mathcal{X}$, until no new states are found, i.e., $\mathcal{X}$ does not change. This *breadth-first* search, requiring d_{max} iterations (each one performing a relational product and a set union), where d_{max} is the largest distance of any reachable state from the initial states, has been experimentally found to suffer from a large *peak size*. In other words, while the final result $\mathcal{X}_{rch}$ might have a compact MDD representation, some intermediate $\mathcal{X}$, corresponding to the reachable states at distance up to d from $\mathcal{X}_{init}$, might require a huge MDD.

The *saturation* algorithm [9], instead, *disjunctively* decomposes $\mathcal{T}$ into a set $\{\mathcal{T}_k : L \geq k \geq 1\}$ of asynchronous events, where $\mathcal{T}_k$ only depends and affects state variable v_k and possibly some of $\{v_{k-1}, ..., v_1\}$. Then, instead of using "global" relational products on the entire MDD, saturation computes "local" fixpoints on the nodes of the initial MDD. More specifically, it computes the fixpoint with respect to $\mathcal{T}_1$ of the nodes associated with v_1 in the MDD encoding $\mathcal{X}_{init}$; then, it computes the fixpoint with respect to $\mathcal{T}_2$ of the nodes associated with v_2, with the proviso that any newly-created node associated with v_1 is immediately saturated by computing its fixpoint with respect to $\mathcal{T}_1$, and so on, until the root node associated with v_L is saturated, at which point it encodes the desired result. This approach tends to create many fewer MDD nodes, each of which is saturated, thus has at least a chance of being in the final MDD (which, encoding a fixpoint, contains only saturated nodes by definition). Empirically, saturation has been shown to build much smaller peak MDDs, sometimes by many orders of magnitude, in turn leading to enormously faster runtimes.

3   A Language to Describe ECA Rules

We now present the syntax and the semantics of our language to define ECA rules and illustrate them with a running example.

3.1   ECA Syntax and Semantics

ECA rules have the format "**on** *events* **if** *condition* **do** *actions*". If the *events* are activated and the boolean *condition* is satisfied, the rule is triggered and its *actions* are performed. In active DBMSs, events are normally produced by explicit database operations such as *insert* and *delete* [1] while, in reactive systems, they are produced by sensors monitoring environment variables [3], e.g., temperature. Many current ECA languages can model the environment and distinguish between **environmental** and **local** variables [2,4,7,17,20,21]. Thus, we designed a language to address these issues, able to handle more general cases and allow different semantics for **environmental** and **local** variables (Fig. 2).

Environmental variables are used to represent environment states that can only be measured by sensors but not *directly* modified by the system. For instance, if we want to increase the temperature in a room, the system may choose to turn on a heater, eventually achieving the desired effect, but it cannot directly change the value of the temperature variable. Thus, environmental variables capture the nondeterminism introduced by the environment, beyond the control of the system. Instead, local variables can be both read and written by the system. These may be associated with an actuator, a record value, or an intermediate value describing part of the system state; we provide operations to set their value to an expression (absolute change), or increase or decrease it by an expression (relative change); these expressions may depend on environmental variables.

Events can be combinations of atomic events activated by environmental or internal changes. We classify them using the keywords **external** and **internal**. An external event can be **activated when** the value of an environmental variable crosses a threshold; at that time, it may take a snapshot of some environmental variables and **read** them into local variables to record their current values. Only the action of an ECA rule can instead **activate** internal events. Internal events are useful to express internal changes or required actions within the system. These two types of events cannot be mixed within a single ECA rule. Thus, rules are *external* or *internal*, respectively. Then, we say that a state is *stable* if only external events can occur in it, *unstable* if actions of external or internal rules are being performed (including the activation of internal events, which may then trigger internal rules). The system is initially stable and, after some

$$env\_vars := \textbf{environmental } env\_var \qquad \text{READ-ONLY BOUNDED NATURAL}$$
$$loc\_vars := \textbf{local } loc\_var \qquad\qquad \text{READ-AND-WRITE BOUNDED NATURAL}$$
$$factor := loc\_var \mid env\_var \mid (\ exp\ ) \mid number$$
$$term := factor \mid term * term \mid term\ /\ term \qquad \text{``/'' IS INTEGER DIVISION}$$
$$exp := exp - exp \mid exp + exp \mid term \qquad \text{``number'' IS A CONSTANT} \in \mathbb{N}$$
$$rel\_op := \ \geq \mid \leq \mid =$$
$$assignment := env\_var \textbf{ into } loc\_var\ [, assignment]$$
$$ext\_ev\_decl := \textbf{external } ext\_ev\ [\ \textbf{activated when } env\_var\ rel\_op\ number\ ]$$
$$[\ \textbf{read } (assignment)\ ]$$
$$int\_ev\_decl := \textbf{internal } int\_ev$$
$$ext\_evs := ext\_ev \mid (ext\_evs \textbf{ or } ext\_evs) \mid (ext\_evs \textbf{ and } ext\_evs)$$
$$int\_evs := int\_ev \mid (int\_evs \textbf{ or } int\_evs) \mid (int\_evs \textbf{ and } int\_evs)$$
$$condition := (condition \textbf{ or } condition) \mid (condition \textbf{ and } condition) \mid$$
$$\textbf{not } condition \mid exp\ rel\_op\ exp$$
$$action := \textbf{increase } (loc\_var,\ exp) \mid \textbf{decrease } (loc\_var,\ exp) \mid$$
$$\textbf{set } (loc\_var,\ exp) \mid \textbf{activate } (int\_ev)$$
$$actions := action \mid (actions \textbf{ seq } actions) \mid (actions \textbf{ par } actions)$$
$$ext\_rule := \textbf{on } ext\_evs\ [\textbf{if } condition]\ \textbf{do } actions$$
$$int\_rule := \textbf{on } int\_evs\ [\textbf{if } condition]\ \textbf{do } actions\ [\textbf{with priority } number]$$
$$system := [env\_vars]^+[loc\_vars]^*[ext\_ev\_decl]^+[int\_ev\_decl]^*$$
$$[ext\_rule]^+[int\_rule]^*$$

Fig. 2. The syntax of ECA rules.

external events trigger one or more external rules, it transitions to unstable states where internal events may be activated, triggering further internal rules. When all actions complete, the system is again in a stable state, waiting for environmental changes that will eventually trigger external events.

The condition portion of an ECA rule is a boolean expression on the value of environmental and local variables; it can be omitted if it is the constant true.

The last portion of a rule specifies which actions must be performed, and in which order. Most actions are operations on local variables which do not directly affect environmental variables, but may cause some changes that will conceivably be reflected in their future values. Thus, all environmental variables are read-only from the perspective of an action. Actions can also **activate** internal events. Moreover, to handle complex action operations, the execution semantics can be specified as any partial order described by a series-parallel graph; this is obtained through an appropriate nesting of **seq** operators, to force a sequential execution, and **par** operators, to allow arbitrary concurrency. The keyword **with priority** enforces a priority for internal rules. If no priority is specified, the default priority of an internal rule is 1, the same as that of external rules.

We now discuss the choices of execution semantics for our language, to support the modeling of reactive systems. The first choice is how to couple the checking of events and conditions for our ECA rules. There are (at least) two options: *immediate* and *deferred*. The event-condition checking is *immediate* if the corresponding condition is immediately evaluated when the events occur, it is *deferred* if the condition is evaluated at the end of a cycle with a predefined frequency. One critical requirement for the design of reactive systems is that the system should respond to external events from the environment [16] as soon as possible. Thus, we choose immediate event-condition checking: when events occur, the corresponding condition is immediately evaluated to determine whether to trigger the rule. We stress that deferred checking can still be modeled using immediate checking, for example by adding an extra variable for the system clock and changing priorities related to rule evaluation to synchronize rule evaluations. However, the drawback of deferred checking is that the design must tolerate false ECA rule triggering or non-triggering scenarios. Since there is a time gap between event activation and condition evaluation, the environmental conditions that trigger an event might change during this period of time, causing rules supposed to be triggered at the time of event activation to fail because the "current" condition evaluation are now inconsistent.

Another important choice is how to handle and model the concurrent and nondeterministic nature of reactive systems. We introduce the concept of *batch* for external events, similar to the concept of transaction in DBMSs. Formally, the boundary of a batch of external events is defined as the end of the execution of all triggered rules. Then, the system starts to receive external events and immediately evaluates the corresponding conditions. The occurrence of an external event closes a batch if it triggers one or more ECA rules; otherwise, the event is added to the current batch. Once the batch closes and the rules to be triggered have been determined, the events in the current batch are cleaned-up, to prevent multiple (and erroneous) triggerings of rules. For example, consider ECA rules r_a: "**on** a **do** $\cdots$" and r_{ac}: "**on** (a **and** c) **do** $\cdots$", and assume that the system finishes processing the last batch of events and is ready to receive external events for the next batch. If external events occur in the sequence "$c, a, \ldots$", event c alone cannot trigger any rule so it begins, but does not complete, the current batch. Then, event a triggers both rules r_a and r_{ac}, closing the current batch. Both rules are triggered and will be executed concurrently. This example shows how, when the system is in a stable state, the occurrence of a single external event may trigger one or more ECA rules, since there is no "contention" within a batch on "using" an external event: rule r_a and r_{ac} share event a and both rules are triggered and executed. If instead the sequence of events is "$a, c, \ldots$", event a by itself constitutes a batch, as it triggers rule r_a. This event is then discarded by the clean-up so, after executing r_a and any internal rule (recursively) triggered by it, the system returns to a stable state and the subsequent events "$c, \ldots$" begin the next batch. Under this semantic, all external events in one *batch* are processed concurrently. Thus, unless there is a termination error, the system will process all triggered rules, including those triggered by the activation of internal events during the current batch, before considering new external events. This batch definition provides maximum nondeterminism on event order, which is useful to discover design errors in a set of ECA rules.

We also stress that, in our semantics, the system is frozen during rule execution and does not respond to external events. Thus, rule execution is instantaneous, while in reality it obviously requires some time. However, from a verification perspective, environmental changes and external event occurrences are nondeterministic and asynchronous, thus our semantic allows the verification process to explore all possible combinations without missing errors due to the order in which events occur and environmental variables change.

3.2 Running Example

We illustrate the expressiveness of our ECA rules on a running example: a light control subsystem in a smart home for senior housing. Figure 3 lists the requirements in natural language (R_1 to R_5). Using motion and pressure sensors, the

environmental	*Mtn, ExtLgt, Slp*
local	*lMtn, lExtLgt, lSlp, lgtsTmr, intLgts*
external	*SecElp* **read** (*Mtn* **into** *lMtn, ExtLgt* **into** *lExtLgt, Slp* **into** *lSlp*)
	MtnOn **activated when** $Mtn = 1$
	MtnOff **activated when** $Mtn = 0$
	ExtLgtLow **activated when** $ExtLgt \leq 5$
internal	*LgtsOff, LgtsOn, ChkExtLgt, ChkMtn, ChkSlp*
(R_1) When the room is unoccupied for 6 minutes, turn off lights if they are on.	
r_1	**on** *MtnOff* **if** ($intLgts > 0$ **and** $lgtsTmr = 0$) **do set** ($lgtsTmr, 1$)
r_2	**on** *SecElp* **if** ($lgtsTmr \geq 1$ **and** $lMtn = 0$) **do increase** ($lgtsTmr, 1$)
r_3	**on** *SecElp* **if** ($lgtsTmr = 360$ **and** $lMtn = 0$) **do** (**set** ($lgtsTmr, 0$) **par activate** (*LgtsOff*))
r_4	**on** *LgtsOff* **do** (**set** ($intLgts, 0$) **par activate** (*ChkExtLgt*))
(R_2) When lights are off, if external light intensity is below 5, turn on lights.	
r_5	**on** *ChkExtLgt* **if** ($intLgts = 0$ **and** $lExtLgt \leq 5$) **do activate** (*LgtsOn*)
(R_3) When lights are on, if the room is empty or a person is asleep, turn off lights.	
r_6	**on** *LgtsOn* **do** (**set** ($intLgts, 6$) **seq activate** (*ChkMtn*))
r_7	**on** *ChkMtn* **if** ($lSlp = 1$ **or** ($lMtn = 0$ **and** $intLgts \geq 1$)) **do activate** (*LgtsOff*)
(R_4) If the external light intensity drops below 5, check if the person is asleep and set the lights intensity to 6. If the person is asleep, turn off the lights.	
r_8	**on** *ExtLgtLow* **do** (**set** ($intLgts, 6$) **par activate** (*ChkSlp*))
r_9	**on** *ChkSlp* **if** ($lSlp = 1$) **do set** ($intLgts, 0$)
(R_5) If the room is occupied, set the lights intensity to 4.	
r_{10}	**on** *MtnOn* **do** (**set** ($intLgts, 4$) **par set** ($lgtsTmr, 0$))

Fig. 3. ECA rules for the light control subsystem of a smart home.

system attempts to reduce energy consumption by turning off the lights in unoccupied rooms or if the occupant is asleep. Passive sensors emit signals when an environmental variable value crosses a significant threshold. The motion sensor measure is expressed by the boolean environmental variable Mtn. The system also provides automatic adjustment for indoor light intensity based on an outdoor light sensor, whose measure is expressed by the environmental variable $ExtLgt \in \{0, ..., 10\}$. A pressure sensor detects whether the person is asleep and is expressed by the boolean environmental variable Slp.

$MtnOn$, $MtnOff$, and $ExtLgtLow$ are external events activated by the environmental variables discussed above. $MtnOn$ and $MtnOff$ occur when Mtn changes from 0 to 1 or from 1 to 0, respectively. $ExtLgtLow$ occurs when $ExtLgt$ drops below 6. External event $SecElp$ models the system clock, occurs every second, and takes a snapshot of the environmental variables into local variables $lMtn$, $lExtLgt$, and $lSlp$, respectively. Additional local variables $lgtsTmr$ and $intLgts$ are used. Variable $lgtsTmr$ is a timer for R_1, to convert the continuous condition "the room is unoccupied for 6 min" into 360 discretized $SecElps$ events. Rule r_1 initializes $lgtsTmr$ to 1 whenever the motion sensor detects no motion and the lights are on. The timer then increases as second elapses, provided that no motion is detected (r_2). If the timer reaches 360, internal event $LgtsOff$ is activated to turn off the lights and to reset $lgtsTmr$ to 0 (r_3). Variable $intLgts$ acts as an actuator control to adjust the internal light intensity.

We use internal events to model events not observable outside. $LgtsOff$, activated by r_3 or r_7, turns the lights off and activates an outdoor light intensity check through $ChkExtLgt$ (r_4). $ChkExtLgt$ activates $LgtsOn$ if $lExtLgt \le 5$ (r_5). $ChkSlp$ is activated by r_8 to check whether a person is asleep, in which case it triggers an action to turn the lights off (r_9). $ChkMtn$, activated by r_6, activates $LgtsOff$ if the room is empty and lights are on, or if the occupant is asleep (r_7).

4   Transforming a Set of ECA Rules into a PN

We now explain how to transform a set of ECA rules into a PN. First, we put each ECA rule into a "regular" form where both the *events* and the *condition* portion of the rule are disjunctions of conjunctions (of events or relational expressions, respectively). All rules of the smart home example in Fig. 3 are in this form. While this transformation may in principle grow exponentially large, each ECA rule usually contains a small number of events and conditions, hence it is not a problem in practice. Due to our immediate event-condition checking assumption, a rule is triggered iff "*trigger $\equiv$ events $\wedge$ condition*" holds.

Next, we map variables and events into places, and use PN transitions to model event testing, condition evaluation, and action execution. Any change in a variable's value is achieved through input and output arcs with appropriate cardinalities. Additional control places and transitions allow the PN behavior to be organized into "phases", as shown next. ECA rules r_1 through r_{10} of Fig. 3 are transformed into the PN of Fig. 4 (dotted transitions and places are duplicated and arcs labeled "*if(cond)*" are present only if *cond* holds).

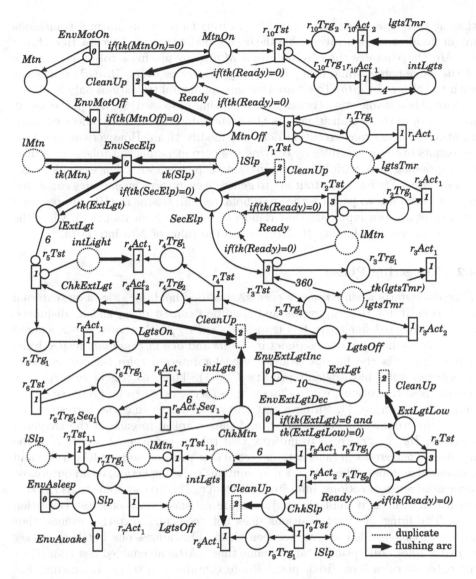

Fig. 4. The PN for ECA rules in Fig. 3.

4.1   Occurring Phase

This phase models the occurrence of external events, due to environment changes over which the system has no control. The PN firing semantics perfectly matches the nondeterministic asynchronous nature of these changes. For example, in Fig. 4, transitions *EnvMotOn* and *EnvMotOff* can add or remove the token in place *Mtn*, to nondeterministically model the presence or absence of people in the room (the inhibitor arc from place *Mtn* back to transition *EnvMotOn* ensures that at most one token resides in *Mtn*). Firing these environmental transitions might nondeterministically enable the corresponding external events. Here, firing *EnvMotOn* generates the external event *MtnOn* by placing a token in the place of the same name, while firing *EnvMotOff* generates event *MtnOff*, consistent with the change in *Mtn*. To ensure that environmental transitions only fire if the system is in a stable state (when no rule is being processed) we assign the lowest priority, 0, to these transitions. As the system does not directly affect environmental variables, rule execution does not modify them. However, we can take snapshots of these variables by copying the current number of tokens into their corresponding local variables using marking-dependent arcs. For example, transition *EnvSecElp* has an output arc to generate event *SecElp*, and arcs connected to local variables to perform the snapshots, e.g., all tokens in *lMtn* are removed by a reset arc (an input arc that removes all tokens from its place), while the output arc with cardinality $tk(Mtn)$ copies the value of *Mtn* into *lMtn*.

4.2   Triggering Phase

This phase starts when $trigger \equiv events \land condition$ holds for at least one external ECA rule. If, for rule r_k, events and condition consist of n_d and n_c disjuncts, respectively, we define $n_d \cdot n_c$ test transitions $r_k Tst_{i,j}$ with priority $P+2$, where i and j are the index of one conjunct in *events* and one in *condition*, respectively, while $P \geq 1$ is the highest priority used for internal rules (in our example, all internal rules have default priority $P = 1$). Then, to trigger rule r_k, only one of these transitions, e.g., $r_7 Tst_{1,1}$ or $r_7 Tst_{1,2}$, needs to be fired (we omit i and j if $n_d = n_c = 1$). Firing a test transition means that the corresponding events and conditions are satisfied, and puts a token in each of the triggered places $r_k Trg_1, \ldots, r_k Trg_N$, to indicate that rule r_k is triggered, where N is the number of outermost parallel actions (recall that **par** and **seq** model parallel and sequential actions). Thus, $N = 1$ if r_k contains only one action, or an outermost sequential series of actions. Inhibitor arcs from $r_k Trg_1$ to test transitions $r_k Tst_{i,j}$ ensure that, even if multiple conjuncts are satisfied, only one test transition fires. The firing of test transitions does not "consume" external events, thus we use double-headed arrows between them. This allows one batch to trigger multiple rules, conceptually "at the same time". After all enabled test transitions for external rules have fired, place *Ready* contains one token, indicating that the current batch of external events can be cleared: transition *CleanUp*, with priority $P+1$, fires and removes all tokens from external and internal event places using reset arcs, since all the rules that can be triggered have been marked. This ends the triggering phase and closes the current batch of events.

4.3   Performing Phase

This phase executes all actions of external rules marked in the previous phase and may further result in triggering and executing internal rules. Transitions in this phase correspond to the actions of rules with priority in $[1, P]$, the same as that of the corresponding rule. An action activates an internal event by adding a token to its place. This token is consumed as soon as a test transition of any internal rule related to this event fires. This is different from the way external rules "use" external events. Internal events not consumed in this phase are cleared when transition *CleanUp* fires in the next batch. When all enabled transitions of the performing phase have fired, the system is in a stable state where environmental changes (transitions with priority 0) can again happen and the next batch starts.

4.4   Translating ECA Rules into a PN

The algorithm in Fig. 5 takes external and internal ECA rules $\mathbf{R}_{ext}$, $\mathbf{R}_{int}$, with priorities in $[1, P]$, environmental and local variables $\mathbf{V}_{env}$, $\mathbf{V}_{loc}$, and external and internal events $\mathbf{E}_{ext}$, $\mathbf{E}_{int}$, and generates a PN. After normalizing the rules and setting P to the highest priority among the rule priorities in $\mathbf{R}_{int}$, it maps environmental variables $\mathbf{V}_{env}$, local variables $\mathbf{V}_{loc}$, external events $\mathbf{E}_{ext}$, and internal events $\mathbf{E}_{int}$, into the corresponding places (Lines 5, 6, and 8). Then, it creates phase control place *Ready*, transition *CleanUp*, and reset arcs for *CleanUp* (Lines 4–5). We use arcs with marking-dependent cardinalities to model expressions. For example, together with inhibitor arcs, these arcs ensure that each variable $v \in \mathbf{V}_{env}$ remains in its range $[v_{min}, v_{max}]$ (Lines 8–10). These arcs also model the **activated when** portion of external events (Line 17), rule conditions (Line 33), and assignments of environmental variables to local variables (Lines 19–20 and Lines 14–15). The algorithm also models external events and environmental changes (Lines 11–24); it connects environmental transitions such as t_{vInc} and t_{vDec} to their corresponding external event places, if any, with an arc whose cardinality evaluates to 1 if the corresponding condition becomes true upon the firing of the transition and the event place does not contain a token already, 0 otherwise (e.g., the arcs from *EnvExtLigDec* to *ExtLgtLow*).

Next, rules are considered (Lines 25–41). A rule with n_d event disjuncts and n_c condition disjuncts generates $n_d \cdot n_c$ testing transitions. To model the parallel-sequential action graph of a rule, we use mutually recursive procedures, one for parallel actions in Fig. 6 and the other for sequential actions in Fig. 7. Procedure *SeqSubGraph* first tests all atomic actions, such as "set", "increase", "decrease", and "activate". Then, it recursively calls *ParSubGraph* at Line 10 if it encounters parallel actions. Otherwise, it calls itself to unwind another layer of sequential actions at Line 12 and Line 15 for the two portions of the sequence. Procedure *ParSubGraph* creates control places and transitions for the two branches of a parallel action and calls *SeqSubGraph* at Line 4.

We use rule r_3: **on** *SecElp* **if** ($lgtsTmr = 360$ **and** $lMtn = 0$) **do** (**set** ($lgtsTmr, 0$) **par activate** (*LgtsOff*)), with default priority $P = 1$, to better illustrate how to transform a rule into our model. Figure 8 shows the resulting PN. Event places *SecElp* and *LgtsOff*, variable places *lMtn* and *lgtsTmr*, control place *Ready*, and control transition *CleanUp*, with priority $P + 1 = 2$, are created during the pre-processing step. The subnets for the external event occurring phase and the event cleanup are also created then. These are shown as dotted places and transitions in Fig. 8.

$TransformECAintoPN$ ($\mathbf{R}_{ext}, \mathbf{R}_{int}, \mathbf{V}_{env}, \mathbf{V}_{loc}, \mathbf{E}_{ext}, \mathbf{E}_{int}$)

1 normalize $\mathbf{R}_{ext}$ and $\mathbf{R}_{int}$ into regular form and set P to the highest rule priority
2 create a place $Ready$ • *to control "phases" of the net*
3 create transition $CleanUp$ with priority $P+1$ and $Ready -[1] \mapsto CleanUp$
4 foreach event $e \in \mathbf{E}_{ext} \cup \mathbf{E}_{int}$ do
5   create place p_e and $p_e -[tk(p_e)] \mapsto CleanUp$
6 create place p_v, for each variable $v \in \mathbf{V}_{loc}$
7 foreach variable $v \in \mathbf{V}_{env}$ with range $[v_{min}, v_{max}]$ do
8   create place p_v and transitions t_{vInc} and t_{vDec} with priority 0
9   create $t_{vDec} -[\text{if}(tk(p_v) > v_{min})1 \text{ else } 0] \mapsto p_v$
10   create $t_{vInc} -[1] \mapsto p_v$ and $p_v -[v_{max}] \!\!-\!\!\circ t_{vInc}$
11 foreach event $e \in \mathbf{E}_{ext}$ **activated when** $v \ op \ val$, for $op \in \{\geq | =\}$ do
12   create $t_{vInc} -[\text{if}(tk(p_v) \ op \ val)1 \text{ else } 0] \mapsto p_e$
13   if e reads $v \in \mathbf{V}_{env}$ into $v' \in \mathbf{V}_{loc}$ then
14   create $p_{v'} -[\text{if}(tk(p_v) \ op \ val)tk(p_{v'}) \text{ else } 0] \mapsto t_{vInc}$
15   create $t_{vInc} -[\text{if}(tk(p_v) \ op \ val)tk(p_v) \text{ else } 0] \mapsto p_{v'}$
16 foreach event $e \in \mathbf{E}_{ext}$ **activated when** $v \ op \ val$, for $op \in \{\leq | =\}$ do
17   create $t_{vDec} -[\text{if}(tk(p_v) \ op \ val)1 \text{ else } 0] \mapsto p_e$
18   if e reads $v \in \mathbf{V}_{env}$ into $v' \in \mathbf{V}_{loc}$ then
19   create $p_{v'} -[\text{if}(tk(p_v) \ op \ val)tk(p_{v'}) \text{ else } 0] \mapsto t_{vDec}$
20   create $t_{vDec} -[\text{if}(tk(p_v) \ op \ val)tk(p_v) \text{ else } 0] \mapsto p_{v'}$
21 foreach event $e \in \mathbf{E}_{ext}$ without an **activated when** portion do
22   create t_e and $t_e -[\text{if}(tk(p_e) = 0)1 \text{ else } 0] \mapsto p_e$
23   if e reads $v \in \mathbf{V}_{env}$ into $v' \in \mathbf{V}_{loc}$ then
24   create $p_{v'} -[tk(p_{v'})] \mapsto t_e$ and $t_e -[tk(p_v)] \mapsto p_{v'}$
25 foreach rule $r_k \in \mathbf{R}_{ext} \cup \mathbf{R}_{int}$ with n_d event disjuncts, n_c condition disjuncts, actions A, and priority $p \in [1, P]$ do
26   create trans. $r_k Tst_{i,j}, i \in [1, n_d], j \in [1, n_c]$,w/priority $P+2$ if $r_k \in \mathbf{R}_{ext}$, else p
27   foreach event e in disjunct i do
28   create $p_e -[1] \mapsto r_k Tst_{i,j}$
29   create $r_k Tst_{i,j} -[1] \mapsto p_e$, if $e \in \mathbf{E}_{ext}$
30   foreach conjunct $v \leq val$ or $v = val$ in disjunct j do
31   create $p_v -[val + \bar{1}] \!\!-\!\!\circ r_k Tst_{i,j}$
32   foreach conjunct $v \geq val$ or $v = val$ in disjunct j do
33   create $p_v -[val] \mapsto r_k Tst_{i,j}$ and $r_k Tst_{i,j} -[val] \mapsto p_v$
34   if actions A is "$(A_1 \ par \ A_2)$" then $n_a = 2$;
35   else $n_a = 1, A_1 = A$;
36   foreach $l \in [1, n_a]$ do
37   create places $r_k Trg_l$ and transitions $r_k Act_l$ with priority p
38   create $r_k Trg_l -[1] \mapsto r_k Act_l$ and $r_k Tst_{i,j} -[1] \mapsto r_k Trg_l$
39     $SeqSubGraph(A_l, "r_k Acl_l", l, p)$
40 foreach $r_k \in \mathbf{R}_{ext}, i \in [1, n_d], j \in [1, n_c]$ do
41   create $r_k Tst_{i,j} -[\text{if}(tk(Ready) = 0)1 \text{ else } 0] \mapsto Ready$ and $r_k Trg_1 -[1] \!\!-\!\!\circ r_k Tst_{i,j}$

Fig. 5. Transforming ECA rules into a PN: $a -[k] \mapsto b$ means "an arc from a to b with cardinality k"; $a -[k] \!\!-\!\!\circ b$ means "an inhibitor arc from a to b with cardinality k".

$ParSubGraph(Pars, Pre, p)$ • *Pars: parallel actions, Pre: prefix*

1 foreach $l \in \{1, 2\}$ do   • *according to the syntax $Pars_2$ has two components*
2   create place $PreAct_l Trg_l Seq_l$ and transition $PreAct_l$ w/priority p
3   create $Pre -[1] \mapsto PreAct_l$ and $PreAct_l -[1] \mapsto PreAct_l Trg_l Seq_l$
4   $SeqSubGraph(Pars_l, "PreAct_l Trg_l Seq_l", l, p)$;

Fig. 6. Processing **par**.

$SeqSubGraph(Seqs, Pre, i, p)$ • *Seqs: sequential actions, Pre: prefix*

1 if *Seqs* **sets** variable v to val then
2   create p_v $-[tk(p_v)] \mapsto Pre$ and $Pre -[val] \mapsto p_v$
3 else if *Seqs* **increases** variable v by val then
4   create $Pre -[val] \mapsto p_v$
5 else if *Seqs* **decreases** variable v by val then
6   create $p_v -[val] \mapsto Pre$
7 else if *Seqs* **activates** an internal event e then
8   create $Pre -[1] \mapsto p_e$
9 else if the outermost operator of *Seqs* is **par** then
10     $ParSubGraph(Seqs, ``Pre", p)$ • *Recursion on parallel part*
11 else if the outermost operator of *Seqs* is **seq** then
12     $SeqSubGraph(Seqs_1, ``Pre", 1, p)$ • *Seqs$_1$ is the first part of Seq*
13   create place $PreTrg_iSeq_1$ and transition $PreAct_iSeq_1$
14   create $Pre -[1] \mapsto PreTrg_iSeq_1$ and $PreTrg_iSeq_1 -[1] \mapsto PreAct_iSeq_1$
15     $SeqSubGraph(Seqs_2, ``PreTrg_iSeq_1", 2, p)$ • *Seqs$_2$ is the second part of Seq*

Fig. 7. Processing **seq**.

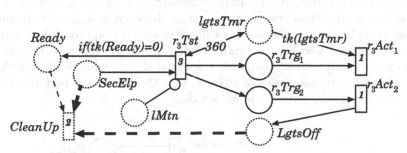

Fig. 8. The PN corresponding to rule r_3

Test transition r_3Tst with priority $P + 2 = 3$ is created for the triggering phase. Place *SecElp* is connected to r_3Tst with an input arc to represent the occurrence of event *SecElp*, while place *lMtn* is connected to r_3Tst with an inhibitor arc and *lgtsTmr* is connected to r_3Tst with both an input and an output arc, with cardinality 360, to represent r_3's triggering condition: $lgtsTmr = 360$ **and** $lMtn = 0$. The PN semantics naturally implements the conjunction of events and conditions. r_3Tst is connected to control place *Ready* with a self-modifying arc having cardinality $if(tk(Ready) = 0)$ to indicate the end of a batch, which enables transition *CleanUp*, that in turn clears up all the tokens in the event places (with the corresponding reset arcs). r_3 has two parallel actions, thus there are two places r_3Trg_1 and r_3Trg_2 that contain a token when r_3 is triggered. Then, two action transitions (r_3Act_1 and r_3Act_2 with priority $P = 1$) are needed for the performing phase. After the event cleanup, when transition *CleanUp* with priority 2 fires, only action transitions (having priority 1) are enabled. r_3Trg_1 is connected to r_3Act_1 and *lgtsTmr* to r_3Act_1 with an arc having cardinality $tk(lgtsTmr)$ to model the action **set** $(lgtsTmr, 0)$. r_3Trg_2 is connected to r_3Act_2 and r_3Act_2 to *LgtsOff* to model action **activate** $(LgtsOff)$.

The translation process we just described generates a PN from a set of ECA rules augmented with an interpretation of the external environment where the value of environmental variables can change asynchronously, nondeterministically, and independently of the values of variables used to define the ECA rules. Because the PN contains additional machinery needed to enforce the semantics of ECA rules (such as the *CleanUp* transition), the two models are only weakly bisimilar, but this is enough to preserve CTL properties [13]

5   Verifying Properties

The first step towards verifying correctness properties is to define $\mathcal{S}_{init}$, the set of initial states, corresponding to all the possible initial combinations of system variables (e.g., *ExtLgt* can initially have any value in $[0, 10]$). One could consider all these possible values by enumerating all legal stable states corresponding to possible initial combinations of the environmental variables, then start the analysis from each of these states, one at a time. However, in addition to requiring the user to explicitly provide the set of initial states, this approach may require enormous runtime, also because many computations are repeated in different runs. Our approach instead computes the initial states symbolically, thanks to the nondeterministic semantics of PNs, so that the analysis is performed once starting from a single, but very large, set $\mathcal{S}_{init}$.

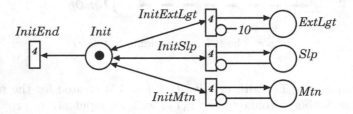

Fig. 9. The initialization phase for the smart home example.

To this end, we add an initialization phase that puts a nondeterministically chosen legal number of tokens in each place corresponding to an environmental variable. This phase is described by a subnet consisting of a transition *InitEnd* with priority $P+3$, a place *Init* with one initial token, and an initializing transition with priority $P+3$ for every environmental variable, to initialize the number of tokens in the corresponding place. Figure 9 shows this subnet for our running example. We initialize the PN by assigning the minimum number of tokens to every environmental variable place and leaving all other places empty, then we let the initializing transitions nondeterministically add a token at a time, possibly up to the maximum legal number of tokens in each corresponding place. When *InitEnd* fires, it disables the initializing transitions, freezes the nondeterministic choices, and starts the system's real execution.

This builds the set of initial states, ensuring that the PN will explore all possible initial states, and avoids the overhead of manually starting the PN from one legal initial marking at a time. Even though the overall state space might be larger (it equals the union of all the state spaces that would be built starting from each individual marking), this is normally not the case. Having to perform just one state space generation is obviously enormously better.

After the initialization step, we proceed with verifying termination and confluence using our tool SMART, which provides symbolic reachability analysis and CTL model checking with counterexample generation [8].

5.1 Termination

Reactive systems constantly respond to external events. However, if the system has a livelock, a finite number of external events can trigger an infinite number of rule executions (i.e, activate a cycle of internal events), causing the system to remain "busy" internally, a fatal design error. When generating the state space, all legal batches of events are considered. Due to the PN execution semantics, we can again avoid the need for an explicit enumeration, this time, of event batches.

Definition 1. A set $\mathcal{G}$ of ECA rules satisfies termination if no infinite sequence of internal events can be triggered in any possible execution of $\mathcal{G}$.   □

In CTL, this can then be expressed as $\neg\mathbf{EF}(\mathbf{EG}(unstable))$, which states that there is no cycle of unstable states reachable from an initial, thus stable, state. Since we observed at the end of Sect. 4.4 that the PN obtained by the translation process is weakly-bisimilar to the ECA rules (plus a representation of the environment), and since weak-bisimilarity preserves CTL properties, termination can be verified directly on the PN. Both traditional breadth-first-search (BFS) and saturation-based [25] algorithms are suitable to compute the **EG** operator. Algorithm *Term* in Fig. 10 uses saturation, which tends to perform much better in both time and memory consumption when analyzing large asynchronous systems. We encode transitions related to external events and environmental variable changes into $\mathcal{N}_{ext}$. Thus, the internal transitions are $\mathcal{N}_{int} = \mathcal{N} \setminus \mathcal{N}_{ext}$. After generating the state space $\mathcal{S}_{rch}$ using constrained saturation [24], we build the set of states $\mathcal{S}_{unst}$ by symbolically intersecting $\mathcal{S}_{rch}$ with the unprimed, or "from", states extracted from $\mathcal{N}_{int}$. Then, we use the CTL operators **EG** and **EF** to identify any nonterminating path (i.e., cycle).

5.2 Confluence

Confluence is another desirable property to ensure consistency in systems exhibiting highly concurrent behavior.

Definition 2. A set $\mathcal{G}$ of ECA rules satisfying termination also satisfies confluence if, for any legal batch b of external events and starting from any particular stable state s, the system eventually reaches a unique stable state.   □

```
bool Term(mdd S_init, mdd2 N_int)
  1   mdd S_rch ← StateSpaceGen(S_init, N_ext ∪ N_int);
  2   mdd S_unst ← Intersection(S_rch, ExtractUnprimed(N_int));
  3   mdd S_p ← EF(EG(S_unst));
  4   if S_p ≠ ∅ then return false              • provide error trace
  5   else return true;
```

```
mdd ExtractUnprimed(mdd2 p)                              • p unprimed
  6   if p = 1 then return 1;
  7   if CacheLookUp(ExtractUnprimedCode, p, r) return r;
  8   foreach i ∈ V_p.v do
  9     mdd r_i ← 0;
 10     if p[i] ≠ 0 then            • p[i] is the node pointed edge i of node p
 11       foreach j ∈ V_p.v s.t. p[i][j] ≠ 0 do
 12         r_i ← Union(r_i, ExtractUnprimed(p[i][j]))
 13   mdd r ← UniqueTableInsert({r_i : i ∈ V_p.v});
 14   CacheInsert(ExtractUnprimedCode, p, r);
 15   return r;
```

Fig. 10. Algorithms to verify the termination property.

Just like termination, confluence can also be expressed in CTL, although in an extremely cumbersome way that we mention simply because, again, this guarantees that it is correct to verify it on the PN. Specifically, if we assume that each stable state s_i is the only one satisfying a special additional atomic proposition p_i, we can express confluence as the (enormous) conjunction over all stable states s_1, s_2, and s_3, with $s_2 \neq s_3$, of the CTL formulas

$$\neg \left(p_1 \wedge \textbf{EX}(unstable \wedge \textbf{E}\ unstable\ \textbf{U}\ p_2) \wedge \textbf{EX}(unstable \wedge \textbf{E}\ unstable\ \textbf{U}\ p_3) \right).$$

We stress that what constitutes a legal batch b of events depends on state s, since the condition portion of one or more rules might affect whether b (or a subset of b) can trigger a rule (thus close a batch). Given a legal batch b occurring in stable state s, the system satisfies confluence if it progresses from s by traversing some (nondeterministically chosen) sequence of unstable states, eventually reaching a stable state uniquely determined by b and s. Checking confluence is therefore expensive [2], as it requires verifying the combinations of all stable states reachable from S_{init} with all legal batches of external events when the system is in that stable state. A straightforward approach enumerates all legal batches of events for each stable state, runs the model, and checks that the set of reachable stable states has cardinality one. We instead only check that, from each reachable unstable state, exactly one stable state is reachable; this avoids enumerating all legal batches of events for each stable state. Since nondeterministic execution in the performing phase is the reason a system may violate confluence, checking the evolution from unstable states suffices.

The brute force algorithm *ConfExplicit* in Fig. 11 enumerates unstable states and generates reachable states only from unstable states using constrained saturation [24]. Then, it counts the stable states in the obtained set. We observe that, starting from an unstable state u, the system may traverse a large set

```
bool ConfExplicit(mdd S_st, mdd S_unst, mdd2 N_int)
1  foreach i ∈ S_unst
2     mdd S_i ← StateSpaceGen(i, N_int);
3     if Cardinality(Intersection(S_i, S_st)) > 1 then
4        return false;                          • provide error trace
5  return true;
```

```
bool ConfExplicitImproved(mdd S_st, mdd S_unst, mdd2 N_int, mdd2 N)

5   mdd S_frontier ← Intersection(RelProd(S_st, N), S_unst);
6   while S_frontier ≠ ∅ do      • if S_frontier is empty, it explores all S_unst
7      pick i ∈ S_frontier;
8      mdd S_i ← StateSpaceGen(i, N_int);
9      if Cardinality(Intersection(S_i, S_st)) > 1 then
10        return false;                         • provide error trace
11     else                        • exclude all unstable states reached by i
12        S_frontier ← S_frontier \ Intersection(S_i, S_unst);
13  return true;
```

Fig. 11. Explicit algorithms to verify the confluence property.

of unstable states before reaching a stable state. If unstable state u is reachable, so are the unstable states reachable from it. Thus, the improved version *ConfExplicitImproved* first picks an unstable state i and, after generating the states reachable from i and verifying that they include only one stable state, it excludes all visited unstable states (Line 11). Furthermore, it starts only from states i in the frontier, i.e., unstable states reachable in one step from stable states (all other unstable reachable states are by definition reachable from this frontier). However, we stress that these, as for all symbolic algorithms, are heuristics, so they are not guaranteed to work better than simpler approaches.

Figure 12 shows a fully symbolic algorithm to check confluence. It first generates the transition transitive closure set from N_{int} using constrained saturation [25], where the "from" states of the closure are in S_{unst} (Line 1). The resulting set encodes the reachability relation from any reachable unstable state without going through any stable state. Then, it filters this relation to obtain the relation from reachable unstable states to stable states by constraining the "to" states to set S_{st}. Thus, checking confluence reduces to verifying whether there exist two different pairs (i, j) and (i, j') in the relation: Procedure *CheckConf* implements this check symbolically. While computing the transitive closure is expensive [25], this approach avoids separate searches from distinct unstable states and is particularly appropriate when S_{unst} is large.

6 Experimental Results

Table 1 reports results for a set of models run on an Intel Xeon 2.53 GHz workstation with 36 GB RAM under Linux. For each model, it shows the state space size ($|S_{rch}|$), the peak memory (M_p), and the final memory (M_f) for each method.

```
bool ConfSymbolic(mdd S_st, mdd S_unst, mdd2 N_int)
  1   mdd2 TC ← ConstraintedTransitiveClosure(N_int, S_unst);
  2   mdd2 TC_u2s ← FilterPrimed(TC, S_st);
  3   return CheckConf(TC_u2s);
```

```
bool CheckConf(mdd2 p)
  4   if p = 1 then return true
  5   if CacheLookUp(CheckConfCode, p, r) return r;
  6   foreach i ∈ V_p.v, s.t. exist j, j' ∈ V_p.v, j ≠ j', p[i][j] ≠ 0, p[i][j'] ≠ 0
      do
  7     foreach j, j' ∈ V_p.v, j ≠ j' s.t. p[i][j] ≠ 0, p[i][j'] ≠ 0 do
  8       if p[i][j] = p[i][j'] return false;           • Confluence does not hold
  9       mdd f_j ← ExtractUnprimed(p[i][j]);            • Result will be cached
 10       mdd f_j' ← ExtractUnprimed(p[i][j']);          • No duplicate
      computation
 11       if Intersection(f_i, f_j') ≠ 0 then return false;
 12     foreach i, j ∈ V_p.v s.t. p[i][j] ≠ 0 do
 13       if CheckConf(p[i][j]) = false return false;
 14     CacheInsert(CheckConfCode, p, true);
 15     return true;
```

Fig. 12. Fully symbolic algorithm to verify the confluence property.

For termination, it shows the time used to verify the property (T_t) and to find the shortest counterexample (T_{sc}). For confluence, it reports the best runtime between our two explicit algorithms (T_{be}) and for our symbolic algorithm (T_s). Memory consumption accounts for both decision diagrams and operation caches.

Net PN_t is the model corresponding to our running example in Fig. 3, and fails the termination check. Even though the state space is not very large, the saturation-based counterexample generation (T_{sc}) is computationally expensive [26] and consumes most of the runtime. The minimal counterexample generated by SMART has a long tail consisting of 1,863 states leading to the 10-state cycle of Fig. 13 (only the non-empty places are listed for each state, and edges are labeled with the corresponding PN transition). The BFS-based algorithm instead first computes set S_{EG} satisfying **EG**(S_{unst}), then it randomly chooses a state s_s in S_{EG}, forms an **EG** witness [26] by randomly selecting successors also in S_{EG}, and generates an **EF** shortest trace from S_{init} to s. This does *not* result in an overall shortest counterexample but, with a reasonable number of attempts, a counterexample with 1,883 states, 12 in the final cycle, is found.

Analyzing the shortest trace provided by the saturation-based algorithm, we can clearly see (in bold) that, when lights are about to be turned off due to the timeout, $lMtn = 0$, and the external light is low, $ExtLgt \leq 5$, the infinite sequence of internal events $(LgtsOff, ChkExtLgt, LgtsOn, ChkMtn)^\omega$ prevents the system from terminating. Thus, rules r_4, r_5, r_6, and r_7 must be investigated. Among the possible modifications, we choose to replace r_5 with r_5' : **on** $ChkExtLgt$ **if** (($intLgts = 0$ **and** $lExtLgt \leq 5$) **and** $lMtn = 1$) **do activate** ($LgtsOn$), resulting in the addition of an input arc from $lMtn$ to $r_5 Tst$. The new corrected model is called PN_c in Table 1, and SMART verifies that it satisfies termination.

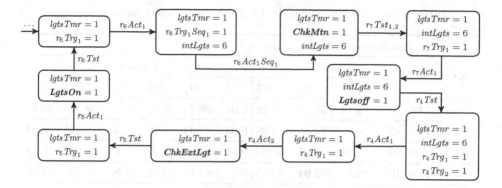

Fig. 13. A termination counterexample (related to rules r_4 to r_7).

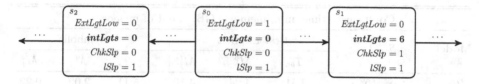

Fig. 14. A confluence counterexample (related to rules r_8 and r_9).

The experimental results for PN_c confirm that verifying termination does not consume much time for either BFS or saturation-based algorithms. However, for PN_t, the saturation-based algorithm finds a minimal counterexample in less time than the random BFS-based algorithm, which does not ensure minimality. In practice, minimal counterexamples are desirable when debugging.

We then run SMART on PN_c to verify confluence, and find 72,644 bad states. Figure 14 shows one of these unstable states, s_0, reaching two stables states, s_1 and s_2. External event $ExtLgtLow$ closes the batch in s_0 and triggers rule r_8, which sets $intLgt$ to 6 and activates internal event $ChkSlp$, which in turn sets $intLgt$ to 0 (we omit intermediate unstable states from s_0 to s_1 and to s_2). Recall rule r_8: **on** $ExtLgtLow$ **do** (**set** ($intLgts$, 6) **par activate** ($ChkSlp$) and rule r_9: **on** $ChkSlp$ **if** ($lSlp = 1$) **do set** ($intLgts$, 0), in Fig. 3. We correct and replace them with r'_8: **on** $ExtLgtLow$ **if** $lSlp=0$ **do set** ($intLgt$, 6) and r'_9: **on** $ExtLgtLow$ **if** $lSlp = 1$ **do set** ($intLgt$, 0); resulting in model PN_{fc}. Checking this new model for confluence, we find that the number of bad states decreases from 72,644 to 24,420. After investigation, we determine that the remaining problem is related to rules r_2 and r_3. After changing rule r_2 to **on** $SecElp$ **if** (($lgtsTmr \geq 1$**and** $lgtsTmr \leq 359$) **and** $lMtn = 0$) **do increase** ($lgtsTmr$, 1), the model passes the check. This demonstrates the effectiveness of counterexamples to help a designer debug a set of ECA rules.

We then turn our attention to larger models, which extend our original model by introducing four additional rules and increasing variable ranges. In PN_1 and PN_2, the external light variable $ExtLgt$ ranges in $[0, 20]$ instead of $[0, 10]$; for

Table 1. Results of verifying the ECA rules for a smart home in Fig. 3.

Model	$|\mathcal{S}_{rch}|$	Termination (time: sec, memory: MB)								
		BFS			Saturation					
		T_b	M_p^b	M_f^b	T_t	M_p^t	M_f^t	T_{sc}	M_p^{sc}	M_f^{sc}
PN_t	$2.66 \cdot 10^6$	8.11	91.85	35.28	0.01	36.25	6.52	7.54	48.41	39.49
PN_c	$2.61 \cdot 10^6$	0.01	31.85	4.28	0.03	32.41	4.48	0	0	0
PN_1	$8.99 \cdot 10^6$	7.98	96.23	36.03	0.04	41.44	6.62	8.08	51.68	41.99
PN_2	$1.78 \cdot 10^7$	15.55	183.04	70.45	0.04	64.00	8.97	16.49	90.14	75.97
PN_3	$2.61 \cdot 10^7$	106.29	554.29	291.11	0.04	155.55	17.29	81.04	356.04	354.94
PN_4	$5.02 \cdot 10^7$	39.33	118.88	41.21	0.04	67.69	8.08	14.54	74.77	58.95

Model	$|\mathcal{S}_{rch}|$	Confluence (time: min, memory: GB, –: out of memory)					
		Best Explicit			Symbolic		
		T_{be}	M_p^{be}	M_f^{be}	T_s	M_p^s	M_f^s
PN_c	$2.38 \cdot 10^6$	4.51	4.24	4.10	5.11	2.02	0.22
PN_1	$8.12 \cdot 10^6$	40.25	14.53	14.33	6.40	2.31	0.27
PN_2	$1.61 \cdot 10^7$	34.40	0.85	0.08	10.11	2.59	0.25
PN_3	$2.33 \cdot 10^7$	> 120.00	–	–	60.09	2.59	0.25
PN_4	$4.55 \cdot 10^7$	> 120.00	–	–	23.33	4.66	0.52

PN_4, it ranges in $[0, 50]$. PN_2 also extends the range of the light timer variable $lgtTmr$ to $[0, 720]$; PN_3 to $[0, 3600]$. For termination, the saturation-based algorithm behaviors much better on the two largest models PN_3 and PN_4 for both time and peak memory consumption. For PN_2 the BFS algorithm happens to a minimal counterexample using less time, but at a cost of twice the peak memory consumption. For smaller models, the requirements for both algorithms are quite acceptable. However, we emphasize that the saturation algorithm guarantees counterexample minimality. We observe that, when verifying confluence, the time and memory consumption tends to increase as the model grows; also, our symbolic algorithm scales much better than the best explicit approach when verifying confluence. For the relatively small state space of PN_t, enumeration is effective, since computing the transitive closure is expensive. However, as the state space grows, enumerating the unstable states becomes unfeasible. We also observe that the supposedly improved explicit confluence algorithm sometimes makes things worse. The reason may lie in the fact that a random selection of a state from the frontier has different statistical properties than the original explicit approach, and in the fact that operation caches save many intermediate results. However, both explicit algorithms run out of memory on PN_3 and PN_4.

Comparing the results for PN_3 and PN_4, we observe that larger state spaces might require fewer resources. With symbolic methods, this might happen if the corresponding MDD is more regular than the one for a smaller state space.

7 Conclusion

Verifying ECA rule bases for reactive systems is challenging due to their highly concurrent and nondeterministic nature. We proposed an approach that transforms an ECA rule base into a self-modifying Petri net with inhibitor arcs and priorities, then uses symbolic verification algorithms. Our approach is general enough to give precise answers to questions about several properties, certainly those that can be expressed in CTL, such as *termination.*

More importantly, we also presented a symbolic *confluence* algorithm, a property that is much more difficult to verify. In principle, this requires us to enumerate "stable" states and show that, from each of them, exactly one stable state can be reached when one or more rules are triggered, even if the sequence of "unstable" states that the system traverses while processing these rules exhibits nondeterminism due to the interleaving of asynchronously triggered actions. As an application, we showed how a light control system can be captured by our approach, and we verified termination and confluence for this model using SMART.

In the future, we would like to improve our approach in the following ways. The confluence algorithm must perform constrained state space generation starting from each unstable state, which is not efficient if $\mathcal{S}_{unst}$ is large. In that case, a simulation-based falsification approach might be more suitable, using intelligent heuristic sampling and searching strategies. However, this approach is sound only if the entire set $\mathcal{S}_{unst}$ is explored. Another direction to extend our work is the inclusion of abstraction techniques to reduce the size of the state space.

Acknowledgment. Work supported in part by UC-MEXUS under grant *Verification of active rule bases using timed Petri nets* and by the National Science Foundation under grant CCF-1442586.

References

1. Abadi, D.J., Carney, D., Çetintemel, U., Cherniack, M., Convey, C., Lee, S., Stonebraker, M., Tatbul, N., Zdonik, S.: Aurora: a new model and architecture for data stream management. VLDB J. **12**(2), 120–139 (2003)
2. Aiken, A., Widom, J., Hellerstein, J.M.: Behavior of database production rules: termination, confluence, and observable determinism. In: Proceedings of the ACM SIGMOD International Conference on Management of Data, pp. 59–68. ACM Press (1992)
3. Augusto, J.C., Nugent, C.D.: A new architecture for smart homes based on ADB and temporal reasoning. In: Toward a Human-Friendly Assistive Environment, vol. 14, pp. 106–113 (2004)

4. Baralis, E., Ceri, S., Paraboschi, S.: Improved rule analysis by means of triggering and activation graphs. In: Sellis, T.K. (ed.) RIDS 1995. LNCS, vol. 985, pp. 163–181. Springer, Heidelberg (1995)
5. Baralis, E., Widom, J.: An algebraic approach to static analysis of active database rules. ACM Trans. Database Syst. **25**(3), 269–332 (2000)
6. Bryant, R.E.: Graph-based algorithms for boolean function manipulation. IEEE Trans. Comput. **35**(8), 677–691 (1986)
7. Choi, E.-H., Tsuchiya, T., Kikuno, T.: Model checking active database rules under various rule processing strategies. IPSJ Digit. Cour. **2**, 826–839 (2006)
8. Ciardo, G., Jones, R.L., Miner, A.S., Siminiceanu, R.I.: Logical and stochastic modeling with SMART. In: Kemper, P., Sanders, W.H. (eds.) TOOLS 2003. LNCS, vol. 2794, pp. 78–97. Springer, Heidelberg (2003)
9. Ciardo, G., Lüttgen, G., Siminiceanu, R.I.: Saturation: an efficient iteration strategy for symbolic state-space generation. In: Margaria, T., Yi, W. (eds.) TACAS 2001. LNCS, vol. 2031, pp. 328–342. Springer, Heidelberg (2001)
10. Ciardo, G., Zhao, Y., Jin, X.: Ten years of saturation: a petri net perspective. In: Jensen, K., Donatelli, S., Kleijn, J. (eds.) ToPNoC V. LNCS, vol. 6900, pp. 51–95. Springer, Heidelberg (2012)
11. Clarke, E.M., Grumberg, O., Peled, D.A.: Model Checking. MIT Press, Cambridge (1999)
12. Comai, S., Tanca, L.: Termination and confluence by rule prioritization. IEEE Trans. Knowl. Data Eng. **15**, 257–270 (2003)
13. French, T.: Decidability of propositionally quantified logics of knowledge. In: Gedeon, T.T.D., Fung, L.C.C. (eds.) AI 2003. LNCS (LNAI), vol. 2903, pp. 352–363. Springer, Heidelberg (2003)
14. Kam, T., Villa, T., Brayton, R.K., Sangiovanni-Vincentelli, A.: Multi-valued decision diagrams: theory and applications. Multiple-Valued Logic **4**(1–2), 9–62 (1998)
15. Kulkarni, K.G., Mattos, N.M., Cochrane, R.: Active database features in SQL3. In: Paton, N.W. (ed.) Active Rules in Database Systems, pp. 197–219. Springer, New York (1999)
16. Lee, E.A.: Computing foundations and practice for cyber-physical systems: a preliminary report. Technical report UCB/EECS-2007-72, University of California, Berkeley, May 2007
17. Li, X., Medina Marín, J., Chapa, S.V.: A structural model of ECA rules in active database. In: Coello Coello, C.A., de Albornoz, Á., Sucar, L.E., Battistutti, O.C. (eds.) MICAI 2002. LNCS (LNAI), vol. 2313, pp. 486–493. Springer, Heidelberg (2002)
18. McCarthy, D., Dayal, U.: The architecture of an active database management system. ACM Sigmod Rec. **18**(2), 215–224 (1989)
19. Murata, T.: Petri nets: properties, analysis and applications. Proc. of the IEEE **77**(4), 541–579 (1989)
20. Nazareth, D.: Investigating the applicability of petri nets for rule-based system verification. IEEE Trans. Knowl. Data Eng. **5**(3), 402–415 (1993)
21. Ray, I., Ray, I.: Detecting termination of active database rules using symbolic model checking. In: Caplinskas, A., Eder, J. (eds.) ADBIS 2001. LNCS, vol. 2151, pp. 266–279. Springer, Heidelberg (2001)
22. Valk, R.: Generalizations of petri nets. In: Gruska, J., Chytil, M.P. (eds.) MFCS 1981. LNCS, vol. 118, pp. 140–155. Springer, Heidelberg (1981)
23. Varró, D.: A formal semantics of uml statecharts by model transition systems. In: Corradini, A., Ehrig, H., Kreowski, H.-J., Rozenberg, G. (eds.) ICGT 2002. LNCS, vol. 2505, pp. 378–392. Springer, Heidelberg (2002)

24. Zhao, Y., Ciardo, G.: Symbolic CTL model checking of asynchronous systems using constrained saturation. In: Liu, Z., Ravn, A.P. (eds.) ATVA 2009. LNCS, vol. 5799, pp. 368–381. Springer, Heidelberg (2009)
25. Zhao, Y., Ciardo, G.: Symbolic computation of strongly connected components and fair cycles using saturation. Innov. Syst. Softw. Eng. **7**(2), 141–150 (2011)
26. Zhao, Y., Xiaoqing, J., Ciardo, G.: A symbolic algorithm for shortest EG witness generation. In: Proceedings of TASE, pp. 68–75. IEEE Computer Society Press (2011)

Tissue Systems and Petri Net Synthesis

Jetty Kleijn[1]([⊠]), Maciej Koutny[2], and Marta Pietkiewicz-Koutny[2]

[1] LIACS, Leiden University, P.O. Box 9512, 2300 RA Leiden, The Netherlands
h.c.m.kleijn@liacs.leidenuniv.nl
[2] School of Computing Science,
Newcastle University, Newcastle upon Tyne NE1 7RU, UK
{maciej.koutny,marta.koutny}@newcastle.ac.uk

Abstract. Tissue systems are a computational abstraction of the chemical reactions and transport of molecules in a tissue. We consider the problem of synthesising tissue systems from specifications of observed or desired behaviour given in the form of transition systems. We demonstrate how a Petri net solution to this problem, based on the notion of regions, yields a method for automated synthesis of tissue systems from transition systems. We first assume that the input of the algorithm contains information about the topology of the system to be constructed, and then discuss the case when such a topology is not known in advance and has yet to be determined.

Keywords: Synthesis · Tissue system · Petri net · Transition system · Region

1 Introduction

Membrane systems and tissue systems are computational models inspired by the functioning of living cells and, in particular, by the way chemical reactions take place in cells and molecules move from one compartment to another [22–25]. Reactions are abstracted to evolution rules that specify which and how many molecules can be produced from given molecules of a certain kind and quantity. Membrane systems model the computational and communication processes within a single cell divided by membranes into compartments; rules belong to compartments and the molecules that are produced either remain in the compartment or can be delivered to a neighbouring (i.e., enclosed or surrounding) compartment. Hence a membrane system has an associated tree-like structure describing the connections that can be used for the transport of molecules. This is generalised in tissue structures to arbitrary graphs allowing communication along all edges. The nodes of the graph associated with a tissue system represent components in a distributed system, (e.g., cells in a tissue) and the edges are the channels along which messages (objects or molecules) are passed. Both membrane and tissue systems are essentially multiset rewriting systems with their dynamic aspects, including potential behaviour (computations), derived from their evolution rules. Consequently, they are intrinsically similar to Petri nets.

© Springer-Verlag Berlin Heidelberg 2014
M. Koutny et al. (Eds.): ToPNoC IX, LNCS 8910, pp. 124–146, 2014.
DOI: 10.1007/978-3-662-45730-6_7

In particular, there exists a canonical way of translating membrane systems into Petri nets with transitions corresponding to evolution rules [14,15]. This translation is faithful in the sense that it relates computation steps at the lowest level and induces in a natural way extensions and interpretations of Petri net structure and behaviour. The membrane structure is translated into *localities* associated with transitions. The locality of a transition represents the compartment to which the corresponding evolution rule belongs. The localities of transitions make it possible to define a *locally maximal* step semantics in addition to the more common sequential semantics and (maximal) step semantics. Locally maximal steps model localised synchronised pulses with maximal concurrency restricted to compartments.

Petri nets are a well-established general model for distributed computation (see, e.g., [5,9,20,26,27] and e.g., [17] for a recent comprehensive overview of applications of Petri nets in systems biology) with an extensive range of tools and methods for construction, analysis, and verification of concurrent systems. The strong semantical link between the two models invites to extend existing Petri net techniques, bringing them to the domain of membrane systems. An example is the process semantics of Petri nets that can help to understand the dynamics and causality in the biological evolutions represented by membrane systems [11,14]. More details on the relationship between Petri nets and membrane systems can be found in, e.g., [12,16].

Here, we focus on the synthesis problem, that is, the problem of the algorithmic construction of a system (of a certain type) from a specification of its (observed or desired) behaviour. Automated synthesis from behavioural specifications is an attractive and powerful way of constructing correct concurrent systems [1,2,4,6–8,19,21]. In [13] the synthesis of membrane systems from (step) transition systems is considered. It is demonstrated there how a solution to the synthesis problem of Petri nets, based on the notion of regions of a transition system, leads to a method for the automated synthesis of membrane systems.

In this paper, we extend this result in two directions. First, we lift the relationship between membrane systems and Petri nets to the level of tissue systems. We then show how the synthesis problem for tissue systems (with locally maximal concurrency) can be solved when the tissue structure of the system to be constructed is given together with the step transition system. Finally, following the ideas developed in [18], we also discuss how the proposed method could be extended to cope with situations when the structure of the target tissue system has to be constructed as well.

The results discussed in this paper have been presented at the workshop Applications of Region Theory (ART) held in Barcelona in July 2013.

2   Preliminaries

Multisets. A multiset over a finite set X is a function $\alpha : X \to \mathbb{N} = \{0, 1, 2, \dots\}$. Such α may be represented by listing its elements with repetitions, e.g., $\alpha = \{y, y, z\}$ is such that $\alpha(y) = 2$, $\alpha(z) = 1$, and $\alpha(x) = 0$ otherwise. The set of all multisets over X will be denoted by $\mathcal{M}(X)$. The size $|\alpha|$ of α is given by $\sum_{x \in X} \alpha(x)$, and $\widehat{\alpha}$ is the set of all the elements occurring in α. Multiset α is said to be empty (and denoted by $\varnothing$) if $\widehat{\alpha} = \varnothing$.

For $\alpha, \beta \in \mathcal{M}(X)$, the sum $\alpha + \beta$ is the multiset given by $(\alpha + \beta)(x) = \alpha(x) + \beta(x)$ for all $x \in X$, and for $k \in \mathbb{N}$ the multiset $k \cdot \alpha$ is given by $(k \cdot \alpha)(x) = k \cdot \alpha(x)$ for all $x \in X$. The difference $\alpha - \beta$ is given by $(\alpha - \beta)(x) = \max\{\alpha(x) - \beta(x), 0\}$ for all $x \in X$. We denote $\alpha \leq \beta$ whenever $\alpha(x) \leq \beta(x)$ for all $x \in X$, and $\alpha < \beta$ whenever $\alpha \leq \beta$ and $\alpha \neq \beta$. The restriction $\alpha|_Z$ of α to a subset $Z \subseteq X$ is given by $\alpha|_Z(x) = \alpha(x)$ for $x \in Z$, and $\alpha|_Z(x) = 0$ otherwise. If $f : X \to Y$ is a function then $f(\alpha)$ is the multiset over Y such that $f(\alpha)(y) = \sum_{x \in f^{-1}(y)} \alpha(x)$, for every $y \in Y$. Moreover, for every $Z \subseteq X$, $f|_Z : Z \to Y$ is the restriction of f to Z.

Step transition systems. A *step transition system* over a finite set (of actions) A is a triple $TS = (Q, \mathscr{A}, q_0)$, where: Q is a set of nodes called *states*; $\mathscr{A}$ is the set of *arcs*, each arc being a triple (q, α, q') such that $q, q' \in Q$ are states and $\alpha \in \mathcal{M}(A)$ is a *step*; and $q_0 \in Q$ is the *initial* state. TS is said to be *finite* if both Q and $\mathscr{A}$ are finite. We may write $q \xrightarrow{\alpha} q'$ whenever (q, α, q') is an arc. For each state $q \in Q$, we introduce the following notation:

- $allSteps_q = \{\alpha \mid \alpha \neq \varnothing \wedge \exists q' : q \xrightarrow{\alpha} q'\}$ are all non-empty steps *enabled at q*;
- $minSteps_q = \{\alpha \in allSteps_q \mid \alpha \neq \varnothing \wedge \neg(\exists \beta \in allSteps_q : \beta < \alpha)\}$ are all non-empty minimal steps enabled at q; and
- T_q are all actions $t \in A$ such that $t \in \widehat{\alpha}$ for some $\alpha \in allSteps_q$.

We additionally assume that:

- if $q \xrightarrow{\alpha} q'$ and $q \xrightarrow{\alpha} q''$ then $q' = q''$;
- for every state $q \in Q$, there is a path from q_0 leading to q;
- for every action $a \in A$, there is a state $q \in Q$ such that $a \in T_q$; and
- for every state $q \in Q$, we have $q \xrightarrow{\varnothing} q'$ iff $q = q'$.

Let $TS = (Q, \mathscr{A}, q_0)$ be a step transition system over a set of actions A, and $TS' = (Q', \mathscr{A}', q_0')$ be a step transition system over a set of actions A'. TS and TS' are *isomorphic* if there are two bijections, $\phi : A \to A'$ and $\nu : Q \to Q'$, such that $\nu(q_0) = q_0'$ and, for all $q, q' \in Q$ and $\alpha \in \mathcal{M}(A)$,

$$(q, \alpha, q') \in \mathscr{A} \iff (\nu(q), \phi(\alpha), \nu(q')) \in \mathscr{A}'.$$

We denote this by $TS \sim_{\phi,\nu} TS'$ or $TS \sim TS'$.

Tissue systems. A *tissue structure* τ (of degree $m \geq 1$) is an undirected graph with m nodes identified with the integers $1, \ldots, m$. For $i, j \in \{1, \ldots, m\}$, we will write $(i, j) \in \tau$ to indicate that there is an edge between i and j, and $i \in \tau$ means that i is a node of τ. We assume that τ has no loops: $(i, j) \in \tau$ implies that $i \neq j$. We will refer to the nodes of a tissue structure as compartments or cells. Figure 1 depicts a tissue structure τ_0 of degree 4 such that $(1, 2) \in \tau_0$ and $(1, 4) \notin \tau_0$.

Let V be a finite set (of *objects*), and τ be a tissue structure of degree m. A *(basic) tissue system* (over V and τ) is a tuple

$$BTS = (V, \tau, w_1^0, \ldots, w_m^0, R_1, \ldots, R_m)$$

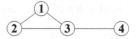

Fig. 1. The tissue structure τ_0 of degree 4.

such that, for every $i \in \tau$, R_i is a finite set of *evolution rules* associated with i and w_i^0 is a multiset of objects from V. Each evolution rule $r \in R_i$ is of the form $r : lhs^r \to rhs^r$, where lhs^r (the left hand side of r) is a non-empty multiset over V, and rhs^r (the right hand side of r) is a multiset over

$$V \cup \{a_{\blacktriangleright j} \mid a \in V \text{ and } (i,j) \in \tau\}.$$

Here the symbol $a_{\blacktriangleright j}$ represents an object a that is sent to compartment j. A *configuration* of BTS is a tuple

$$C = (w_1, \ldots, w_m)$$

of multisets of objects, and $C_0 = (w_1^0, \ldots, w_m^0)$ is the *initial* configuration. Figure 2 shows a tissue system over $V = \{a, b, c\}$ and the tissue structure depicted in Fig. 1.

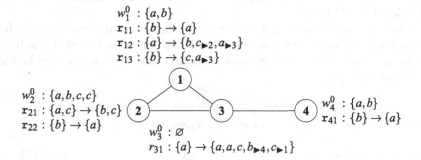

Fig. 2. The tissue system BTS_0.

A tissue system evolves from configuration to configuration as a consequence of the application of evolution rules. There are different *execution modes* ranging from fully synchronous — as many applications of rules as possible — to sequential — a single application of a rule at a time. We distinguish two modes based on the notion of a vector multi-rule.

A *vector multi-rule* of BTS is a tuple $\mathbf{r} = \langle \mathbf{r}_1, \ldots, \mathbf{r}_m \rangle$ where, for each compartment i of τ, $\mathbf{r}_i$ is a multiset of rules from R_i. For such a vector multi-rule, we denote by $lhs_i^{\mathbf{r}}$ the multiset

$$\sum_{r \in R_i} \mathbf{r}_i(r) \cdot lhs^r$$

in which all objects in the left hand sides of the rules in $\mathbf{r}_i$ are accumulated, and by $rhs_i^{\mathbf{r}}$ the multiset

$$\sum_{r \in R_i} \mathbf{r}_i(r) \cdot rhs^r$$

of all (indexed) objects in the right hand sides. The first multiset specifies how many objects are needed in each compartment for the simultaneous execution of all the instances of evolution rules in $\mathbf{r}$.

A vector multi-rule $\mathbf{r}$ of BTS is *enabled* at a configuration C if $lhs_i^{\mathbf{r}} \leq w_i$, for each i. If $\mathbf{r}$ is enabled at a configuration C, then C has in each compartment i enough copies of objects for the application of the multiset of evolution rules $\mathbf{r}_i$.

When vector multi-rule $\mathbf{r}$ is enabled at C, this configuration can *evolve* to the configuration $C' = (w_1', \ldots w_m')$ such that, for each i and object a:

$$w_i'(a) = w_i(a) - lhs_i^{\mathbf{r}}(a) + rhs_i^{\mathbf{r}}(a) + \sum_{(i,j) \in \tau} rhs_j^{\mathbf{r}}(a_{\blacktriangleright i}) .$$

A vector multi-rule $\mathbf{r} = \langle \mathbf{r}_1, \ldots, \mathbf{r}_m \rangle$ enabled at C, is said to be *locally maximal enabled*, or lmax-enabled for short, if no non-empty $\mathbf{r}_i$ can be extended in such a way that the resulting vector multi-rule is enabled at C. In this case, each compartment is either not involved or uses a maximal multiset of rules. For example, in Fig. 2, $\langle \{\mathbf{r}_{11}, \mathbf{r}_{12}\}, \varnothing, \varnothing, \varnothing \rangle$ is lmax-enabled at the initial configuration. We denote by $C \xrightarrow{\mathbf{r}}_{lmax} C'$ the evolution of an lmax-enabled vector multi-rule $\mathbf{r}$ from C to C'.

An *lmax-computation* is a finite sequence of lmax-evolutions starting from the initial configuration; any configuration which can be obtained through such a computation is called *lmax-reachable*. For the tissue system depicted in Fig. 2 we have, for example:

$$C_0 \xrightarrow{\langle \{\mathbf{r}_{11}, \mathbf{r}_{12}\}, \varnothing, \varnothing, \varnothing \rangle}_{lmax} (\{a, b\}, \{a, b, c, c, c\}, \{a\}, \{a, b\}) .$$

The *lmax-concurrent reachability graph* of BTS is given by:

$$CRG_{lmax}(BTS) = ([C_0\rangle_{lmax} \, , \, \{(C, \sum_{i=1}^{m} \mathbf{r}_i, C') \mid C \in [C_0\rangle_{lmax} \wedge C \xrightarrow{\langle \mathbf{r}_1, \ldots, \mathbf{r}_m \rangle}_{lmax} C'\} \, , \, C_0),$$

where $[C_0\rangle_{lmax}$ is the set of all lmax-reachable configurations which are the nodes of the graph; C_0 is the initial node; and the arcs between the nodes are labelled by multisets of evolution rules involved in the executed vector multi-rule.[1]

---

[1] Though it may be that rules from different compartments are the same in terms of the multisets defining their left hand and right hand sides, we assume here that evolution rules associated with different compartments can be distinguished, e.g., by giving them each their own name (an injective label).

Petri nets. A *Place/Transition net* (or *pt*-net) is specified as a tuple $PT = (P, T, W, M_0)$, where: P and T are finite disjoint sets of respectively *places* and *transitions*; $W : (T \times P) \cup (P \times T) \to \mathbb{N}$ is the *arc weight function*; and $M_0 : P \to \mathbb{N}$ is the *initial marking* (in general, any multiset of places is a marking). We say that a place p is a *pre-place* (or *post-place*) of a transition t if $W(p, t) > 0$ (resp. $W(t, p) > 0$). We use the standard graphical representation of nets and their markings.

A *step* α of PT is a multiset of transitions. Its *pre-multiset* and *post-multiset* of places, ${}^\bullet\alpha$ and $\alpha^\bullet$, are respectively given by ${}^\bullet\alpha(p) = \sum_{t \in T} \alpha(t) \cdot W(p, t)$ and $\alpha^\bullet(p) = \sum_{t \in T} \alpha(t) \cdot W(t, p)$, for each place p. Step α is *enabled* at a marking M if ${}^\bullet\alpha \leq M$. We denote this by $M[\alpha\rangle$. A single transition t is said to be enabled at M if the step $\{t\}$ is enabled at M. If $M[\alpha\rangle$, then α can be *executed* leading to the marking M' given by $M' = M - {}^\bullet\alpha + \alpha^\bullet$. We denote this by $M[\alpha\rangle M'$.

Two transitions, $t \neq t' \in T$ are in *potential conflict* if they share a pre-place; moreover, they are in *conflict at a marking* M if $M[\{t\}\rangle$ and $M[\{t'\}\rangle$, but $M[\{t, t'\}\rangle$ does not hold. Notice that being in conflict implies being in potential conflict, but not necessarily vice versa as two transitions sharing a pre-place can be executed together, if this pre-place holds enough tokens for both of them.

Petri nets with localities. *pt*-nets are a general model of concurrent computation. To capture the compartmentalisation of membrane systems, [14,15] add explicit localities to transitions. Here, as a notational convenience, we associate localities also to places.

A *pt-net with localities* (or *ptl*-net for short) is a tuple $PTL = (P, T, W, \ell, M_0)$ such that (P, T, W, M_0) is a *pt*-net, and $\ell : P \cup T \to \{1, 2, \ldots, m\}$ where $m \geq 1$ is the *location mapping* of PTL. We refer to $\{1, 2, \ldots, m\}$ as the *localities* of PTL, and we call x and z *co-located* if $\ell(x) = \ell(z)$. In diagrams, nodes representing co-located transitions and/or places will be shaded in the same way, as shown in Fig. 3. Notions and notations introduced for *pt*-nets are inherited by *ptl*-nets through their underlying *pt*-net. Moreover, in the remainder of this paper, we will consider only *ptl*-nets in which all transitions have at least one pre-place, *ensuring that the lmax firing rule defined next is sound.*

Co-locating transitions makes it possible to introduce another concept of enabling for steps of transitions. We say that a *step* α of PTL is *locally maximal enabled*, or lmax-enabled for short, at a marking M if $M[\alpha\rangle$ and α cannot be extended by a transition co-located with a transition in α to yield a step which is enabled at M; i.e., there is no $t \in T$ such that $\ell(t) \in \ell(\widehat{\alpha})$ and $M[\alpha + \{t\}\rangle$. We denote this by $M[\alpha\rangle_{lmax}$, and then denote the locally maximal execution (lmax-execution) of α by $M[\alpha\rangle_{lmax} M'$, where $M' = M - {}^\bullet\alpha + \alpha^\bullet$. Locally maximal concurrency (lmax-concurrency) is similar to maximal concurrency (in which all localities which have enabled transitions, should be involved), but now only active localities[2] cannot execute further transitions. For the *ptl*-net in Fig. 3, $\{t_1^{r11}, t_1^{r12}\}$ is lmax-enabled at the given marking, but $\{t_1^{r11}\}$ is not.

An *lmax-step sequence* is a finite sequence of lmax-executions starting from the initial marking, and an *lmax-reachable* marking is any marking resulting from

---

[2] By active localities of a step α we mean the localities of transitions present in α.

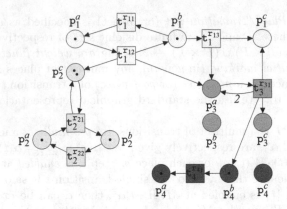

Fig. 3. The *ptl*-net PTL_0 corresponding to the basic tissue system BTS_0, where $\ell(x_i^z) = i$, for each node of the form x_i^z. Note that, e.g., transitions $\mathbf{t}_1^{r11}$, $\mathbf{t}_1^{r12}$ and $\mathbf{t}_1^{r13}$ are co-located.

the execution of such a sequence. Moreover, the *lmax-concurrent reachability graph* of *PTL* is the step transition system:

$$CRG_{lmax}(PTL) = (\ [M_0\rangle_{lmax}\ ,\ \{(M, \alpha, M') \mid M \in [M_0\rangle_{lmax} \wedge M[\alpha\rangle_{lmax} M'\}\ ,\ M_0\ ),$$

where $[M_0\rangle_{lmax}$ is the set of all lmax-reachable markings which are the nodes of the graph; M_0 is the initial node; and the arcs between the nodes are labelled by lmax-executed steps of transitions. Such reachability graphs provide complete representations of the dynamic behaviour of *ptl*-nets.

Finally, a *ptl*-net $PTL = (P, T, W, \ell, M_0)$ is *spanned* over a tissue structure τ of degree m if $\ell : P \cup T \to \{1, 2, \ldots, m\}$ and the following hold, for all $p \in P$ and $t \in T$:

(i) if $W(p, t) > 0$ then $\ell(p) = \ell(t)$; and
(ii) if $W(t, p) > 0$ then $\ell(p) = \ell(t)$ or $(\ell(p), \ell(t)) \in \tau$.

The *ptl*-net of Fig. 3 is spanned over the tissue structure depicted in Fig. 1. A fragment of its lmax-concurrent reachability graph is shown in Fig. 4.

Note that if two transitions of a *ptl*-net spanned over a tissue structure share a pre-place (i.e., are in potential conflict), then they are co-located. Hence, in *ptl*-nets spanned over tissue structures, transitions that are not co-located are never in conflict.

3   Tissue Systems and Petri Nets

We now demonstrate how a tissue system $BTS = (V, \tau, w_1^0, \ldots, w_m^0, R_1, \ldots, R_m)$ over a tissue structure τ of degree m, can be translated into a *ptl*-net $PTL(BTS) = (P, T, W, \ell, M_0)$ spanned over the same tissue structure and faithfully reflecting the dynamics of BTS. The ptl-net $PTL(BTS)$ has distinct places $\mathbf{p}_j^a$ with $\ell(\mathbf{p}_j^a) = j$, for each object $a \in V$ and compartment j, and distinct transitions $\mathbf{t}_i^r$ with $\ell(\mathbf{t}_i^r) = i$, for each rule r and i such that r is a rule associated with compartment i. The initial marking inserts $w_j^0(a)$ tokens into each place $\mathbf{p}_j^a$. The connectivity between transition $t = \mathbf{t}_i^r$ and place $p = \mathbf{p}_j^a$ is given by:

$$W(p,t) = \begin{cases} lhs^r(a) & \text{if } i = j \\ 0 & \text{otherwise} \end{cases} \quad \text{and} \quad W(t,p) = \begin{cases} rhs^r(a) & \text{if } i = j \\ rhs^r(a_{\blacktriangleright j}) & \text{if } (i,j) \in \tau. \\ 0 & \text{otherwise.} \end{cases}$$

Figure 3 shows the result of the above translation for the tissue system in Fig. 2.

To capture the very close relationship between BTS and $PTL(BTS)$, we define two bijective mappings, ν and ϕ:

- for every marking M of $PTL(BTS)$, we let $\nu(M) = (w_1, \dots, w_m)$ be the configuration given by $w_i(a) = M(\mathbf{p}_i^a)$, for every object a and every i.
- for every transition t_i^r, we set $\phi(t_i^r) = r$.

Similar to the case of membrane systems as discussed in [13], this allows us to formulate a direct relationship between the basic dynamics of a tissue system and the ptl-net obtained from it through the above translation.

In particular, the evolution in BTS of a vector multi-rule $\mathbf{r} = \langle \mathbf{r}_1, \dots, \mathbf{r}_m \rangle$ leading from a configuration C to a configuration C' corresponds to the execution of the step $\alpha_{\mathbf{r}} = \phi^{-1}(\mathbf{r}_1) + \cdots + \phi^{-1}(\mathbf{r}_m)$ at $\nu^{-1}(C)$ and leading to $\nu^{-1}(C')$. Moreover, if $\mathbf{r}$ is lmax-enabled at C, then $\alpha_{\mathbf{r}}$ is lmax-enabled at $\nu^{-1}(C)$.

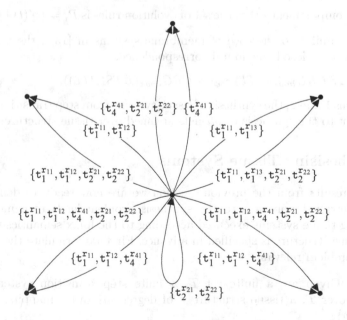

Fig. 4. A fragment of the lmax-concurrent reachability graph $CRG_{lmax}(PTL_0)$ of the ptl-net PTL_0 of Fig. 3, showing all the arcs outgoing from the initial state.

Conversely, whenever $M[\alpha\rangle M'$ in $PTL(BTS)$, we let $\mathbf{r}_\alpha = \langle \mathbf{r}_1, \ldots, \mathbf{r}_m \rangle$ be the vector multi-rule defined by $\mathbf{r}_i = \phi(\alpha_i)$ for all $i \in \{1, \ldots, m\}$, where α_i is α restricted to $\{t \in T \mid \ell(t) = i\}$; then $\mathbf{r}_\alpha$ is enabled at $\nu(M)$ in BTS and evolves to $\nu(M')$. Also, if α is lmax-enabled at M, then $\mathbf{r}_\alpha$ is lmax-enabled at $\nu(M)$.

Since $\nu(M_0) = C_0$, the lmax-concurrent reachability graphs of BTS and $PTL(BTS)$ are isomorphic step transition systems.

Theorem 1. $CRG_{lmax}(PTL(BTS)) \sim_{\phi,\nu} CRG_{lmax}(BTS)$. $\hfill\square$

By the requirement that the left-hand sides of evolution rules be non-empty multisets, the translation yields ptl-nets in which indeed every transition has at least one pre-place, as required. Moreover, also a reverse translation can be provided.

Let $PTL = (P, T, W, \ell, M_0)$ be a ptl-net spanned over a tissue structure τ of degree m. We construct the corresponding tissue system $BTS(PTL)$ over τ in the following way:

- P is the set of objects of $BTS(PTL)$;
- its initial configuration is $\nu'(M_0)$, where $\nu'(M) = (M|_{\ell^{-1}(1) \cap P}, \ldots, M |_{\ell^{-1}(m) \cap P})$, for every marking M of PTL;
- for each transition $t \in T$ with $\{t\}^\bullet = \{p^1, \ldots, p^k\}$, $BTS(PTL)$ has a corresponding evolution rule $\phi'(t)$ of the form $\phi'(t) : {}^\bullet\{t\} \to \{a_1, \ldots, a_k\}$ where, for $i \leq k$,
$$a_i = \begin{cases} p^i & \text{if } \ell(p^i) = \ell(t) \\ p^i_{\blacktriangleright \ell(p^i)} & \text{if } (\ell(t), (\ell(p^i)) \in \tau . \end{cases}$$

- for each compartment $i \in \tau$, the set of evolution rules is $R_i = \{\phi'(t) \mid \ell(t) = i\}$.

Again, and similar to the case of membrane systems in [13] , the translation results in a very close behavioural correspondence.

Theorem 2. $CRG_{lmax}(PTL) \sim_{\phi',\nu'} CRG_{lmax}(BTS(PTL))$. $\hfill\square$

By Theorems 1 and 2, the synthesis of tissue systems from step transition systems is equivalent to the synthesis of ptl-nets spanned over tissue structures.

4   Synthesising Tissue Systems

Using the results from the previous section we are now ready to demonstrate how the Petri net approach to the synthesis problem leads to a method for synthesising tissue systems executed according to the lmax semantics when the desired tissue structure is specified in advance. First we formulate the Petri net synthesis problem relevant here.

Problem 1. Given are a finite set T, a finite step transition system $TS = (Q, \mathscr{A}, q_0)$ over T, a tissue structure τ of degree m, and a mapping $\ell : T \to \{1, 2, \ldots, m\}$.

Construct a ptl-net $PTL = (P, T, W, \ell', M_0)$ spanned over τ such that $CRG_{lmax}(PTL) \sim TS$ and $\ell = \ell'|_T$.

As demonstrated in [4], synthesis problems like Problem 1 can be solved using techniques from the theory of regions of transition systems (see, e.g., [1,7,19]) and its extension dealing with firing policies such as the lmax executions [4].

Intuitively, a region represents a place in the hypothetical net that generates the given transition system. Regions are used both to check whether a net satisfying the conditions can be constructed at all and, if the answer turns out to be positive, some of them can be used to construct such net.

Since our aim here is to synthesize a *ptl*-net which is underpinned by a *pt*-net, a *region* of a step transition system TS as specified above consists of three mappings

$$reg = (\ \sigma : Q \to \mathbb{N}\ ,\ \imath : T \to \mathbb{N}\ ,\ \omega : T \to \mathbb{N}\ ) \tag{1}$$

such that, for every arc $q \xrightarrow{\alpha} q'$ of TS,

$$\sigma(q) \geq \omega(\alpha) \quad \text{and} \quad \sigma(q') = \sigma(q) - \omega(\alpha) + \imath(\alpha)\ . \tag{2}$$

Here $\omega(\alpha) = \sum_{t \in T} \alpha(t) \cdot \omega(t)$ and similarly $\imath(\alpha) = \sum_{t \in T} \alpha(t) \cdot \imath(t)$. In a region of the form (1) representing a place p, $\sigma(q)$ is the number of tokens in p in the marking corresponding to the node q, $\omega(t)$ represents the weight of the arc from p to transition t, and $\imath(t)$ represents the weight of the arc from t to p. Requirement (2) then specifies that p contains enough tokens not to block the step α executed at state (the marking corresponding to) q, and also ensures that the number of tokens in p before and after executing α is consistent with the total arc weight of the step α in relation to p.

In addition, the target *ptl*-net must be spanned over τ. We call the combination of a region reg as in (1) with a location $i_{reg} \in \tau$ *compatible* (with the given tissue structure τ and the mapping ℓ) if the following hold, for every $t \in T$:

- if $\omega(t) > 0$ then $\ell(t) = i_{reg}$; and
- if $\imath(t) > 0$ then $\ell(t) = i_{reg}$ or $(\ell(t), i_{reg}) \in \tau$.

Note that if reg is compatible with i_{reg}, then $i_{reg} = \ell(t)$ for all $t \in T$ such that $\omega(t) > 0$. If there is no $t \in T$ such that $\omega(t) > 0$, but $\imath(t) > 0$ for some $t \in T$, then we can choose i_{reg} to be the smallest k such that for all $t \in T$ with $\imath(t) > 0$ either $\ell(t) = k$ or $(\ell(t), k) \in \tau$. Otherwise we can arbitrarily set i_{reg} to be 1 (in fact, any value from τ would be fine since if reg is turned into a place it would be isolated). All this implies that we will leave i_{reg} implicit (and if reg is turned into a net place p, we set $\ell'(p) = i_{reg}$). The set of all regions compatible with τ and ℓ will be denoted by $\mathbf{P}_{\tau,\ell}$.

Finally, Problem 1 should be feasible in the first place, in the sense that the transition system TS can be realised by a finite *ptl*-net with some compatible regions as its places. There are two necessary and sufficient conditions for realisability (see [1,4,7]): (i) *state separation*: for every pair of distinct states of the transition system, there is a compatible region (a marked place) distinguishing between them; and (ii) *forward closure*: there are sufficiently many places defined by compatible regions to disallow steps in the *ptl*-net that would not correspond to steps in the transition system.

We will now outline the synthesis procedure. We begin by describing how those places can be found that potentially provide a solution to Problem 1; in other words, all compatible regions of the form (1) of the transition system TS.

Finding compatible regions. Let T, τ, ℓ, and $TS = (Q, \mathscr{A}, q_0)$ be as in Problem 1. Assume that $Q = \{q_0, \ldots, q_h\}$ and $T = \{t_1, \ldots, t_n\}$. We use three vectors of non-negative variables: $\mathbf{x} = x_0 \ldots x_h$, $\mathbf{y} = y_1 \ldots y_n$ and $\mathbf{z} = z_1 \ldots z_n$. We also denote $\mathbf{p} = \mathbf{xyz}$ and define a homogeneous linear system

$$\mathscr{P} : \begin{cases} x_i \geq \alpha \cdot \mathbf{z} \\ x_j = x_i + \alpha \cdot (\mathbf{y} - \mathbf{z}) \end{cases} \qquad \text{for all } q_i \xrightarrow{\alpha} q_j \text{ in } TS \qquad (3)$$

where $\alpha \cdot \mathbf{z}$ denotes $\alpha(t_1) \cdot z_1 + \cdots + \alpha(t_n) \cdot z_n$ and similarly for $\alpha \cdot (\mathbf{y} - \mathbf{z})$.

The regions of TS are then determined by the integer solutions $\mathbf{p}$ of the system $\mathscr{P}$ assuming that, for $0 \leq i \leq h$ and $1 \leq j \leq n$, $\sigma(q_i) = x_i$, $\iota(t_j) = y_j$ and $\omega(t_j) = z_j$.

The set of rational solutions of $\mathscr{P}$ forms a polyhedral cone in $\mathbb{Q}^{h+2n+1}$. As described in [3], one can effectively compute <u>finitely</u> many integer generating rays $\mathbf{p}^1, \ldots, \mathbf{p}^k$ of this cone such that any integer solution $\mathbf{p}$ of $\mathscr{P}$ can be expressed as a linear combination of the rays with non-negative rational coefficients,

$$\mathbf{p} = \sum_{l=1}^{k} c_l \cdot \mathbf{p}^l.$$

Such rays $\mathbf{p}^l = \mathbf{x}^l \mathbf{y}^l \mathbf{z}^l$ are fixed and (some of them) may be turned into net places if Problem 1 has a solution. More precisely, if $\mathbf{p}^l$ is turned into a place, then

$$M_0(\mathbf{p}^l) = x_0^l \qquad W(t_i, \mathbf{p}^l) = y_i^l \qquad W(\mathbf{p}^l, t_i) = z_i^l \qquad (4)$$

where M_0 is the initial marking of the target net, and $t_i \in T$.

Clearly, not all such rays can be used to define a place in the net being constructed, as they have to be compatible with τ and ℓ. This is easily checked. Having thus found the set $\mathbf{R}_{\tau,\ell}$ of generating rays compatible with τ and ℓ, we obtain the following.

Fact 1. *Each region* $\mathbf{p} \in \mathbf{P}_{\tau,\ell}$ *is a non-negative linear combination of rays in* $\mathbf{R}_{\tau,\ell}$.

The converse does not hold, i.e., a non-negative linear combination of compatible regions need not be compatible. We then check whether Problem 1 is feasible.

Checking state separation. Let $TS = (Q, \mathscr{A}, q_0)$ be as in Problem 1. We take in turn each pair of distinct states, q_i and q_j, of Q and decide whether there exists $\mathbf{p} = (\sigma, \iota, \omega) \in \mathbf{P}_{\tau,\ell}$ with coefficients $c_1, \ldots, c_k$ such that $\sigma(q_i) = x_i \neq x_j = \sigma(q_j)$. Since the latter is equivalent to

$$\sum_{l=1}^{k} c_l \cdot x_i^l \neq \sum_{l=1}^{k} c_l \cdot x_j^l ,$$

it follows from Fact 1 that it suffices to check whether there exists at least one $\mathbf{p}^l \in \mathbf{R}_{\tau,\ell}$ (called a *witness* [6]) such that $x_i^l \neq x_j^l$.

Checking forward closure. Let T, τ, ℓ, and $TS = (Q, \mathscr{A}, q_0)$ again be as in Problem 1. First, we take in turn each state q_i of Q, and calculate the set of steps that are *region enabled* w.r.t. τ and ℓ at q_i, denoted by $regSteps_{\tau,\ell}^{q_i}$. Intuitively, such steps can actually occur in the net under construction (if it exists) without taking into account the lmax execution rule. Formally, a step $\alpha \in \mathscr{M}(T)$ belongs to $regSteps_{\tau,\ell}^{q_i}$ if $\sigma(q_i) \geq w(\alpha)$, for all compatible regions $(\sigma, \imath, w) \in \mathbf{P}_{\tau,\ell}$. Note that according to the lmax-semantics not all steps, which do not occur in the transition system TS, need to be disallowed by constraints introduced by places of the net being constructed. Some will be ruled out by the way lmax-semantics chooses steps for execution.

To build $regSteps_{\tau,\ell}^{q_i}$ one only needs to consider non-empty steps $\alpha \in \mathscr{M}(T)$ with $|\alpha| \leq m \cdot Max$, where Max is the maximum size of the steps labelling arcs in TS. The reason is that for all $i \in \tau$, there exists a compatible region $(\sigma, \imath, w) \in \mathbf{P}_{\tau,\ell}$ (again referred to as a *witness* which, in a successful construction, provides a pre-place for each t with $\ell(t) = i$) such that, for all $q \in Q$, $\sigma(q) = Max$ and, for every $t \in T$,

$$w(t) = \iota(t) = \begin{cases} 1 & \text{if } \ell(t) = i \\ 0 & \text{otherwise} . \end{cases} \tag{5}$$

Consequently, no step α with $|\alpha| > m \cdot Max$ can belong to $regSteps_{\tau,\ell}^{q_i}$.

For each non-empty step α with $|\alpha| \leq m \cdot Max$ it is the case that $\alpha \notin regSteps_{\tau,\ell}^{q_i}$ iff for some $\mathbf{p} \in \mathbf{P}_{\tau,\ell}$ with coefficients $c_1, \ldots, c_k$ we have $x_i < \alpha \cdot \mathbf{z}$. Since the latter is equivalent to $\sum_{l=1}^{k} c_l \cdot (x_i^l - \alpha \cdot \mathbf{z}^l) < 0$, it follows from Fact 1 that it suffices to check whether there exists at least one $\mathbf{p}^l \in \mathbf{R}_{\tau,\ell}$ (again a *witness*) such that $x_i^l - \alpha \cdot \mathbf{z}^l < 0$.

Having determined the steps in $regSteps_{\tau,\ell}^{q_i}$, in order to establish forward closure under the assumed lmax semantics, we need to verify that, for every state $q \in Q$,

$$allSteps_q = \{\alpha \in regSteps_{\tau,\ell}^{q} \mid \neg \exists t \in T : \alpha + \{t\} \in regSteps_{\tau,\ell}^{q} \wedge \ell(t) \in \ell(\widehat{\alpha})\} .$$

Constructing the solution net. If the above checks for the feasibility of Problem 1 are successful, one can construct a solution *ptl*-net spanned over τ by taking all the witnesses, rays and regions, and treating them as places in the way indicated in (4). By the results of [4], the constructed net PTL satisfies $CRG_{lmax}(PTL) \sim TS$.

Example 1. Consider the set of five transitions $T = \{t_1, t_2, t_3, t_4, t_5\}$, step transition system TS_1 and tissue structure τ_1 as shown in Fig. 5, and a mapping $\ell : T \to \{1, 2, 3\}$ assigning localities to transitions so that $\ell(t_1) = 1$, $\ell(t_2) = 3$ and $\ell(t_3) = \ell(t_4) = \ell(t_5) = 2$.

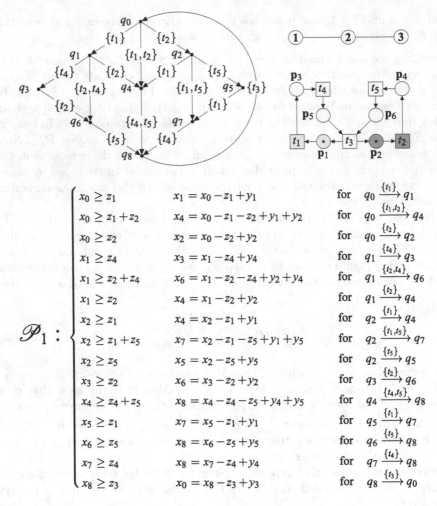

Fig. 5. A step transition system TS_1 together with the induced homogenous linear system $\mathscr{P}_1$, a tissue structure τ_1, and a *ptl*-net PTL_1 spanned over τ_1 generating TS_1.

Figure 5 shows the homogenous linear system $\mathscr{P}_1$, as defined in (3), induced by the transition system TS_1. The following six vectors are integer solutions of $\mathscr{P}_1$:

$$
\begin{array}{l}
\quad\ x_0\ x_1\ x_2\ x_3\ x_4\ x_5\ x_6\ x_7\ x_8 \quad y_1\ y_2\ y_3\ y_4\ y_5 \quad z_1\ z_2\ z_3\ z_4\ z_5 \\
\mathbf{p}_1 =\ 1\ \ 0\ \ 1\ \ 0\ \ 0\ \ 1\ \ 0\ \ 0\ \ 0 \quad\ \ 0\ \ 0\ \ 1\ \ 0\ \ 0 \quad\ \ 1\ \ 0\ \ 0\ \ 0\ \ 0 \\
\mathbf{p}_2 =\ 1\ \ 1\ \ 0\ \ 1\ \ 0\ \ 0\ \ 0\ \ 0\ \ 0 \quad\ \ 0\ \ 0\ \ 1\ \ 0\ \ 0 \quad\ \ 0\ \ 1\ \ 0\ \ 0\ \ 0 \\
\mathbf{p}_3 =\ 0\ \ 1\ \ 0\ \ 0\ \ 1\ \ 0\ \ 0\ \ 1\ \ 0 \quad\ \ 1\ \ 0\ \ 0\ \ 0\ \ 0 \quad\ \ 0\ \ 0\ \ 0\ \ 1\ \ 0 \\
\mathbf{p}_4 =\ 0\ \ 0\ \ 1\ \ 0\ \ 1\ \ 0\ \ 1\ \ 0\ \ 0 \quad\ \ 0\ \ 1\ \ 0\ \ 0\ \ 0 \quad\ \ 0\ \ 0\ \ 0\ \ 0\ \ 1 \\
\mathbf{p}_5 =\ 0\ \ 0\ \ 0\ \ 1\ \ 0\ \ 0\ \ 1\ \ 0\ \ 1 \quad\ \ 0\ \ 0\ \ 0\ \ 1\ \ 0 \quad\ \ 0\ \ 0\ \ 1\ \ 0\ \ 0 \\
\mathbf{p}_6 =\ 0\ \ 0\ \ 0\ \ 0\ \ 0\ \ 1\ \ 0\ \ 1\ \ 1 \quad\ \ 0\ \ 0\ \ 0\ \ 0\ \ 1 \quad\ \ 0\ \ 0\ \ 1\ \ 0\ \ 0
\end{array} \tag{6}
$$

We further observe that all the $\mathbf{p}_i$'s are generating rays of the set of solutions of the system $\mathscr{P}_1$ defining regions of TS_1, each such ray being compatible with the tissue structure τ_1. Moreover, the localities of the regions in (6) are determined as follows: $\ell(\mathbf{p}_1) = 1$, $\ell(\mathbf{p}_2) = 3$ and $\ell(\mathbf{p}_3) = \ell(\mathbf{p}_4) = \ell(\mathbf{p}_5) = \ell(\mathbf{p}_6) = 2$. It turns out that the $\mathbf{p}_i$'s are sufficient to establish the state separation and forward closure properties for the considered instance of Problem 1 (in particular, regions constructed as in (5) for the general case are not needed). One can therefore construct a solution, and the resulting *ptl*-net PTL_1 is shown in Fig. 5.

Remark 1. One can check that all the $\mathbf{p}_i$'s in (6) are indeed generating rays of the system $\mathscr{P}_1$ of Fig. 5. Consider, for example, $\mathbf{p}_3$ and assume that it can be represented as a positive linear combination $\mathbf{p}_3 = c \cdot \mathbf{p} + \ldots$ of some integer generating rays. In terms of Petri nets, a generating ray $\mathbf{p}$ must be of the following form, where $k = x_0$ is the number of tokens in $\mathbf{p}$ in the initial marking:

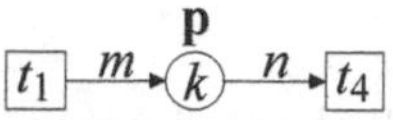

$$\boxed{t_1}\; \overset{m}{\longrightarrow}\; \overset{\mathbf{p}}{\textstyle\bigcirc\!\!k}\; \overset{n}{\longrightarrow}\; \boxed{t_4}$$

Our first observation is that according to TS_1 it is possible to execute a step sequence $\{t_2\}\{t_5\}\{t_1\}\{t_4\}\{t_3\}$, returning back to the initial marking. Hence we must have $k - n + m = k$, implying $m = n$. Moreover, $k = 0$ as otherwise the initial marking of $\mathbf{p}_3$ would have to be nonempty. Hence $\mathbf{p} = m \cdot \mathbf{p}_3$, and so $\mathbf{p}_3$ is a generating ray. $\qquad\square$

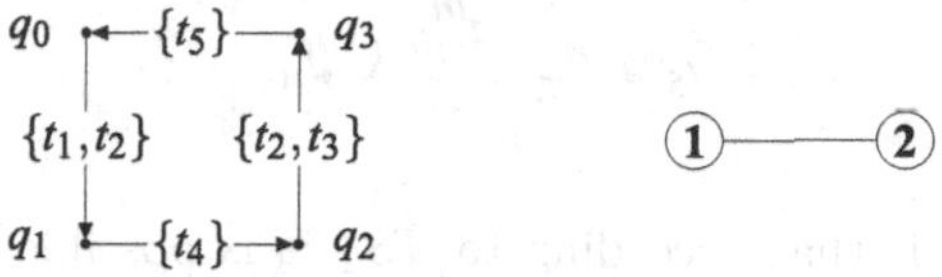

$$
\begin{array}{ccc}
q_0 & \xleftarrow{\;\{t_5\}\;} & q_3 \\[2pt]
\{t_1,t_2\}\!\downarrow & \quad \uparrow\{t_2,t_3\} & \\[2pt]
q_1 & \xrightarrow{\;\{t_4\}\;} & q_2
\end{array}
\qquad\qquad
\textcircled{1}\!\!-\!\!-\!\!-\!\!\textcircled{2}
$$

$$
\mathscr{P}_2 : \begin{cases}
x_0 \geq z_1 + z_2 & x_1 = x_0 - z_1 - z_2 + y_1 + y_2 & \text{for} \quad q_0 \xrightarrow{\{t_1,t_2\}} q_1 \\
x_1 \geq z_4 & x_2 = x_1 - z_4 + y_4 & \text{for} \quad q_1 \xrightarrow{\{t_4\}} q_2 \\
x_2 \geq z_2 + z_3 & x_3 = x_2 - z_2 - z_3 + y_2 + y_3 & \text{for} \quad q_2 \xrightarrow{\{t_2,t_3\}} q_3 \\
x_3 \geq z_5 & x_0 = x_3 - z_5 + y_5 & \text{for} \quad q_3 \xrightarrow{\{t_5\}} q_0
\end{cases}
$$

Fig. 6. A step transition system TS_2 together with the induced homogenous linear system $\mathscr{P}_2$, and a tissue structure τ_2.

Example 2. Consider the set of five transitions $T = \{t_1, t_2, t_3, t_4, t_5\}$, step transition system TS_2 and tissue structure τ_2 as shown in Fig. 6, and a mapping $\ell : T \to \{1, 2\}$ assigning localities to transitions such that $\ell(t_1) = \ell(t_2) = \ell(t_3) = 1$ and $\ell(t_4) = \ell(t_5) = 2$. Figure 6 shows the homogenous linear system $\mathscr{P}_2$, as defined in (3), induced by the transition system TS_2 depicted in Fig. 6. Following the synthesis approach described above, one can construct a solution for the considered instance of Problem 1, and the resulting *ptl*-net PTL_2 is shown in Fig. 7.

This example becomes more interesting if, instead of the tissue structure τ_2, we consider τ_1 depicted in Fig. 5 together with the following mapping assigning localities to transitions: $\ell(t_1) = \ell(t_2) = \ell(t_3) = 2$, $\ell(t_4) = 1$ and $\ell(t_5) = 3$. The point is that in such a case the generating ray:

$$\mathbf{p}_{conflict} = \begin{array}{cccc|ccccc|ccccc} x_0 & x_1 & x_2 & x_3 & y_1 & y_2 & y_3 & y_4 & y_5 & z_1 & z_2 & z_3 & z_4 & z_5 \\ 0 & 1 & 0 & 1 & 0 & 1 & 0 & 0 & 0 & 0 & 0 & 0 & 1 & 1 \end{array}$$

used in the construction of the *ptl*-net PTL_2 of Fig. 7 ceases to be compatible (as t_4 and t_5 have different localities). However, a suitable solution *ptl*-net PTL_3 can still be constructed using the remaining generating rays, as shown in Fig. 7. This is a fortunate situation, where the non-compatibility of some of the generating rays still allows one to construct a solution net. Our next example shows that this is not always the case.

Remark 2. One can check that all the regions used in the construction of PTL_2 are indeed generating rays of the system $\mathscr{P}_2$. Consider, in particular, $\mathbf{p}_{conflict}$ and assume that it can be represented as a positive linear combination $\mathbf{p}_{conflict} = c \cdot \mathbf{p} + \ldots$ of some integer generating rays. In terms of Petri nets, and given that $x_0 = 0$ in $\mathbf{p}_{conflict}$, such a generating ray $\mathbf{p}$ (denoted $\mathbf{p}_{mnk}$) must be of the following form in the initial marking:

$$\mathbf{p}_{mnk}$$

Our first observation is that according to TS_2 it is possible to execute a step sequence $\{t_1, t_2\}\{t_4\}\{t_2, t_3\}\{t_5\}$, returning back to the initial marking. Hence we must have $m - k + m - n = 0$, implying $m = \frac{k+n}{2}$. Hence $m > 0$ and $k + n > 0$ as $\mathbf{p}_{mnk}$ is a non-zero vector. Then we observe that $n > 0$ since otherwise $\mathbf{p}_{mnk}$ would contain $m = \frac{k}{2} > 0$ tokens after executing $\{t_1, t_2\}$ making it impossible to execute t_4 which needs k tokens. The situation where $k = 0$ is, on the other hand possible, and it leads (after normalisation) to a generating ray $\mathbf{p}_{120}$. Suppose then that $k > 0$. It then follows that $\mathbf{p}_{mnk} = \mathbf{p}_{conflict} + \mathbf{p}_{(m-1)(n-1)(k-1)}$, and so $\mathbf{p}_{mnk}$ can be a generating ray only if $\mathbf{p}_{(m-1)(n-1)(k-1)}$ and $\mathbf{p}_{conflict}$ are co-linear. This is only possible when $\mathbf{p}_{(m-1)(n-1)(k-1)} = (m-1) \cdot \mathbf{p}_{conflict}$, and so $\mathbf{p}_{mnk} = m \cdot \mathbf{p}_{conflict}$. It therefore follows that the only positive linear combination $\mathbf{p}_{conflict} = c \cdot \mathbf{p} + \ldots$ must be of the form $\mathbf{p}_{conflict} = c \cdot \mathbf{p}_{conflict} + c' \cdot \mathbf{p}_{120}$. This however, is impossible. Hence $\mathbf{p}_{conflict}$ is a generating ray. $\square$

Example 3. Consider the set of three transitions $T = \{t_1, t_2, t_3\}$, step transition system TS_3 as shown in Fig. 8, a trivial tissue structure consisting of just one node, and a mapping $\ell : T \rightarrow \{1\}$ assigning localities to transitions so that $\ell(t_1) = \ell(t_2) = \ell(t_3) = 1$.

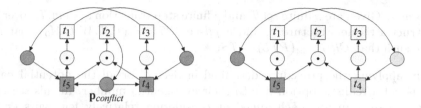

Fig. 7. Two *ptl*-nets generating the step transition system TS_2 of Fig. 6: PTL_2 spanned over the tissue structure τ_2 of Fig. 6 (left); and PTL_3 spanned over τ_1 of Fig. 5 (right).

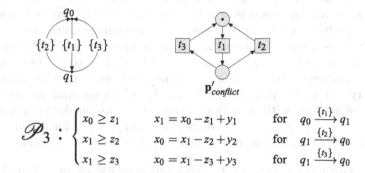

$$\mathscr{P}_3 : \begin{cases} x_0 \geq z_1 & x_1 = x_0 - z_1 + y_1 & \text{for} \quad q_0 \xrightarrow{\{t_1\}} q_1 \\ x_1 \geq z_2 & x_0 = x_1 - z_2 + y_2 & \text{for} \quad q_1 \xrightarrow{\{t_2\}} q_0 \\ x_1 \geq z_3 & x_0 = x_1 - z_3 + y_3 & \text{for} \quad q_1 \xrightarrow{\{t_3\}} q_0 \end{cases}$$

Fig. 8. A step transition system TS_3 together with the induced homogenous linear system $\mathscr{P}_3$, and a *ptl*-net PTL_4 generating TS_3, where all the transitions and places are co-located.

Figure 8 shows the homogenous linear system $\mathscr{P}_3$ induced by TS_3 and, following the synthesis approach described above, one can construct a solution to the considered instance of Problem 1 (see *ptl*-net PTL_4 of Fig. 8).

Consider now the tissue structure τ_1 shown in Fig. 5 together with the following mapping assigning localities to transitions: $\ell(t_1) = 1$, $\ell(t_2) = 2$ and $\ell(t_3) = 3$. In this case, the generating ray:

$$\begin{array}{cccccccc} & x_0 \; x_1 & y_1 \; y_2 \; y_3 & z_1 \; z_2 \; z_3 \\ \mathbf{p}'_{conflict} = & 0 \quad 1 & 1 \quad 0 \quad 0 & 0 \quad 1 \quad 1 \end{array}$$

used in the construction of the *ptl*-net PTL_4 is no longer compatible (as t_2 and t_3 have different localities), and the considered instance of Problem 1 has no solutions at all.

5 Synthesis Without Knowing the Tissue Structure

The synthesis procedure outlined above works only when in addition to the step transition system, a tissue structure τ together with a location mapping ℓ are given as input. Suppose now that this is not the case, and the latter must be 'discovered' by the synthesis procedure. In other words, the synthesis problem we want to consider can now be formulated as follows.

Problem 2. Given are a finite set T and a finite step transition system TS over T. Construct a tissue structure τ, and a *ptl*-net $PTL = (P, T, W, \ell, M_0)$ spanned over τ such that $CRG_{lmax}(PTL) \sim TS$.

Simply applying the procedure described in Sect. 4 for all the potential pairs (τ, ℓ) is not a realistic option due to their exponential number. In this section, we will present an approach aimed at considering relatively few pairs (τ, ℓ), by adopting ideas from [18]. First of all, we will assume from here on that the unknown tissue structure τ is a clique. This can be done without loss of generality, because whenever PTL is a *ptl*-net spanned over a tissue structure τ, then PTL is also spanned over any tissue structure τ' obtained from τ by adding extra edges. As a consequence of this assumption, any unknown pair (τ, ℓ) can be considered as a *co-location* relation: an equivalence relation $\backsimeq$ over T such that, for all $u, v \in T$, we have $u \backsimeq v$ iff $\ell(u) = \ell(v)$. Conversely, any equivalence relation $\backsimeq$ over T can be viewed as a co-location relation by assuming an arbitrary but fixed enumeration $T_1, \ldots, T_m$ of its equivalence classes and letting $\tau_{\backsimeq}$ be a clique with m nodes (a tissue structure of degree m), and the mapping $\ell_{\backsimeq} : T \to \{1, 2, \ldots, m\}$ be defined by $\ell_{\backsimeq}(T_i) = \{i\}$, for $i \leq m$.

We can now introduce two new versions of the synthesis problem.

Problem 3. Given are a finite set T, a co-location relation $\backsimeq$ over T, and a finite step transition system TS over T.

Construct a *ptl*-net $PTL = (P, T, W, \ell, M_0)$ spanned over $\tau_{\backsimeq}$ such that $CRG_{lmax}(PTL) \sim TS$ and $\ell_{\backsimeq} = \ell|_T$.

Problem 4. Given are a finite set T, and a finite step transition system TS over T.

Construct a co-location relation $\backsimeq$ over T and a *ptl*-net $PTL = (P, T, W, \ell, M_0)$ spanned over $\tau_{\backsimeq}$ such that $CRG_{lmax}(PTL) \sim TS$ and $\ell_{\backsimeq} = \ell|_T$.

To solve Problem 3, the procedure described in Sect. 4 can be applied with $\tau = \tau_{\backsimeq}$ and $\ell = \ell_{\backsimeq}$. Problem 4 is more complicated as it requires one to construct a suitable co-location relation as well.

5.1   Co-location Relations

We start by investigating co-location relations in step transition systems and in particular in lmax-concurrent reachability graphs of *ptl*-nets spanned over tissue structures.

Let $\backsimeq$ be a co-location relation over the finite set T. For $t \in T$ and a multiset α over T, we will denote $t \backsimeq \alpha$ whenever there is at least one $u \in \widehat{\alpha}$ satisfying $t \backsimeq u$. Clearly, each *ptl*-net $PTL = (P, T, W, \ell, M_0)$ induces a unique co-location relation $\backsimeq_{PTL}$ over T defined by $u \backsimeq_{PTL} v$ iff $\ell(u) = \ell(v)$, for all $u, v \in T$.

The next result captures a key property of the co-location relations induced by *ptl*-nets spanned over tissue structures. It is a direct consequence of the fact that only co-located transitions can be in conflict.

Proposition 1. *Let q be a state of the lmax-concurrent reachability graph TS of a ptl-net PTL spanned over a tissue structure.*

1. *If $\alpha \in allSteps_q$ and γ is a non-empty maximal sub-multiset of α containing only co-located transitions, then $\gamma \in minSteps_q$.*
2. *If $\alpha \in minSteps_q$, then all the transitions in α are co-located w.r.t. $\simeq_{PTL}$.*

Proof. (1) Note that q is a marking of PTL.

Suppose that $\gamma \notin allSteps_q$. Since $\gamma \leq \alpha$ and α is enabled at q, γ is also enabled at q. Then, as $\gamma \notin allSteps_q$, there is $t \in T$ such that $t \simeq_{PTL} \gamma$ and $\gamma + \{t\}$ is enabled at q. On the other hand, as α is lmax-enabled at q and $t \simeq_{PTL} \alpha$ (since $t \simeq_{PTL} \gamma$ and $\gamma \leq \alpha$), $\alpha + \{t\}$ is not enabled at q. This and $\alpha \in allSteps_q$ means that there is a pre-place p of t such that $^\bullet(\alpha + \{t\})(p) > q(p)$. From the assumption that γ is a maximal sub-multiset of α containing only co-located transitions, the fact that $t \simeq_{PTL} \gamma$, and the fact that p is a pre-place of t, it follows that $^\bullet\alpha(p) = {}^\bullet\gamma(p)$. Hence we obtain

$$^\bullet(\gamma + \{t\})(p) = {}^\bullet\gamma(p) + {}^\bullet\{t\}(p) = {}^\bullet\alpha(p) + {}^\bullet\{t\}(p) = {}^\bullet(\alpha + \{t\})(p) > q(p).$$

Therefore $\gamma + \{t\}$ is not enabled at q, leading to a contradiction.

Hence $\gamma \in allSteps_q$ and so, since all the transitions in γ are co-located w.r.t. $\simeq_{PTL}$, $\gamma \in minSteps_q$.

(2) follows immediately from (1). □

We then obtain a complete characterisation of the co-location relation restricted to transitions in steps labelling arcs outgoing from a given node.

Theorem 3. *Let q be a state of the lmax-concurrent reachability graph TS of a ptl-net PTL spanned over a tissue structure. Then two distinct transitions in T_q are co-located w.r.t. $\simeq_{PTL}$ iff either there is no step in $allSteps_q$ to which the two transitions belong, or there is a step in $minSteps_q$ to which the two transitions belong.*

Proof. Let t and u be distinct transitions in T_q.

($\Longrightarrow$) Suppose that $t \simeq_{PTL} u$ and there is $\alpha \in allSteps_q$ such that $t, u \in \widehat{\alpha}$. Let γ be the (non-empty) maximal sub-multiset of α comprising the transitions co-located with t and u. Then $t, u \in \widehat{\gamma}$ and, by Proposition 1(1), we have $\gamma \in minSteps_q$.

($\Longleftarrow$) If there is no $\alpha \in allSteps_q$ such that $t, u \in \widehat{\alpha}$, then t and u must be in conflict at q. Hence $t \simeq_{PTL} u$. If there is $\alpha \in minSteps_q$ such that $t, u \in \widehat{\alpha}$, we apply Proposition 1(2). □

Corollary 1. *Let q be a state of the lmax-concurrent reachability graph TS of a ptl-net PTL spanned over a tissue structure. Then $\simeq_{PTL} |_{T_q \times T_q}$ is equal to $\simeq_{TS}^q$, where:*

$$\simeq_{TS}^q = \bigcup_{\alpha \in minSteps_q} \widehat{\alpha} \times \widehat{\alpha} \;\cup\; \left((T_q \times T_q) \setminus \bigcup_{\alpha \in allSteps_q} \widehat{\alpha} \times \widehat{\alpha} \right). \tag{7}$$

Proof. Follows from Theorem 3 and the observation that, by Proposition 1(1), for every transition $t \in T_q$, there is $\alpha \in minSteps_q$ such that $t \in \widehat{\alpha}$. Hence $\simeq^q_{TS}$ is reflexive. □

It should be stressed that the above characterisation of $\simeq_{PTL} |_{T_q \times T_q}$ *does not depend* on PTL, but only on TS, and so it can be used in a synthesis algorithm.

5.2   Synthesis with an Unknown Co-location Relation

We can now discuss the solvability of Problem 4. Let T be a finite set of transitions and let $TS = (Q, \mathscr{A}, q_0)$ be a finite step transition system TS over T, both fixed for the rest of this section. We define two relations on the transitions in T:

$$\sim_{ok} = \bigcup_{q \in Q} \simeq^q_{TS} \quad \text{and} \quad \sim_{no} = \bigcup_{q \in Q} (T_q \times T_q) \backslash \simeq^q_{TS} .$$

It follows from Corollary 1 that if $\simeq$ is part of a solution to Problem 4, then $\sim_{ok}$ is a subset of $\simeq$, and $\sim_{no}$ is disjoint with $\simeq$. What is more, as co-location is an equivalence relation, the reflexive transitive closure $\simeq_{ok}$ of $\sim_{ok}$ is also a subset of $\simeq$.

It further follows from Corollary 1 that if there exists a $q \in Q$ such that $\simeq^q_{TS}$ is different from $\simeq_{ok} |_{T_q \times T_q}$, then the instance of Problem 4 we are dealing with has no solution (as we would then have $\simeq^q_{TS} \subset \simeq_{ok} |_{T_q \times T_q} \subseteq \simeq |_{T_q \times T_q} = \simeq^q_{TS}$). If there is no such q, then any co-location relation that would be part of a solution to Problem 4 belongs to the set Δ_{TS} of all co-location relations $\simeq$ over T such that: (i) $\simeq_{ok} \subseteq \simeq$; and (ii) $\simeq$ and $\sim_{no}$ are disjoint.

From (i) and (ii) above as well as from the assumption that $\simeq^q_{TS} = \simeq_{ok} |_{T_q \times T_q}$, for all $q \in Q$, we obtain

Fact 2. *Let $\simeq$ and $\simeq'$ be two co-location relations in Δ_{TS}. Then $\simeq |_{T_q \times T_q} = \simeq' |_{T_q \times T_q}$, for all $q \in Q$.*

One can then enumerate all co-location relations $\simeq$ in Δ_{TS} and check the solvability of Problem 3 for each such $\simeq$. This can be done by following the procedure described in Sect. 4 for $\tau = \tau_{\simeq}$ and $\ell = \ell_{\simeq}$.

What is more, by the next result, one can restrict this check to the largest (in terms of set inclusion) co-location relations in Δ_{TS}.

Theorem 4. *Let $\simeq$ and $\simeq'$ be two co-location relations in Δ_{TS} such that $\simeq \subseteq \simeq'$. If Problem 4 has a solution with $\simeq$, then it also has a solution with $\simeq'$.*

Proof. Assume that a *ptl*-net $PTL = (P, T, W, \ell, M_0)$ with $\ell|_T = \ell_{\simeq}$ is a solution to Problem 4.

Let us consider $PTL' = (P, T, W, \ell', M_0)$ where $\ell'|_T = \ell_{\simeq'}$ and $\ell'(p) = \ell'(t)$ whenever $\ell(p) = \ell(t)$, for all $p \in P$ and $t \in T$. Since $\simeq \subseteq \simeq'$, PTL' is a *ptl*-net spanned over $\tau_{\simeq'}$. Hence, to show the result, it suffices to demonstrate that PTL and PTL' have the same lmax-concurrent reachability graphs. Moreover, since the underlying *pt*-nets of PTL and PTL' are the same, all we need to show is that at each lmax-reachable marking of PTL the sets of lmax-enabled steps are identical for both ptl-nets.

Let us consider any lmax-reachable marking M of PTL. Clearly, such a marking corresponds to a unique state $q \in Q$. We then observe that:

(1) α is enabled at M in PTL *iff* α is enabled at M in PTL'; and
(2) if α and $\{t\}$ are steps enabled at M (in PTL or PTL'), then $t \simeq \alpha$ *iff* $t \simeq' \alpha$.

Note that (2) above follows from the fact that if β is a step enabled at M, then there is a step γ which is lmax-enabled at M and $\beta \leq \gamma$ (as each transition has at least one pre-place). It therefore follows that $\{t\} \cup \widehat{\alpha} \subseteq T_q$. Hence, by Fact 2, $t \simeq \alpha$ *iff* $t \simeq' \alpha$.

We now observe that, by (1) and (2) above, the sets of lmax-enabled steps at M are identical for both ptl-nets.   □

The problem of finding (the largest) co-location relations in Δ_{TS} is related to the minimum clique cover problem (MCC). To see this consider the undirected graph $\mathscr{G}$ such that its vertices are the equivalence classes of $\simeq_{ok}$. Moreover, two such equivalence classes, c and c', are joined by an edge in $\mathscr{G}$ if $(c \times c') \cap \sim_{no} = \varnothing$. It then follows that the co-location relations in Δ_{TS} are in one-to-one correspondence with the clique covers of $\mathscr{G}$. Furthermore, a minimal clique cover of $\mathscr{G}$ (i.e., one with a minimal number of cliques) corresponds to a largest co-location relation in Δ_{TS}. However, the converse does not in general hold as MCC looks for covers with the least possible number of cliques, whereas Δ_{TS} corresponds to covers which cannot be 'improved upon' by joining together some of the cliques. The two problems are therefore very close but not equivalent. Consider, for example, the following graph $\mathscr{G}$:

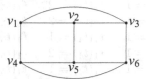

In this case, MCC would return just one cover $(\{v_1, v_2, v_3\}, \{v_4, v_5, v_6\})$, whereas Δ_{TS} would also consider $(\{v_1, v_4\}, \{v_2, v_5\}, \{v_3, v_6\})$. Having said that, we conjecture that practical solutions developed for MCC can be suitably adopted to work also for the problem of finding the largest co-location relations in Δ_{TS}. Finally, although the MCC problem is NP-complete [10], we feel that in practice this should not be a major issue as the number of vertices in $\mathscr{G}$ will often be much smaller than the number of transitions in T.

Examples. We end this section discussing a couple of instances of Problem 4. First we consider again the step transition system TS_1 shown in Fig. 5. In this case, $\sim_{ok} = \simeq_{ok}$ and $\sim_{no}$ are respectively as follows:

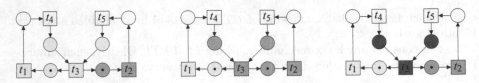

Fig. 9. Three solutions to the synthesis problem with unknown tissue structure for TS_1 of Fig. 5.

Hence there are exactly four possible ways of assigning localities to transitions in this example:

$$
\begin{array}{llll}
\ell_1(t_1) = 1 & \ell_1(t_2) = 2 & \ell_1(t_4) = \ell_1(t_5) = 3 & \ell_1(t_3) = 1 \\
\ell_2(t_1) = 1 & \ell_2(t_2) = 2 & \ell_2(t_4) = \ell_2(t_5) = 3 & \ell_2(t_3) = 2 \\
\ell_3(t_1) = 1 & \ell_3(t_2) = 2 & \ell_3(t_4) = \ell_3(t_5) = 3 & \ell_3(t_3) = 3 \\
\ell_4(t_1) = 1 & \ell_4(t_2) = 2 & \ell_4(t_4) = \ell_4(t_5) = 3 & \ell_4(t_3) = 4
\end{array}
$$

The *ptl*-net corresponding to ℓ_3 was shown in Fig. 5. The remaining three possible solutions are depicted in Fig. 9.

Finally, we consider the step transition system TS_2 shown in Fig. 6. In this case $\sim_{no}$ is empty whereas $\sim_{ok}$ and $\simeq_{ok}$ look as follows:

This leads to the following possible assignments of localities:

$$
\begin{array}{lll}
\ell_1(t_1) = \ell_1(t_2) = \ell_1(t_3) = 1 & \ell_1(t_4) = 2 & \ell_1(t_5) = 3 \\
\ell_2(t_1) = \ell_2(t_2) = \ell_2(t_3) = 1 & \ell_2(t_4) = 2 & \ell_2(t_5) = 2 \\
\ell_1(t_1) = \ell_1(t_2) = \ell_1(t_3) = 1 & \ell_1(t_4) = 1 & \ell_1(t_5) = 2 \\
\ell_1(t_1) = \ell_1(t_2) = \ell_1(t_3) = 1 & \ell_1(t_4) = 2 & \ell_1(t_5) = 1 \\
\ell_1(t_1) = \ell_1(t_2) = \ell_1(t_3) = 1 & \ell_1(t_4) = 1 & \ell_1(t_5) = 1
\end{array}
$$

6   Concluding Remarks

In this paper, we developed, through Theorems 1 and 2, arguably the strongest (step transition system based) kind of semantical equivalence between tissue systems and the class of *ptl*-nets spanned over tissue structures. Moreover, we provided mappings which can be used to move freely between these two types of models of dynamic systems. As a direct consequence of this result, the problem of synthesis of tissue systems from step transition systems is equivalent to the problem of synthesis of *ptl*-nets spanned over tissue structures. In the second part of the paper we therefore concentrated on the latter problem. We first lifted the synthesis method introduced in [13] to *ptl*-nets spanned over tissue structures. After that, by applying ideas from [18], we proposed an approach for the synthesis of *ptl*-nets spanned over tissue structures which can be applied if the tissue structure is not given in advance.

To summarise, we have described how one can adapt a solution to the Petri net synthesis problem based on regions of step transition systems, so that the resulting method can be used to construct tissue systems with a specific behaviour. There are other synthesis results developed for Petri nets which can be employed to extend the proposed solution in several directions. In particular evolution rules equipped with promoters and inhibitors directly lead to Petri nets extended with inhibitor and activator arcs (see [12,16] for suitable translations). Another direction is to consider synthesis of tissue systems from infinite transition systems, or from execution scenarios.

Finally, we would like to emphasize that this paper presents a general and abstract solution to a synthesis problem and potential applications of the theory presented go far beyond biologically inspired systems. In fact, thanks to the extension to arbitrary topologies, our results apply to general (globally asynchronous locally synchronous) distributed systems with communicating components. An interesting problem to investigate in the future could be the issue of reducing the number of connections in the clique structure we are constructing in our current approach.

Acknowledgements. We are grateful to the reviewers for their useful comments and suggestions.

This research was supported by the 973 Program Grant 2010CB328102, NSFC Grant 61133001, and EPSRC GAELS and UNCOVER projects.

References

1. Badouel, E., Darondeau, P.: Theory of regions. In: Reisig, W., Rozenberg, G. (eds.) APN 1998. LNCS, vol. 1491, pp. 529–586. Springer, Heidelberg (1998)
2. Bernardinello, L.: Synthesis of net systems. In: Ajmone Marsan, M. (ed.) ICATPN 1993. LNCS, vol. 691, pp. 89–105. Springer, Heidelberg (1993)
3. Chernikova, N.: Algorithm for finding a general formula for the non-negative solutions of a system of linear inequalities. USSR Comput. Math. Math. Phys. **5**, 228–233 (1965)
4. Darondeau, P., Koutny, M., Pietkiewicz-Koutny, M., Yakovlev, A.: Synthesis of nets with step firing policies. Fundam. Inform. **94**(3–4), 275–303 (2009)
5. Desel, J., Juhás, G.: What is a Petri net? In: Ehrig, H., Juhás, G., Padberg, J., Rozenberg, G. (eds.) APN 2001. LNCS, vol. 2128, pp. 1–25. Springer, Heidelberg (2001)
6. Desel, J., Reisig, W.: The synthesis problem of Petri nets. Acta Inf. **33**(4), 297–315 (1996)
7. Ehrenfeucht, A., Rozenberg, G.: Partial (set) 2-structures. Part I: basic notions and the representation problem. Acta Inf. **27**(4), 315–342 (1990)
8. Ehrenfeucht, A., Rozenberg, G.: Partial (set) 2-structures. Part II: state spaces of concurrent systems. Acta Inf. **27**, 343–368 (1990)
9. Jensen, K., van der Aalst, W.M.P., Balbo, G., Koutny, M., Wolf, K. (eds.): Transactions on Petri Nets and Other Models of Concurrency VII. LNCS, vol. 7480. Springer, Heidelberg (2013)

10. Karp, R.M.: Reducibility among combinatorial problems. In: Miller, R.E., Thatcher, J.W. (eds.) Complexity of Computer Computations. The IBM Research Symposia Series, pp. 85–103. Plenum Press, New York (1972)
11. Kleijn, J., Koutny, M.: Processes of membrane systems with promoters and inhibitors. Theor. Comput. Sci. **404**(1–2), 112–126 (2008)
12. Kleijn, J., Koutny, M.: Petri nets and membrane computing. In: Păun, G., Rozenberg, G., Salomaa, A. (eds.) The Oxford Handbook of Membrane Computing, pp. 389–412. Oxford University Press, Oxford (2010)
13. Kleijn, J., Koutny, M., Pietkiewicz-Koutny, M., Rozenberg, G.: Membrane systems and Petri net synthesis. In: Ciobanu, G. (ed.) MeCBIC. EPTCS, vol. 100, pp. 1–13 (2012)
14. Kleijn, J., Koutny, M., Rozenberg, G.: Process semantics for membrane systems. J. Autom. Lang. Comb. **11**(3), 321–340 (2006)
15. Kleijn, J., Koutny, M., Rozenberg, G.: Towards a Petri net semantics for membrane systems. In: Freund, R., Păun, G., Rozenberg, G., Salomaa, A. (eds.) WMC 2005. LNCS, vol. 3850, pp. 292–309. Springer, Heidelberg (2006)
16. Kleijn, J., Koutny, M., Rozenberg, G.: Petri nets for biologically motivated computing. Sci. Ann. Comp. Sci. **21**(2), 199–225 (2011)
17. Koch, I., Reisig, W., Schreiber, F. (eds.): Modeling in Systems Biology – The Petri Net Approach. Springer, London (2011)
18. Koutny, M., Pietkiewicz-Koutny, M.: Synthesis of Petri nets with localities. Sci. Ann. Comp. Sci. **19**, 1–23 (2009)
19. Mukund, M.: Petri nets and step transition systems. Int. J. Found. Comput. Sci. **3**(4), 443–478 (1992)
20. Petri, C.A.: Kommunikation mit Automaten. Ph.D. thesis (1962)
21. Pietkiewicz-Koutny, M.: The synthesis problem for elementary net systems with inhibitor arcs. Fundam. Inform. **40**(2–3), 251–283 (1999)
22. Păun, G.: Computing with membranes. J. Comput. Syst. Sci. **61**(1), 108–143 (2000)
23. Păun, G.: Membrane Computing, An Introduction. Springer, Heidelberg (2002)
24. Păun, G., Rozenberg, G.: A guide to membrane computing. Theor. Comput. Sci. **287**(1), 73–100 (2002)
25. Păun, G., Rozenberg, G., Salomaa, A. (eds.): The Oxford Handbook of Membrane Computing. Oxford University Press, Oxford (2010)
26. Reisig, W., Rozenberg, G. (eds.): APN 1998. LNCS, vol. 1491. Springer, Heidelberg (1998)
27. Reisig, W., Rozenberg, G. (eds.): APN 1998. LNCS, vol. 1492. Springer, Heidelberg (1998)

A Coloured Petri Net Approach to the Functional and Performance Analysis of SIP Non-INVITE Transaction

Junxian Liu[1]([⊠]) and Lin Liu[2]

[1] Science and Technology on Information Systems Engineering Laboratory,
National University of Defense Technology, Changsha 410073, Hunan,
People's Republic of China
allenliu_gfkd@163.com
[2] School of Information Technology and Mathematical Sciences,
University of South Australia, Mawson Lakes, SA 5095, Australia
Lin.Liu@unisa.edu.au

Abstract. With the increasing popularity of Voice over IP, the Session Initiation Protocol (SIP), a protocol for session creation and management, has become more and more important. This paper is focused on SIP non-INVITE transaction (NIT) and analyzes its functional correctness and performance. We firstly propose an extension to a Coloured Petri Net (CPN) based protocol verification methodology with a performance analysis component. Following the extended methodology, CPN models for NIT are created, verified and simulated. Functional verification shows that NIT contains no livelock and dead code, but it is not free of deadlock. Simulation analysis indicates that channel loss has a signifcant impact on bandwidth consumption by NIT, and when channel loss rate is less than 20 %, the delay by the server generating its final response has great influence on NIT performance. The outcome of this research also demonstrates the effectiveness of CPN for both functional and performance analysis of network protocols.

Keywords: SIP · Coloured Petri nets · Protocol verification · Functional analysis · Performance analysis

1 Introduction

Many Internet applications, such as voice calls and multimedia distributions, require that a session is established and maintained for the exchange of data between the participants. The Session Initiation Protocol (SIP) was developed by the Internet Engineering Task Force (IETF), as a general-purpose signalling protocol for creating, maintaining and terminating Internet sessions. The specification of SIP was first published as RFC 2543 [1] in 1999, and the second version (RFC 3261 [2]) was released in 2002. Over the years, SIP has gained increasing popularity in many Internet applications and has become the predominant

© Springer-Verlag Berlin Heidelberg 2014
M. Koutny et al. (Eds.): ToPNoC IX, LNCS 8910, pp. 147–177, 2014.
DOI: 10.1007/978-3-662-45730-6_8

signalling protocol for Voice over IP (VoIP). At the same time SIP has been undergoing continuous development and has been the topic of many studies.

Early research publications on SIP were mainly focused on introducing the features of SIP to the broad community and comparing or interconnecting SIP with other multimedia networking standards, such as H.323 [3–5]. Great efforts have also been made on studying or extending the applicability of SIP in various environments, such as wireless [6,7] and peer-to-peer [8] networks. Recently security analysis of SIP has also attracted more research [9–11].

Along with the above research directions, there have been a large number of studies addressing performance issues of SIP. The research broadly falls into two categories: (1) Performance analysis with analytical approaches. Wu et al. analyzed the performance of SIP for carrying telephony information in terms of queuing delay and delay variations [12]; Subramanian and Dutta [13] proposed a performance model for the SIP proxy servers and studied some of the key performance benchmarks such as server utilization, queue size and memory utilization; Sisalem et al. studied the effects of message loss, transmission delays and server load on the performance of SIP [14]; In [15] the reliability of a SIP server was studied. (2) Performance evaluation using software tools or test beds, or via prototyping. In [16] Rohricht and Bless analyzed how the resource reservation request interacts with SIP signalling requests based on a prototype implementation of SIP, and evaluated the duration of the overall signalling process; Sari and Wirya used an open source network emulation tool in the study of a SIP based VoIP application [17]; Chebbo et al. presented a modeling tool for estimating the number of required SIP entities for supporting certain traffic [9].

Interestingly although it would not be logical to evaluate the performance of a protocol without the knowledge of its functional correctness, much less attention has been paid to analyzing the functions of SIP since the protocol was first released. Only until recent years, a few studies of functional verification of SIP were undertaken by researchers in the Petri net community. In [18] a Petri net model was created for the SIP service, reachability analysis was conducted on the service model. In [19], the authors modeled a SIP-based discovery protocol for the Multi-Channel Service Oriented Architecture, which uses SIP as one of its basic components for web services in a mobile environment. Gehlot and Nigro presented a Coloured Petri net model of SIP in [20]. In [21,22], functional properties of SIP were analyzed using Coloured Petri nets.

From the perspective of protocol engineering [23,24], it is ideal to use the same formal technique to analyze both functional properties and performance of a protocol. In this way, functional correctness of the protocol is verified firstly, then performance analysis can be conducted on a more solid ground and can be based on the same model (possibly with minor modifications), therefore to achieve a set of formal, coherent and comprehensive analysis results on the protocol. However, based on our knowledge, there has not been such work done on SIP. In this paper, we aim at narrowing the gap with respect to SIP analysis.

The challenge is that most formal techniques do not provide the same level of support for functional and performance analysis. One technique may possess the strength in functional analysis or in performance analysis, but not in both. So for one protocol, different techniques have to be used for the two types of analysis. Therefore extra modeling effort must be made and it is difficult to relate the models and results of functional analysis to those of performance analysis.

Coloured Petri net (CPN) [25] is a graphical language for modeling and analyzing complex concurrent systems, and it is the combination of Petri nets and the ML programming language. CPN has been shown to be an effective technique for the formal specification and analysis of network protocols [26–31]. In the past two decades, CPN and its software tools (e.g. CPN Tools [32]) have evolved to provide better support for performance analysis using timed CPN and automatic simulations. However, up to now the majority of applications of CPNs in the field of protocol analysis are on functional analysis [33]. Very limited work has been found in using CPNs for protocol performance analysis, and even less work on using CPNs for both functional and performance analysis. Recently, some preliminary research was presented in [34] regarding the integration of CPN state space analysis and simulation based performance analysis for protocol analysis. In this paper, we will follow the same direction to apply CPN to analyze SIP.

In [35], a CPN based protocol verification methodology is presented and it has been used in analyzing the functional properties of many protocols [26–30]. A highlight of these is the work in [31], which has made real-life impact on the development of the Datagram Congestion Control Protocol [36]. Given its success in protocol functional analysis, in this paper, we extend this methodology with a performance analysis component. Then we apply the extended methodology to conduct both functional and performance analysis of SIP.

Transactions are the most important components of SIP and they are used for controlling SIP message exchanges. Two types of SIP transactions are defined in RFC 3261 [2]: INVITE transaction for setting up a session, and non-INVITE transaction (NIT) for terminating a session or other SIP functions such as a client registering its contact information with a SIP registrar. In this paper, we focus on SIP NIT, because as mentioned earlier, there have been a few studies concentrating on the functional verification of SIP INVITE transaction with CPNs [21,22], but very little work was done for analyzing SIP NIT.

The contribution of this paper is thus twofold: (1) a formal and complete analysis of the functions and performance of SIP NIT; (2) proposing an extension to the CPN based methodology [34] for both functional and performance analysis of protocols and demonstrating the effectiveness of the methodology with the SIP NIT case study.

The rest of the paper is organized as follows. Section 2 introduces the CPN based protocol verification methodology in [35] and proposes the extension to it. Section 3 introduces SIP and SIP NIT. The modeling and functional analysis of SIP NIT are presented in Sects. 4 and 5 respectively. In Sect. 6, after proposing a set of metrics for evaluating the performance of NIT, timed CPN simulations are used to analyze the performance of SIP NIT. Finally Sect. 7 concludes the paper and discusses future work.

2 The CPN Approach to Protocol Analysis

In this section we firstly introduce the methodology in [35] for functional analysis of protocols. Then we propose the extension to formalize a complete CPN approach for both functional and performance analysis of protocols.

The methodology in [35] comprises two types of analysis: verification against service specification and verification of general properties (see Fig. 1).

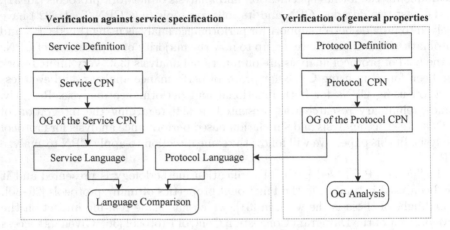

Fig. 1. Protocol verification methodology using CPNs [35]

The goal of the verification against service specification is to examine whether or not a protocol has fulfilled the service requirements given in the service definition. After a CPN model of the service definition is created, the state space (Occurrence Graph or OG) of the CPN is generated. From the state space, the expected sequences of service primitives (known as service language) are obtained. As in the service CPN model, service primitives are modeled with CPN transitions and the state space includes all the possible occurrence sequences of the CPN transitions, it is possible to reduce the state space while preserving service primitive sequences. In the next step, the protocol language is generated in a similar way, and it contains the sequences of service primitives produced by the protocol's operation. The two languages are then compared to detect any inconsistency between them.

Apart from meeting service requirements, for a protocol to function correctly, it must possess the important general properties [37], namely it must not contain any deadlocks or livelocks. It is also of interest to check if a protocol design contains dead code, i.e. actions that are never been carried out. These properties can be analyzed using CPN state space analysis (we will show how this is done in detail in Sect. 5 with the analysis of SIP NIT). As presented in Fig. 1, a CPN model of the protocol definition is created and its state space is generated. State space analysis is then conducted to obtain information about the dynamic behavior and properties of the protocol.

As mentioned in the Introduction section, it is ideal to use the same formal technique to analyze both the functional properties and performance of a protocol. The above methodology, however, only covers functional verification. On the other hand, CPNs and the CPN tools [32] have provided good support for simulation based performance. Therefore, we extend this methodology with the steps required for performance analysis. As indicated in Fig. 2, we have kept the verification of general properties and link it to the steps of simulation based performance analysis. Note that the verification against service specification is not included in the extended methodology because in practice, most protocol standards, especially Internet protocols developed by IETF, do not provide service definitions of protocols. Furthermore, it is the verification of general properties that is the basis for performance analysis.

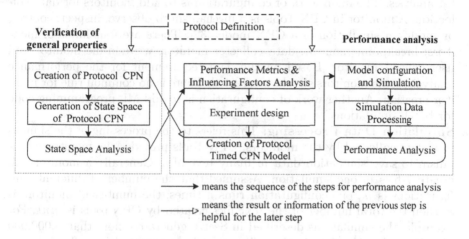

Fig. 2. Extended methodology using CPNs

In the following, we describe the main steps for performance analysis shown in Fig. 2.

1. **Performance Metrics and Influencing Factors Analysis:** This involves analyzing the protocol definition and proposing a set of metrics for evaluating the protocol's performance. The metrics may be related to the rate of successful termination of the protocol, time taken to terminate, delays in message transmissions, and the usage of network resources (bandwidth). Factors possibly affecting the metrics also need to be identified during this step. The results of state space analysis can be helpful with finding these factors. During this step, analytical study of the relationship between the metrics and the identified factors may be conducted, which gives theoretical analysis result of the protocol's performance. Also the result can be compared with the outcome of simulation based performance analysis.

2. **Experiment Design:** The main work of this step is to analyze the importance of the factors identified in Step 1 and classify them into parameters/variables or constants. For each parameter, select some typical values

within its range. For each constant, select a typical value to be used in simulations. Then we need to take into account the values of all parameters, and design the experiment using some experimental design methods, e.g. multi-factor and multi-level orthogonal experimental design approaches [38].

3. **Creation of Protocol Timed CPN Model:** In this step, we modify the protocol CPN model previously created for general property analysis, by adding time information. As after time information is appended to the CPN model, the behavior of the model may change, some new places or transitions may need to be added.

4. **Model Configuration and Simulation:** After the timed CPN model is obtained, we configure the model according to the experiment designed in Step 2, run CPN simulations using CPN Tools and collect simulation data for analysis. The main work of configuration is to add monitors for data collection. A monitor in CPN Tools is a mechanism to observe, inspect, control, or modify a simulation of a CPN model [32]. There are four kinds of monitors: breakpoint monitor, data collector monitor, write-in-file monitor and user-defined monitor. Based on the data requirement for the performance analysis, some monitors should be created. There is no common rule for monitor creation. Another work of configuration is to add ML programming code for batch simulations.

5. **Simulation Data Processing:** This refers to the processing of the simulation data collected by the monitors. CPN Tools provides the monitor mechanism to save simulation data in many text files. Generally a monitor will create 7 files in one simulation. Assumed that the number of different configurations is m, one configuration runs n times, the number of monitors is k, then the total number of the text files created by CPN tools is mnk. For example, the simulations described in Sect. 6 generated more than 6,000,000 files. Therefore the data in these files must be processed in an effective way, which can be done by programming.

6. **Performance Analysis:** In the last step, we analyze the impact of the factors on the metrics and find out the key factors. Based on the analysis result, propose the changes to the design and implementation of the protocol. The difficulty of the analysis is how to identify the combined impact of several factors on one metric, and how to determine the most important factors on all of the metrics.

In the following sections after introducing SIP and SIP NIT, we will apply the extended methodology to analyze the general or functional properties and performance of SIP NIT.

3   Overview of SIP and SIP NIT

3.1   SIP Messages, Layers and Transactions

There are two types of SIP messages: requests and responses. A request is sent from a client to a server to invoke a particular operation on the server. RFC 3261

[2] defines 6 classes of requests: INVITE, ACK, OPTIONS, BYE, CANCEL, and REGISTER, for initiating, modifying, tearing down a session or communicating with a SIP registrar. A response is sent from a server to a client to indicate the status of a request. There are 6 classes of responses and they are distinguished from each other by a 3-digit integer status code. When the details of a response are not essential, for simplicity, a response with a status code between 100 and 199 is referred as a "1xx response", a response with a status code between 200 and 299 is referred as a "2xx response", and so on. A 1xx response is known as a provisional response, which is used to indicate that the server is performing some further action. A response with a status code between 200 to 699 is a final response, where a 2xx response indicates the request was successful; a 3xx response gives the redirection information about the server; 4xx and 5xx responses are used to indicate client or server errors; and a 6xx response reflects a global error.

SIP is organized into four functional layers [2]: syntax and encoding layer, transport layer, transaction layer, and transaction user (TU) layer. The top layer (TU layer) controls the creation and cancellation of SIP transactions sitting in the transaction layer, and the transactions in turn control the exchange of messages between the client and server under the instructions of their TUs. How SIP elements send and receive messages over the network is defined in the transport layer. The lowest layer (syntax and encoding layer) specifies the format and structure of SIP messages.

As SIP transactions govern SIP message exchanges between the participants of a session, the transaction layer plays the most essential role in SIP operations. A SIP transaction involves a series of SIP messages, generally a request followed by one or more responses. A SIP transaction that starts with an INVITE request is known as an INVITE transaction, and any other transaction is called a non-INVITE transaction. Each SIP transaction comprises a client transaction and a server transaction at the client and server sides respectively.

This paper concerns about the analysis of SIP non-INVITE transaction, which is introduced in more detail in the next section.

3.2   SIP Non-INVITE Transaction

A non-INVITE transaction (NIT) is started when the TU at the client slide initiates a request other than INVITE or ACK and passes the request to the transaction. The non-INVITE client transaction (NICT) and non-INVITE server transaction (NIST) provide their functions by each maintaining a state machine as shown in Fig. 3.

Referring to Fig. 3(a), NICT has four states: *Trying, Proceeding, Completed* and *Terminated*. The *Trying* state is entered when NICT is initiated with a request from its TU and the request is passed to SIP transport layer for transmission. When entering the *Trying* state, NICT sets Timer F to fire in $64T1$ s, where $T1$ is the estimated round trip delay between the client and the server. The default value for $T1$ is 500 ms as specified in RFC 3261. Timer E is also set

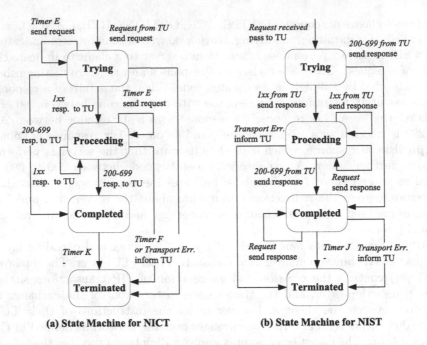

Fig. 3. State machines of NIT

if an unreliable transport is used. The interval of Timer E starts at $T1$ and is doubled until it hits $T2$ (whose default value is $8T1$).

When NICT is in its *Trying* state, one of the following events can occur: (1) Timer E fires. Then the timer is reset and the request is retransmitted; (2) Timer F fires. In this case NICT enters its *Terminated* state; (3) A provisional response is received. The NICT needs to pass the response to its TU and enter the *Proceeding* state; (4) A final response is received. Then NICT passes the response to its TU and enters the *Completed* state; (5) A transport error is reported by SIP transport layer. Upon receiving the report, NICT informs its TU and enters the *Terminated* state.

In the *Proceeding* state, the same events can happen and the corresponding actions are taken as those in the *Trying* state, except that when a provisional response is received, NICT remains in current state instead of moving to a new state.

Once NICT enters its *Completed* state, Timer K is set to fire in $T4$ s for unreliable transport, and zero seconds for reliable transport. $T4$ represents the amount of time for NICT to absorb retransmitted responses and its default value is $10T1$ s. When Timer K fires, NICT enters its *Terminated* state.

The state machine for the server transaction (NIST) is shown in Fig. 3(b). NIST also has four states. It is initialized in the *Trying* state upon receiving a request other than INVITE or ACK. This request is then passed to its TU for processing.

When NIST is in its *Trying* state, one of the two events may occur: (1) Receiving a provisional response from its TU. NIST then passes the response to SIP transport layer for transmission and enters its *Proceeding* state; (2) Receiving a final response from its TU. Then NIST passes the response to the SIP transport layer for transmission and enters its *Completed* state.

When NIST is *Proceeding*, as in the *Trying* state, it may receive a provisional or final response from its TU, and the response is passed to the SIP transport layer for transmission. Additionally in the *Proceeding* state, NIST may receive a retransmitted request. In this case, it re-sends the provisional response. If a transport error is reported by the SIP transport layer when NIST is in the *Proceeding* state, NIST informs its TU and enters the *Terminated* state.

When NIST enters its *Completed* state, it sets Timer J to fire in $64T1$ s for unreliable transport, and zero seconds for reliable transport. While in the *Completed* state, one of the following events can occur: (1) Receiving a retransmitted request. NIST then re-sends the final response; (2) Receiving a final response from its TU. In this case, NIST discards the response; (3) A transport error is reported by SIP transport layer. NIST then needs to inform its TU and enters its *Terminated* state; (4) Timer J fires, which will cause NIST to enter its *Terminated* state.

For either NICT or NIST, once entering the *Terminated* state, it is destroyed by its TU immediately.

4   Modeling SIP NIT with CPN

4.1   Modeling Assumptions

The CPN model of NIT is based on the state machines of the transaction (Fig. 3). For the convenience of modeling, or to eliminate the ambiguity of the state machines, the following assumptions are made when we create the CPN model:

1. A state machine must have an initial state which provides a starting point. The initial states of the state machines of NICT and NIST are missing, so we add the *Initial* state to the CPN models of NICT and NIST respectively.
2. Based on the firing intervals between Timer E and Timer F, the maximum number of the retransmissions of a request is 10.
3. NICT discards any responses received when it is *Completed*. NIST discards any request retransmissions when it is *Trying*.
4. There are no proxies between the client and server.

4.2   The Top Level CPN Model for NIT

Figure 4 shows the top level model for NIT. Place *TU_Req* represents the request by the client TU. Place *TU_Resp* represents the responses by the server TU. The four substitution transitions, *Client_Transaction*, *Server_Transaction*, *Client_Transport_Layer* and *Server_Transport_Layer*, each corresponds to a CPN module. Places *Requests*, *Responses*, *Received_Request*, *Received_Responses*,

TP_Error_C and *TP_Error_S* are socket places, modeling the information exchanged between SIP transaction layer and transport layer. Places *Channel_C2S*, *Channel_S2C*, transitions *Loss_C2S*, *Loss_S2C* and their guards, as well as the inscriptions, model the behavior of the channel between the client and server.

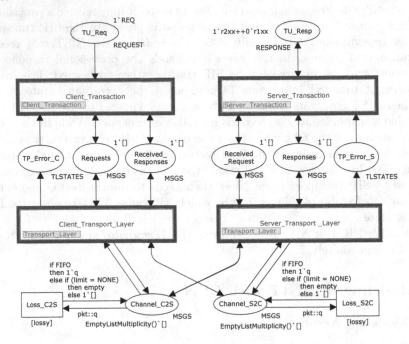

Fig. 4. Top level CPN model for NIT

In the following sections, we introduce the CPN declaration used in the top level model and the lower level models one by one.

4.3 Definition of Colour Sets, Variables, Constants and Functions

Referring to Table 1, *STATE* is an enumeration colour set which defines the states of NICT and NIST. The request and response are defined as enumeration colour sets *REQUEST* and *RESPONSE* respectively. The response messages are named as follows: r1xx for a provisional response, and r2xx for a final response. Colour set *MSG* is defined as the union of *REQUEST* and *RESPONSE* and *MSGS* represents the lists of requests or responses.

Table 2 shows the declaration of the variables and constants. m_rt represents the maximum number of (re)transmissions of a request. *limit*, *lossy* and *FIFO* are used for configuring the properties of the communication channel. *limit* is an optional integer by using the keyword SOME. $limit = NONE$ means that the capacity of the channel is unbounded. $limit = SOME\ 11$ means that the capacity of the channel is bounded to 11 which is equal to m_rt. When the model is for

Table 1. Colour sets used in the top level CPN model

No.	Definition
1	colset INT = int with 0..11;
2	colset BOOL = bool;
3	colset STATE = with initial |trying |proceeding |completed |terminated;
4	colset REQUEST = with REQ;
5	colset RESPONSE = with r1xx |r2xx;
6	colset TLSTATES = with tlnormal |tlerror;(*transport layer status*)
7	colset MSG = union response:RESPONSE + request:REQUEST;
8	colset MSGS = list MSG;

the transaction operating over a reliable medium, we set $FIFO = true$ and $lossy = false$. In other combinations of the values of the two variables, the model is for the transaction operating over an unreliable medium, indicating that the channel may either reorder or lose messages. We select three cases in the analysis (see Sect. 5.3): (1) the value of $FIFO$ is $true$, and $lossy$ is a boolean variable with its value ($true$ or $false$) randomly selected in simulation; (2) Both the values of $FIFO$ and $lossy$ are $false$; (3) the value of $FIFO$ is $false$ and $lossy$ is a boolean variable.

Table 2. Variables and constants used in the top level CPN model

No.	Definition	No.	Definition
1	val m_rt = 11;	7	var req: REQUEST;
2	val limit = SOME 11;	8	var res: RESPONSE;
3	var lossy: BOOL;	9	var pkt: MSG;
4	var FIFO: BOOL;	10	var ress, reqs: MSGS;
5	var sc, ss: STATE;	11	var q,qs,qr: MSGS;
6	var tperror: BOOL;		

Table 3 lists 4 functions. $EmptyListMultiplicity()$ is used to set the initial marking of $Channel\_C2S$ and $Channel\_S2C$. $ClientStateChange()$ is used to determine the state of NICT after a response is passed to its TU. $SendResponse1()$ and $SendResponse2()$ are used to determine the response to be sent.

4.4 CPN Model for NICT

According to the state machine of NICT (Fig. 3(a)) and following the modeling assumption, the CPN model for NICT is created and shown in Fig. 5. Places

Table 3. Functions used in the top level CPN model

No.	Definition
1	*fun EmptyListMultiplicity () =*
	if (FIFO orelse limit=NONE) then 1 else valOf(limit)
2	*fun ClientStateChange (sc, res) =*
	if ((sc=trying) orelse (sc=proceeding)) andalso (res=r2xx) then completed
	else if (res=r1xx) andalso (sc=trying) then proceeding else sc
3	*fun SendResponse1 (ss, ress) =*
	if (ss=proceeding) then ress^^[response r1xx]
	else if (ss=completed) then ress^^[response r2xx] else ress
4	*fun SendResponse2 (res, ress) = ress^^[response res]*

Requests, Received_Responses, TU_Request and *TP_Error_C* are input or output ports. The state of NICT is modeled by place *Client*, which is typed with *STATE*. Place *Count* is used to record the number of retransmissions of a request. Transition *Request_from_TU* models how NICT receives a request from its TU and passes to the transport layer. *Timer_E_Fire* models how NICT retransmits the request. *Timer_F_Fire* and *Timer_K_Fire* model how NICT changes its state when Timer F or Timer K fires. *Inform_TU* models the changing of the state of NICT when a transport layer error occurs. *Resp_to_TU* models how NICT passes a response to its TU.

4.5   CPN Model for NIST

Figure 6 shows the model for NIST. Places *Received_Requests, Responses, TU_Resp* and *TP_Error_S* are input/output ports. *TU_Resp* is typed with *RESPONSE* and is used to model the responses generated by the server TU. The state of NIST is modeled by the place *Server*, which is typed with *STATE*. Four transitions are connected to this place, where *Pass_to_TU* models how NIST receives the request from the transport layer and passes it to its TU, *Response_from_TU* models how NIST deals with a response from its TU, *Timer_J_Fire* models the state change of NIST when Timer J fires, and *Terminate_Server* represents the terminating of NIST.

4.6   CPN Model for SIP Transport Layer

The CPN model for SIP transport layer includes five places and three transitions (Fig. 7). Transitions *Send* and *Receive* models the main functions of SIP transport layer. The interpretation of the related arc inscriptions can be found in [39]. The model combines reordering and FIFO channels when loss is only from the head of the FIFO queue. When *FIFO = true*, the channel will be FIFO, otherwise it operates as a reordering channel. *limit* is used to configure the channel capacity. When *limit* is *NONE* the channel is unlimited. Transition *Transport_Error* models the occurrence of a transport error and how the error is reported to the transaction. Places *MSGs, Received_MSGs, Channel1* and *Channel2* are input/output ports interact with other models (see Fig. 4).

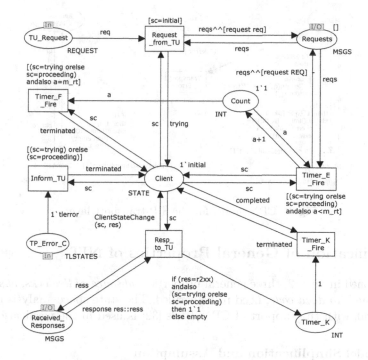

Fig. 5. CPN model for NICT

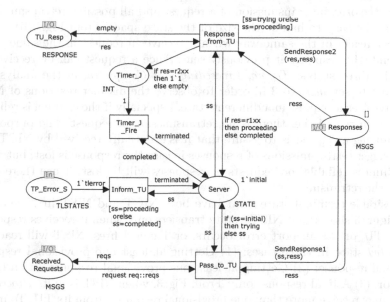

Fig. 6. CPN model for NIST

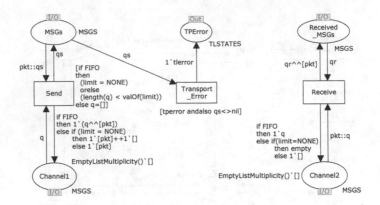

Fig. 7. CPN model for the SIP transport layer

5   Verification of General Properties of NIT

As mentioned in Sect. 2, three general properties, *absence of livelocks*, *absence of deadlock* and *no dead code*, need to be verified. The state space analysis method of CPN [40] with the support of CPN Tools [32] is used in the verification.

5.1   Model Simplification and Assumption

According to the description of NIT, NICT can retransmit a request up to 10 times over an unreliable medium. In state space analysis, if we set $m\_rt = 11$ to represent the original transmission of a request and all possible retransmissions, it may not be easy to handle the size of the state space. From Fig. 3(b) we see that NIST reacts in the same way when it receives a request in the same state, i.e. re-sends the response it previously sent. Since a request can be received in one of the three states: *Trying*, *Proceeding* and *Completed*, in the analysis, it is sufficient to set m_rt to 3 in order to observe the distinct reactions of NIST when it receives a request in a different state. Especially if the channel is reliable, we can let $m\_rt = 1$, i.e. there is no retransmission of request. The purpose of retransmitting a request is to assure that it is eventually received by NICT and also to trigger retransmissions of responses in case the response is lost, but when the medium is reliable, no requests or responses will be lost, hence there is no need for the retransmission.

A desirable terminal state must have both NICT and NIST in *Terminated* state. Figure 3 shows that NIST's state transfers only when it receives responses from its TU, or a transport error occurs, or Timer J fires. NIST will reach its *Terminated* state in three cases: (1) Getting at least one provisional response and a final response; (2) Getting at least one provisional response and a transport error; (3) A final response only. From Fig. 3, when NIST is in its *Proceeding* state, it may receive more than one provisional responses from its TU. To model this, we let place *TU_Resp* be the input place as well as the output place of transition *Response_from_TU*, so that the response token can be "reused". To reduce the size of state space without loss of generality, we also alter the inscription of the arc from transition *Response_from_TU* to place *TU_Resp* into *"empty"* and analyze the state space under several initial markings of place *TU_Resp*, including *2`r1xx++1`r2xx, 1`r1xx++1`r2xx, 2`r1xx, 1`r1xx and 1`r2xx*.

In the following analysis, we take an incremental approach, i.e. we firstly verify the model operating over a reliable medium, then the model operating over an unreliable medium.

5.2   Verification of General Properties for Reliable Medium

In the case of NIT operating over a reliable medium, we let *FIFO* be *true*, *lossy* be *false* in the CPN model. According to the assumption m_rt is set to 1.

The state space reports under different initial markings were generated using CPN Tools. The numbers of nodes and arcs of the full State Spaces and Strongly Connected Components (SCC) Graphs are listed in Table 4, in which the column "Initial Markings" contains the initial markings of place *TU_Resp*.

Table 4. State space statistics for reliable medium

Initial markings	SS Nodes	SS Arcs	SCC Nodes	SCC Arcs
2`r1xx + +1`r2xx	272	659	272	659
1`r1xx + +1`r2xx	111	226	111	226
2`r1xx	58	106	58	106
1`r1xx	24	33	24	33
1`r2xx	36	57	36	57

We see that for each of the initial markings, the numbers of nodes and arcs of the SCC graph are the same as those of the state space. This implies that the state space has no cycles. Therefore NIT operating over a reliable medium has no livelocks, as a livelock is shown as a cycle in the state space that once entered, can never escape from [35].

The property of *absence of deadlocks* is analyzed by examining the dead markings. If NIT works well, both NICT and NIST must be in the *Terminated* state when they complete. Hence a desirable dead marking is a marking in which places *Client* of model *Client_Transaction* (Fig. 5) and *Server* of model *Server_Transaction* (Fig. 6) each has a token with colour *terminated*. The result of dead markings is summarized in Table 5, in which K_1 is the total number of dead markings, K_2 is the number of dead markings in which places *Client* and *Server* are both *terminated*, column "Undesirable Dead Markings" lists the dead markings which are undesirable (only the tokens of places *Client* and *Server* are shown) and K_3 is the number of the undesirable dead markings.

Table 5. Dead markings for reliable medium

Initial markings	K_1	K_2	Undesirable dead markings	K_3
$2`r1xx + + 1`r2xx$	16	14	(*terminated, initial*)	2
$1`r1xx + + 1`r2xx$	11	9	(*terminated, initial*)	2
$2`r1xx$	5	2	(*terminated, initial*)	2
			(*terminated, proceeding*)	1
$1`r1xx$	4	1	(*terminated, initial*)	2
			(*terminated, proceeding*)	1
$1`r2xx$	6	4	(*terminated, initial*)	2

From Table 5 we can see that there are 3 kinds of dead markings:

1. *Client* of model *Client_Transaction* has a token with colour *terminated*, so does the *Server* of *Server_transaction*. This kind of dead markings are desirable.
2. *Client* of model *Client_Transaction* has a token with colour *terminated* and *Server* of model *Server_transaction* has a token with colour *initial*, indicating that NIST does not receive any requests. The shortest paths from the initial marking to these dead markings are then analyzed, and the paths show that transport error of the client side (when sending the request) is the cause of the dead markings, so they are undesirable but reasonable and acceptable.
3. *Client* of model *Client_Transaction* has a token *terminated* and *Server* of model *Server_transaction* has a token *proceeding*. This kind of dead markings appears when the initial marking of place *TU_Resp* only includes "*r1xx*", therefore they are caused by the inadequate response from the server TU and are not desirable.

Therefore the CPN model of NIT operating over a reliable medium does not satisfy the property *absence of deadlocks*. When the TU of NIST misbehaves and never responds with a final response, NIT will fall into a deadlock, where NIST can never be terminated. Therefore it wound be suitable to use a timer in this case to terminate NIST.

Dead code of a protocol appear as dead transitions of the CPN model of the protocol. We found five dead transitions in the CPN model of NIT (Table 6): *Loss_C2S* and *Loss_S2C* in top level model, *Timer_E_Fire* and *Timer_K_Fire* in model *Client_Transaction*, and *Timer_J_Fire* in model *Server_Transaction*. As we set *lossy = false* for the case of reliable medium, *Loss_C2S* and *Loss_S2C* cannot be enabled (see Fig. 4), so it is expected for the two transitions to be dead. As *m_rt* is set to 1 to reduce state space in the case of reliable medium, no retransmission of request is possible, so Timer E can never be enabled, therefore it is expected to be dead too. From Table 5, *Timer_K_Fire* and *Timer_J_Fire* are dead when the initial marking of place *TU_Resp* does not contain "*r2xx*". This indicates that if the server TU never generates a final response, the two timers never fire, hence they are dead code of NIT in this case.

Table 6. Dead transitions for reliable medium

Initial markings	Dead transitions
2`r1xx + +1`r2xx	Loss_C2S; Loss_S2C; Timer_E_Fire
1`r1xx + +1`r2xx	Loss_C2S; Loss_S2C; Timer_E_Fire
2`r1xx	Loss_C2S; Loss_S2C; Timer_E_Fire; Timer_K_Fire; Timer_J_Fire
1`r1xx	Loss_C2S; Loss_S2C; Timer_E_Fire; Timer_K_Fire; Timer_J_Fire
1`r2xx	Loss_C2S; Loss_S2C; Timer_E_Fire

5.3   Verification of General Properties for Unreliable Medium

To analyze the properties of NIT operating over an unreliable medium, we conduct the analysis for the following three cases:

– *FIFO* is *true*, *lossy* is a boolean variable;
– *FIFO* is *false*, *lossy* is a boolean variable;
– *FIFO* is *false*, *lossy* is false;

The state space reports under different configurations were generated using CPN Tools. The numbers of nodes and arcs in the State Space and the SCC Graph are listed in Table 7. As the numbers of nodes and arcs contained in the SCC graph are the same as that in the state space graph, the state space has no cycles, so NIT operating over an unreliable medium has no livelocks.

Table 7. State space statistics for unreliable medium

FIFO	Lossy	Initial markings	SS Nodes	SS Arcs	SCC Nodes	SCC Arcs
true	boolean	2`r1xx + +1`r2xx	11174	48788	11174	48788
		1`r1xx + +1`r2xx	4534	18041	4534	18041
		2`r1xx	1546	5834	1546	5834
		1`r1xx	544	1690	544	1690
		1`r2xx	1007	3418	1007	3418
false	boolean	2`r1xx + +1`r2xx	16696	75312	16696	75312
		1`r1xx + +1`r2xx	6080	25123	6080	25123
		2`r1xx	1546	5834	1546	5834
		1`r1xx	544	1690	544	1690
		1`r2xx	1007	3418	1007	3418
false	false	2`r1xx + +1`r2xx	14753	53557	14653	53557
		1`r1xx + +1`r2xx	5517	18763	5517	18763
		2`r1xx	1426	4495	1426	4495
		1`r1xx	500	1317	500	1317
		1`r2xx	944	2744	944	2744

The dead markings of the model are listed in Table 8, in which the meaning of K_1, K_2 and K_3 is the same as that in Table 5. The kinds of the dead markings are the same as those in the case of a reliable medium, and only numbers of each kind of dead markings are different. Hence the conclusion is same, i.e. when the TU of NIST does not respond with a final response, NIT will reach a deadlock.

Table 8. Dead markings for unreliable medium

FIFO	Lossy	Initial markings	K_1	K_2	Undesirable dead markings	K_3
true	boolean	$2\,`r1xx + +1\,`r2xx$	120	115	(*terminated, initial*)	5
		$1\,`r1xx + +1\,`r2xx$	79	74	(*terminated, initial*)	5
		$2\,`r1xx$	25	16	(*terminated, initial*)	5
					(*terminated, proceeding*)	4
		$1\,`r1xx$	17	8	(*terminated, initial*)	5
					(*terminated, proceeding*)	4
		$1\,`r2xx$	38	33	(*terminated, initial*)	5
false	boolean	$2\,`r1xx + +1\,`r2xx$	120	115	(*terminated, initial*)	5
		$1\,`r1xx + +1\,`r2xx$	79	74	(*terminated, initial*)	5
		$2\,`r1xx$	25	16	(*terminated, initial*)	5
					(*terminated, proceeding*)	4
		$1\,`r1xx$	17	8	(*terminated, initial*)	5
					(*terminated, proceeding*)	4
		$1\,`r2xx$	38	33	(*terminated, initial*)	5
false	false	$2\,`r1xx + +1\,`r2xx$	119	115	(*terminated, initial*)	4
		$1\,`r1xx + +1\,`r2xx$	78	74	(*terminated, initial*)	4
		$2\,`r1xx$	24	16	(*terminated, initial*)	4
					(*terminated, proceeding*)	4
		$1\,`r1xx$	16	8	(*terminated, initial*)	4
					(*terminated, proceeding*)	4
		$1\,`r2xx$	37	33	(*terminated, initial*)	4

As shown in Table 9, there are four dead transitions: *Loss_C2S* and *Loss_C2S* in the top level model, *Timer_K_Fire* in *Client_Transaction*, and *Timer_J_Fire* in *Server_Transaction*. *Loss_C2S* and *Loss_S2C* are dead when the channel has no loss, which is expected as in the case of reliable medium, so they are not dead code. *Timer_K_Fire* and *Timer_J_Fire* are dead when the initial marking of *TU_Resp* does not contain "*r2xx*", which is similar to the case of reliable medium, i.e. if the server TU never generates a final response, then the two timers are dead code.

Table 9. Dead transitions for unreliable medium

FIFO	Lossy	Initial markings	Dead transitions
true	boolean	$2\,{}^{\backprime}r1xx + +1\,{}^{\backprime}r2xx$	*none*
		$1\,{}^{\backprime}r1xx + +1\,{}^{\backprime}r2xx$	*none*
		$2\,{}^{\backprime}r1xx$	*Timer_K_Fire; Timer_J_Fire*
		$1\,{}^{\backprime}r1xx$	*Timer_K_Fire; Timer_J_Fire*
		$1\,{}^{\backprime}r2xx$	*none*
false	boolean	$2\,{}^{\backprime}r1xx + +1\,{}^{\backprime}r2xx$	*none*
		$1\,{}^{\backprime}r1xx + +1\,{}^{\backprime}r2xx$	*none*
		$2\,{}^{\backprime}r1xx$	*Timer_K_Fire; Timer_J_Fire*
		$1\,{}^{\backprime}r1xx$	*Timer_K_Fire; Timer_J_Fire*
		$1\,{}^{\backprime}r2xx$	*none*
false	false	$2\,{}^{\backprime}r1xx + +1\,{}^{\backprime}r2xx$	*Loss_C2S; Loss_S2C*
		$1\,{}^{\backprime}r1xx + +1\,{}^{\backprime}r2xx$	*Loss_C2S; Loss_S2C*
		$2\,{}^{\backprime}r1xx$	*Loss_C2S; Loss_S2C;*
			Timer_K_Fire; Timer_J_Fire
		$1\,{}^{\backprime}r1xx$	*Loss_C2S; Loss_S2C;*
			Timer_K_Fire; Timer_J_Fire
		$1\,{}^{\backprime}r2xx$	*Loss_C2S; Loss_S2C*

5.4 Summary of the Verification of General Properties

Based on the state space analysis, we can conclude that SIP NIT operating over a reliable medium or an unreliable medium is free of livelocks, but the final state of NIST is determined by the server TU's response and the quality of the medium. If the TU of NIST does not generate any final response, NIST may stay in its *Proceeding* state, which is a deadlock. A fix to this would be to add a timer for the *Proceeding* state of NIST or to require the TU to destroy the transaction if the TU decides to not send a final response. However, the timers are dead code only for the specific case when the server TU does not give a final response, as they are used when a final response is generated by the server TU.

6 Analyzing the Performance of NIT

In this section, we evaluate the performance of NIT on the basis of the NIT CPN model created in Sect. 4. Following the extended methodology (Fig. 2), firstly the performance metrics and the possible factors influencing the measures are identified. Then the CPN model is augmented with time information and CPN simulation is conducted to assess NIT performance using the metrics. To be more generic in performance analysis, we assume that an unreliable transport medium is used, i.e. a message may be lost or reordered.

6.1   Performance Metrics and Influencing Factors

To evaluate the performance of SIP NIT, we propose the following three classes of metrics.

The first class of metrics measures the performance of NIT with respect to its termination. According to RFC 3261 [2], when NIT is terminated desirably, its NICT and NIST both enter the *Terminated* states. If the termination is a result of NICT receiving a final response, NIT is considered to be terminated successfully. Therefore we use the following two termination related metrics:

- **TR** (*Termination Rate*): the probability that NIT is terminated desirably.
- **SR** (*Success Rate*): the probability that NIT is terminated successfully [41]. Clearly $SR \leq TR \leq 1$.

The second class of metrics relates to the duration of NIT and the delays for NICT and NIST to receive a response and request, respectively, including:

- **TTC** (*Termination Time of NICT*), the time interval from the start of NIT till its NICT is terminated.
- **TTS** (*Termination Time of NIST*), the time interval from the start of NIT till its NIST is terminated.
- **RD** (*Request Delay*), the time interval from NICT sending a request for the first time till the request or a retransmission of the request being received by NIST for the first time.
- **pRpD** (*Provisional Response Delay*), the time interval from NICT sending a request for the first time till a provisional response or a retransmission of the response being received by NICT for the first time [41].
- **fRpD** (*Final Response Delay*), the time interval from NICT sending a request for the first time till a final response or a retransmission of the response is received by NICT for the first time [41].

The third class of metrics relates to the resource consumption by NIT, which include:

- **RT** (*Requests Transmitted*), the total number of requests sent by NICT [41], including the initially transmitted request and its retransmissions.
- **pRpT** (*Provisional Responses Transmitted*), the total number of provisional responses (the initial transmission and its retransmissions) sent by NIST [41].
- **fRpT** (*Final Responses Transmitted*), the total number of final responses (the initial transmission and its retransmissions) sent by NIST [41].
- **BC** (*Bandwidth Consumption*), the number of request and response messages transmitted per second in the duration of NIT, i.e. $BC = (fRpT + pRpT + RT)/max(TTC, TTS)$.

From the results of functional verification, the performance of NIT is affected by the server TU's response and the quality of medium. Assumed that transport error does not happen and the server TU responds normally (i.e. it always generates a final response), we can identify the following factors or parameters that may affect the performance of NIT:

- **pPD** (*Provisional Response Processing Delay*), the time required by server TU to process a request and create a provisional response [41].
- **fPD** (*Final Response Processing Delay*), the time required by server TU to process a request and create a final response.
- **LRC** (*Loss Rate of Channel*), the probability of losing a packet by medium.
- **TD** (*Transmission Delay*), the end-to-end delay of the channel.

Obviously RD (*Request Delay*) is not relevant to fPD and it is affected by LRC only. From the definition of TTC (*Termination Time of NICT*) $TTC = min(32\,s, fRpD)$, where $32\,s$ (i.e. $64T1$) is the firing interval of Timer F. The definition of TTS (*Termination Time of NIST*) implies that $TTS = (RD + fPD + 32)$ *seconds*, where $32\,s$ is the firing interval of Timer J. Therefore TTC is always less than $32\,s$ and TTS is always larger than $32\,s$, indicating that NICT always terminates earlier than NIST.

In the following, we will use CPN simulation based method to analyze how possibly these factors would affect the performance of NIT, i.e. to find out the relationships between the factors and the defined performance metrics.

6.2   Experiment Settings

In order to identify the relationships between the factors and the performance metrics, we need to conduct a series of simulation experiments for different values of the factors. So firstly we determine the possible values of the factors as follows:

- Referring to Fig. 3, as the duration of Timer F is $64T1$, NICT will eventually enter its *Completed* state within $64T1$, either because it receives a final response before Timer F fires or Timer F fires. Furthermore any response received by NICT will be discarded when it is in the *Completed* state, so if it takes the server TU more than $64T1$ to generate a final response, i.e. $fPD > 64T1$, the response will be useless anyway. Therefore, in our experiments, we assume that the value of fPD is in the range of $[0, 64T1]$.
- As NIT needs to complete rapidly, it is reasonable to consider that if the server TU generates a provisional response, it should generate the response without any delay, i.e. we assume that the provisional response processing delay, $pPD = 0\,s$.
- Obviously, the value of LRC is in $[0, 1]$.
- In general the transmission delay, TD is about half of the RTT, i.e. $T1/2$, which is much smaller comparing to other delays. So for the convenience of analysis, we assume that $TD = 0\,s$.

After having determined the values of the factors, we design the series of experiments by varying the values of fPD and TD. Specifically, in the experiments the following values of fPD are used: 0, 3, 6, ..., 63. Note that the unit for these values is $T1$. The values chosen for LRC are: 0, 0.05, 0.1, ..., 0.95. We call a combination of the values of fPD and LRC an experiment schema, denoted as (fPD, LRC). Therefore all the experiment schemas as stated above, can be represented as a set, $S_{exp} = \{(fPD, LRC)|fPD = 0, 3, 6, \ldots, 63;\ LRC = 0, 0.05, 0.1, \ldots, 0.95\}$.

6.3   Timed CPN Model Creation and Configuration

To obtain the timed CPN model for simulation analysis, *RESPONSE* and *STATE* in Table 1 are each modified to a timed colour set, and then the models in Figs. 4, 5, 6 and 7 are modified with time information. In these models we use one CPN time unit to represent $T1$ (500 ms). The main modifications include:

- Three changes to the CPN model for NICT (Fig. 8). The arc from place *Count* to transition *Time_F_Fire* is deleted (refer to Fig. 5), and a new arc is added to connect *Request_from_TU* and *Count*. A new place *Time_F* is added and connected to *Time_F_Fire* and *Request_from_TU*. Then the time information related to Timers E, F, and K are added into the inscriptions of the new arcs and other two arcs: the arc from *Timer_E_Fire* to *Count* and the arc from *Resp_to_TU* to *Timer_K*. As the retransmissions are controlled by simulation clock, the limitation of *m_rt* is removed from the guard functions of the transitions *Inform_TU* and *Timer_E_Fire*.
- Two modifications on the arc inscriptions of NIST model (see Fig. 9). The inscription of the arc from *Response_from_TU* to *TU_Resp* is modified with a timestamp *fPD* to represent the delay in using the final response. A timestamp is added into the inscription of the arc from *Response_from_TU* to *Time_J* to determine the firing time of Timer J.
- In the model for SIP transport layer, the inscription of the arc from *Receive* to *received_MSGs* is modified to model the loss of the channel (Fig. 10).

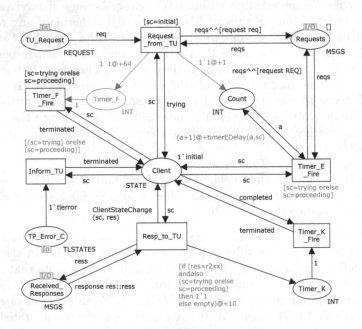

Fig. 8. Modified model for NICT

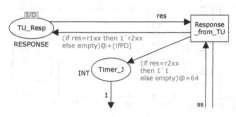

Fig. 9. Modified model for NIST (part)

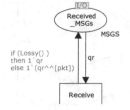

Fig. 10. Modified model for SIP transport layer (part)

To collect simulation data, seven data collection monitors are added to the model (Table 10). The monitor CTT records the terminate time of NICT and is used to calculate the value of *TTC*. The monitors RD, pRpD, fRpD, RT, pRpT and fRpT are used to record the values of the corresponding (same named) metrics as specified in Sect. 6.1. The metric *TR* can be calculated by monitor RD as a NIT will terminate desirably if the value recorded by the monitor RD is larger than zero. The metric *SR* can be calculated based the monitor fRpD, as a NIT will terminate successfully if the value recorded by fRpD is larger than zero. The metric *TTS* can be calculated based on the metric *RD*. *BC* is a composite metric so that it can be calculated based the values recorded by the monitors RT, pRpT, fRpT, RD and CTT.

Table 10. Data collection monitors of the CPN model

Name	Model	Node	Metrics using the monitor
CTT	*Client_Transaction*	place *Client*	*TTC, BC*
RD	*Server_Transaction*	transition *Pass_to_TU*	*RD, TTS, BC, TR*
pRpD	*Client_Transaction*	transition *Resp_to_TU*	*pRpD*
fRpD	*Client_Transaction*	transition *Resp_to_TU*	*fRpD, SR*
RT	*Client_Transaction*	place *Count*	*RT, BC*
pRpT	*Server_Transaction*	transition *Pass_to_TU*	*pRpT, BC*
fRpT	*Server_Transaction*	transition *Pass_to_TU*	*fRpT, BC*

6.4 Simulation Results and Analysis

For each experiment schema described in Sect. 6.2, 400 runs of simulations are done using CPN Tools. The average values of the metrics *TR*, *SR*, *TTS*, *RT*, *pRpT*, *fRpT* and *BC* are then calculated based on the simulation data. The relationship between the average value of a metric and each of the two factors, *fPD* and *LRC*, is plotted and shown in Figs. 11, 12, 13, 14, 15, 16 and 17, one figure for one metric. In each of the figures, sub-figure (a) shows the relationship between the metric and the factors *fPD* and *LRC* as a three-dimensional graph, sub-figures (b) and (c) are the two-dimensional projections for the metric and one single factor.

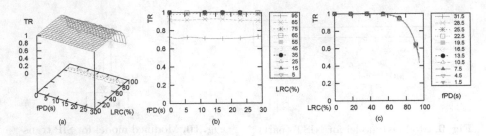

Fig. 11. Termination Rate (TR)

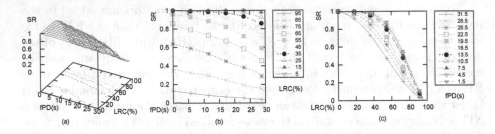

Fig. 12. Success Rate (SR)

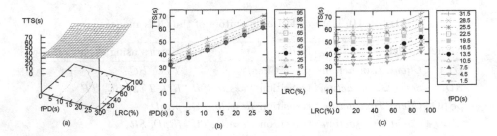

Fig. 13. Termination time of NIST (TTS)

Figure 11 shows that the influence of *fPD* on *TR* (*Termination Rate*) is negligible, and *LRC* significantly impacts on *TR* only when it is greater than 50 %,. From Fig. 12, we see that on *SR* (*Success Rate*), *LRC* has greater impact than *fPD*.

Figure 13 shows that the impact of *fPD* and *LRC* on *TTS*, from which we know that the impact of *fPD* is significant than that of *LRC*, and *TTS* is a linear function of *fPD* when *LRC* is fixed.

Figures 14, 15, 16 and 17 show how the factors affect the metrics related to the bandwidth consumption. From Fig. 14, *RT* (*Requests Transmitted*) increases when *LRC* or *fPD* increases. The longer the delay at the server TU (*fPD*) or the more messages are lost by the channel (*LRC*), the later the time when NICT receives a final response, hence bigger *RT*, i.e. more requests are retransmitted.

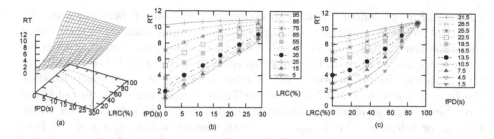

Fig. 14. Requests Transmitted (RT)

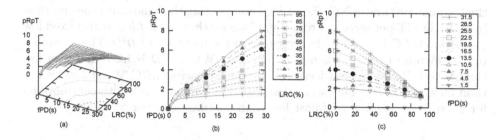

Fig. 15. Provisional Responses Transmitted (pRpT)

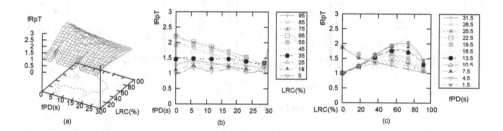

Fig. 16. Final Responses Transmitted (fRpT)

When *fPD* or *LRC* increases, the impact of *LRC* or *fPD* on *RT* decreases. Figure 15 shows that *pRpT* (*Provisional Responses Transmitted*) increases with the increase of *fPD* and it decreases with the increase of *LRC*.

Figure 16 shows that *fRpT* (*Final Responses Transmitted*) is much less than *pRpT* and *RT*. When *LRC* is larger than 35 %, the impact of *fPD* on *fRpT* is significant, otherwise the impact is not significant. For a fixed *fPD*, the relationships between *fRpT* and *LRC* are convex functions, the curvature of the functions decreases when *fPD* decreases. There are exceptions when *fPD* equals to 4.5, 16.5 or 28.5 s. In these cases the value of *fPD* is coincident with the firing time of Timer E in simulation. When the simulation clock is 9, 33 and 57 units (corresponding to 4.5, 16.5 and 28.5 s respectively), transition

Timer_E_Fire of model *Client_Transaction* and transition *Response_from_TU* of model *Server_Transaction* are both enabled without conflict. If they fire at the same time, NICT and NIST will enter their *Completed* states, so when the request and response reach their destinations, the server will still retransmit the final response. In other words, if the value of *fPD* was a bit small, to allow the final response to reach NICT before Timer E fires, the response would not have been retransmitted as a result of the retransmitted request when Timer E fires; or if it was a bit larger, the retransmission of the request would have caused a retransmission of the provisional response instead of a final response. In both situations, the value of *fRpT* would not be affected.

The metric *BC* (*Bandwidth Consumption*) is related to *pRpT*, *fRpT*, *RT* and the termination time of NIT (i.e. *TTS*), representing the bandwidth consumption by a single NIT per second. From Fig. 17 we see that when *LRC* is at a fixed low (high) level, *BC* increases (decreases) with the increases of *fPD*. This is caused by the increase of *TTS* when *fPD* increases. When *fPD* is fixed and at a low (high) level, *BC* increases (decreases) by the increase of *LRC*. When *LRC* is less than 50 % and *fPD* is not larger than 20 s, the average bandwidth consumption for a single transaction is almost less than 0.3 (messages per seconds).

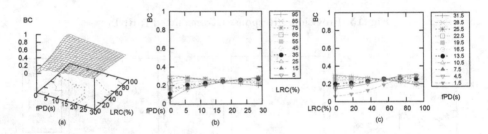

Fig. 17. Bandwidth Consumption (BC)

6.5 Summary of the Simulation Analysis

From the experiment results in Sect. 6.4, Comparing to *fPD*, channel loss rate (*LRC*) has more significant influence on the successful termination of NIT. However, taking into account that *LRC* is normally below 20 % in reality, NIT will terminate successfully with over 90 % probability, regardless of the value of *fPD*. Therefore NIT can perform effectively to successful termination in practice.

The termination time of NIT is influenced by the final response processing delay directly. The bigger *fPD* is, the longer NIT lasts. The influence of *LRC* on termination time gradually increases with increase of *LRC*, and the influence is very little when *LRC* < 20 %.

The bandwidth consumption for different values of *LRC* and *fPD* vary in a very small range and overall the bandwidth consumption of NIT is at a low level. However considering the termination time increases along with the increases of *LRC* or *fPD*, the bandwidth consumption in fact increases. This means that

NIT consumes more network resource. Figure 14, 15, and 16 show that most of the bandwidth is consumed by the retransmissions of the request and provisional responses, hence most of the request retransmissions are wasted, because NICT could terminate even without any provisional response. Therefore when the quality of transport medium is good enough (low loss rate and short transmitted delay), a long processing delay of the final response at the server will result in big bandwidth consumption, and the less the final response processing delay is, the better.

7 Conclusions and Future Work

In this paper, firstly the CPN based protocol verification methodology [39] is extended by including the steps for performance analysis. The extended methodology is then used to analyze the functions and performance of SIP NIT.

Functional verification shows that NIT behaves well in most cases. NIT operating over an unreliable medium or a reliable medium is both free of livelocks, but it is not free of deadlock. NICT will always terminate, but NIST may stay in its *Proceeding* state instead of eventually moving to the *Terminated* state. The final state of NIST is determined by the TU's response and the quality of the underlying channel. NIST will stay in the *Proceeding* state if its TU does not generate any final response.

Based on the result of functional verification, a set of performance metrics and their influencing factors are proposed for analyzing the performance of NIT, including the metrics reflecting the termination degree of NIT, time-related metrics, and bandwidth consumption related metrics. The simulation results show that if the channel loss rate (LRC) is reasonable, i.e. less than 20 %, NIT performs well and all metrics have acceptable values. Most retransmissions of request are wasted because NICT can terminate successfully even without any provisional response. Due to the retransmitted requests or provisional responses, a long processing delay of the final response leads to big bandwidth consumption.

The risk of a long final response processing delay is that NIT may encounter a so-called "race condition", in which the final response generated by the server may not reach the client before the timer of the client transaction expires [42]. If NIT loses the race, i.e. NICT does not receive any final response before Timer F expires, the client and server will have conflicting views about the NIT: the server believes that the transaction has succeeded as it responded to the request with a 2xx response, but the client believes that the transaction has failed since the final response reached the client after NICT had been terminated. The consequence of losing a race is that the server will be temporarily blacklisted by the client.

The reasons for NIT losing the race are various, e.g. the server takes too long to generate a final response, or the channel loss rate is too high to get a final response through in time. From the simulation analysis we know that the usage of retransmitted request is a primary cause, too many retransmissions of the request are used to trigger the retransmissions of the provisional responses. This finding is consistent with what is stated in RFC 4320, an update to SIP

RFC 3261 for solving the "losing race" problem. The main idea of the update is to limit the use of provisional responses. However, very little work was done to evaluate the efficiency of the update, and this may be a possible future work.

The study of this paper also shows that CPN is a valid and powerful formal technique for protocol verification and performance analysis. The general properties of a protocol, including absence of deadlocks, absence of livelock, and absence of dead event, can be verified using CPN. The performance of a protocol can be analyzed using timed CPN simulation, as demonstrated by the findings with SIP NIT. Additionally, given the graphical representation of CPNs and good support of CPN Tools for state space and simulation analysis, we hope that the proposed methodology is easy and intuitive to use,comparing to some other similar model checking methods.

The methodology presented in this paper is not perfect yet, for example the procedures of performance analysis may not be general enough to guide the performance analysis for other protocols. Hence there is still lots of work to do to improve the methodology, including refining the procedures, generalizing and formalizing the methods for analyzing the impact of the influencing factors on the performance metrics and to compare the impacts of different factors [43].

Acknowledgments. The first author (Dr Junxian Liu) would like to thank Professor Jonathan Billington and the University of South Australia for inviting him to conduct collaborative research on verification of the Session Initiation Protocol. Both authors are grateful to Professor Jonathan Billington for providing them valuable guidance on this work.

This work was supported in part by the National Natural Science Foundation of China under Grant No 71171196.

References

1. Handley, M., Schulzrinne, H., Schooler, E., Rosenberg, J.: SIP: Session Initiation Protocol. RFC 2543 (Proposed Standard, obsoleted by RFC 3261), March 1999
2. Rosenberg, J., Schulzrinne, H., Camarillo, G., Johnston, A., Peterson, J., Sparks, R., Handley, M., Schooler, E.: SIP: Session Initiation Protocol (2002)
3. Glasmann, J., Kellerer, W., Muller, H.: Service development and deployment in H.323 and SIP. In: Proceedings of the Sixth IEEE Symposium on Computers and Communications, pp. 378–385 (2001)
4. Glasmann, J., Kellerer, W., Muller, H.: Service architectures in H.323 and SIP: a comparison. IEEE Commun. Surv. Tutorials **5**(2), 32–47 (2003)
5. Wang, L., Agarwal, A., Atwood, J.: Modelling and verification of interworking between SIP and H.323. Comput. Netw. **45**(2), 77–98 (2004)
6. 3GPP: 3GPP Website - Technologies. http://www.3gpp.org/Technologies. Accessed: 20 January 2013
7. Camarillo, G., García-Martín, M.: The 3G IP Multimedia Subsystem (IMS): Merging the Internet and the Cellular Worlds. Wiley, New York (2011)
8. Rosenberg, J., Schulzrinne, H., Huitema, C., Gurle, C.: Session Initiation Protocol (SIP) Extension for Instant Messaging. RFC 3428, December 2002

9. Chebbo, H., Wilson, M.: Traffic and load modelling of an IP mobile network. In: 4th International Conference on 3G Mobile Communication Technologies, 3G 2003, (Conf. Publ. No. 494), pp. 423–427 (2003)
10. Schmidt, H., Dang, C.T., Hauck, F.: Proxy-based security for the session initiation protocol (SIP). In: Second International Conference on Systems and Networks Communications, ICSNC 2007, p. 42 (2007)
11. Geneiatakis, D., Lambrinoudakis, C., Kambourakis, G., Kafkalas, A., Ehlert, S.: A first order logic security verification model for SIP. In: IEEE International Conference on Communications, ICC '09, pp. 1–6 (2009)
12. Wu, J.S., Wang, P.Y.: The performance analysis of SIP-T signaling system in carrier class VoIP network. In: 17th International Conference on Advanced Information Networking and Applications, AINA 2003, pp. 39–44 (2003)
13. Subramanian, S., Dutta, R.: Performance and scalability of M/M/c based queuing model of the SIP proxy server - a practical approach. In: 2009 Australasian Telecommunication Networks and Applications Conference (ATNAC), pp. 1–6 (2009)
14. Sisalem, D., Liisberg, M., Rebahi, Y.: A theoretical model of the effects of losses and delays on the performance of SIP. In: Global Telecommunications Conference, IEEE GLOBECOM 2008, pp. 1–6. IEEE (2008)
15. Gurbani, V.K., Jagadeesan, L.J., Mendiratta, V.B.: Characterizing session initiation protocol (SIP) network performance and reliability. In: Malek, M., Nett, E., Suri, N. (eds.) ISAS 2005. LNCS, vol. 3694, pp. 196–211. Springer, Heidelberg (2005)
16. Rohricht, M., Bless, R.: Advanced quality-of-service signaling for the session initiation protocol (SIP). In: 2012 IEEE International Conference on Communications (ICC), pp. 6987–6992 (2012)
17. Sari, R., Wirya, P.: Performance analysis of session initiation protocol on emulation network using NIST NET. In: The 9th International Conference on Advanced Communication Technology, vol. 1, pp. 506–510 (2007)
18. Peng, Y., Zhanting, Y., Jizeng, W.: Petri net model of session initiation protocol and its verification. In: International Conference on Wireless Communications, Networking and Mobile Computing, WiCom 2007, pp. 1861–1864 (2007)
19. Gehlot, V., Hayrapetyan, A.: A formalized and validated executable model of the SIP-based presence protocol for mobile applications. In: ACM Southeast Regional Conference, pp. 185–190. ACM (2007)
20. Gehlot, V., Nigro, C.: Colored Petri net model of the session initiation protocol (SIP). In: IECON 2010–36th Annual Conference on IEEE Industrial Electronics Society, pp. 2150–2155 (2010)
21. Ding, L.G., Liu, L.: Modelling and analysis of the INVITE transaction of the session initiation protocol using coloured Petri nets. In: van Hee, K.M., Valk, R. (eds.) PETRI NETS 2008. LNCS, vol. 5062, pp. 132–151. Springer, Heidelberg (2008)
22. Liu, L.: Verification of the SIP transaction using coloured Petri nets. In: Proceedings of the Thirty-Second Australasian Computer Science Conference (ACSC 2009), Computer Science 2009. CRPIT, Wellington, New Zealand, 19–23 January, 2009, vol. 91, pp. 63–72. Australian Computer Society (2009)
23. Billington, J., Wilbur-Ham, M.C., Bearman, M.Y.: Automated protocol verification. In: Proceedings of the IFIP WG6.1 Fifth International Conference on Protocol Specification, Testing and Verification V, pp. 59–70. North-Holland Publishing Co., Amsterdam (1985)

24. Billington, J.: Specification of protocols: protocol engineering. In: Kent, A., Williams, J., Kent, R. (eds.) Encyclopedia of Microcomputers, vol. 7, pp. 299–314. Marcel Dekker, New York (1991)
25. Jensen, K., Kristensen, L.M.: Coloured Petri Nets - Modelling and Validation of Concurrent Systems. Springer, Berlin (2009)
26. Gordon, S.D.: Verification of the WAP transaction layer using coloured Petri nets. Ph.D. thesis, Telecommunications Research and Computer Systems Engineering Centre, University of South Australia, November 2001
27. Han, B.: Formal specification of the TCP service and verification of TCP connection management. Ph.D. thesis, School of Electrical and Information Engineering, University of South Australia, December 2004
28. Ouyang, C., Billington, J.: Formal analysis of the internet open trading protocol. In: Núñez, M., Maamar, Z., Pelayo, F.L., Pousttchi, K., Rubio, F. (eds.) FORTE 2004. LNCS, vol. 3236, pp. 1–15. Springer, Heidelberg (2004)
29. Tokmakoff, A., Billington, J.: An approach to the analysis of interworking traders. In: Donatelli, S., Kleijn, J. (eds.) ICATPN 1999. LNCS, vol. 1639, pp. 127–146. Springer, Heidelberg (1999)
30. Villapol, M.E., Billington, J.: A coloured Petri net approach to formalising and analysing the resource reservation protocol. CLEI Electron. J 6(1), 1–25 (2003)
31. Vanit-Anunchai, S., Billington, J., Kongprakaiwoot, T.: Discovering chatter and incompleteness in the datagram congestion control protocol. In: Wang, F. (ed.) FORTE 2005. LNCS, vol. 3731, pp. 143–158. Springer, Heidelberg (2005)
32. CPN Group: CPN Tools homepage (2012)
33. Kristensen, L.M., Simonsen, K.I.F.: Applications of coloured Petri nets for functional validation of protocol designs. In: Jensen, K., van der Aalst, W.M.P., Balbo, G., Koutny, M., Wolf, K. (eds.) ToPNoC VII. LNCS, vol. 7480, pp. 56–115. Springer, Heidelberg (2013)
34. Liu, J., Ye, X., Li, J.: Analyzing performance for complex protocol using validated CP-nets models. In: Proceedings of the 2010 10th IEEE International Conference on Computer and Information Technology, CIT '10, pp. 377–384. IEEE Computer Society, Washington, DC (2010)
35. Billington, J., Gallasch, G.E., Han, B.: A coloured Petri net approach to protocol verification. In: Desel, J., Reisig, W., Rozenberg, G. (eds.) ACPN 2003. LNCS, vol. 3098, pp. 210–290. Springer, Heidelberg (2004)
36. Kohler, E., Handley, M., Floyd, S.: Datagram Congestion Control Protocol (DCCP). RFC 4340 (Proposed Standard), March 2006. Updated by RFCs 5595, 5596
37. Holzmann, G.J.: Design and Validation of Computer Protocols. Prentice-Hall Inc., Upper Saddle River (1991)
38. Diamond, W.: Practical Experiment Designs: For Engineers and Scientists. Industrial Engeneering/Quality Management. Wiley, New York (2001)
39. Billington, J., Vanit-Anunchai, S., Gallasch, G.E.: Parameterised coloured Petri net channel models. In: Jensen, K., Billington, J., Koutny, M. (eds.) ToPNoC III. LNCS, vol. 5800, pp. 71–97. Springer, Heidelberg (2009)
40. Jensen, K., Kristensen, L.M., Wells, L.: Coloured Petri Nets and CPN Tools for Modelling and Validation of Concurrent Systems. STTT 9(3–4), 213–254 (2007)
41. Happenhofer, M., Egger, C., Reichl, P.: Quality of signalling: a new concept for evaluating the performance of non-INVITE SIP transactions. In: 2010 22nd International Teletraffic Congress (ITC), pp. 1–8, September 2010

42. Sparks, R.: Problems Identified Associated with the Session Initiation Protocol's (SIP) Non-INVITE Transaction. RFC 4321 (Informational), January 2006
43. Babich, F., Deotto, L.: Formal methods for specification and analysis of communication protocols. IEEE Commun. Surv. Tutorials 4(1), 2–20 (2002)

Author Index

Printed in the United States
By Bookmasters